Fifth Edition

CONTENT AREA LITERACY

TOOLKIT OF DISCIPLINARY STRATEGIES FOR MIDDLE AND HIGH SCHOOL

Jerry L. Johns
Paula Di Domenico
Rachel Lesinski-Roscoe

Kendall Hunt
publishing company

Book Team

Chairman and Chief Executive Officer Mark C. Falb
President and Chief Operating Officer Chad M. Chandlee
Vice President, Higher Education David L. Tart
Director of Publishing Partnerships Paul B. Carty
Senior Developmental Coordinator Angela Willenbring
Project Coordinator Charmayne McMurray
Permissions Editor Caroline Kieler
Cover Designer Heather Richman

Author Information for Correspondence, Professional Development, and Workshops

Jerry L. Johns, Ph.D.
Northern Illinois University
Distinguished Professor Emeritus
E-mail: *jjohns@niu.edu*

Paula DiDomenico, Ed.D.
E-mail: *pmdidomenico@gmail.com*
@pmdidomenico

Rachel Lesinski-Roscoe, Ed.D.
E-mail: *rlesinski02@gmail.com*
@RachelLesinski

Ordering Information

Address: Kendall Hunt Publishing Company
4050 Westmark Drive
Dubuque, IA 52004-1840
Telephone: 800-247-3458, ext. 5
Website: www.kendallhunt.com
Fax: 800-772-9165

Websites and applications were active when the book went to press.

Cover image by © Shutterstock, Inc.

Kendall Hunt
publishing company
www.kendallhunt.com
Send all inquiries to:
4050 Westmark Drive
Dubuque, IA 52004-1840

ISBN 979-8-7657-0699-2

Printed in the United States of America
10 9 8 7 6 5 4 3 2 1

Dedications

I wish to dedicate this book in honor and loving memory of my brother Tom (born 9/11/1948) who died suddenly on March 7, 2021. Tom was a substitute teacher in Washington and Michigan. He also had numerous seasonal jobs that included picking fruit and working in an Alaskan fish factory. He volunteered at the library and loved reading, nature, and gardening. He was a quietly intense environmentalist famous for his fresh salads. Tom was an accomplished artist in pottery, silk screening, and printmaking. He was a compassionate caregiver for our mom and a fun companion to sister Nancy. He was humble, kind, conscientious, steadfast, and absurdly frugal. Tom's surprisingly loud voice, exceptional Scrabble skills, gentle countenance, and captivating smile will be missed.

~Brother Jerry

To my colleagues who inspire me and Luca, Milo, and Olivia who remind me how important it is that I continue to stretch and grow.

~Paula

To my children, G, V, A, & A, and to my students because learning, laughing, and reading with you have been life's most perfect gifts. You are my inspiration. To Mom, Dad, and Sarah, my first teachers; Neil, my first student; and Danny, for learning alongside me every day. To my literacy friends, who always listen and challenge me to think differently.

~Love, Rachel, Mom, Mrs. L

Contents

Acknowledgments

We would like to acknowledge Dr. Jerry Johns for his relentless and picky pursuit of perfection. We would like to extend our gratitude to the amazing professors we had at Northern Illinois University who prepared us for all academic adventures. Thank you to the educators who are reading this book and trying new strategies with their students. And finally, we are proud to teach at schools with colleagues and administrators who are always looking out for us. A special appreciation to Daniel Landau for his contributions to the Spider Discussion strategy.

About the Authors

Jerry L. Johns has been recognized as a distinguished teacher and writer who has made presentations for professional conferences and school districts. He has taught students from kindergarten through graduate school. Jerry taught in the public schools and spent his career at Northern Illinois University. He was also a visiting professor at Western Washington University and the University of Victoria. He was president of the International Reading (now Literacy) Association, the Association of Literacy Educators and Researchers, the Illinois Reading Council, and was a member of the board of the American Reading Forum. Jerry has authored or coauthored nearly 300 books, articles, monographs, and research studies. Several recent titles include the 7th edition of *Improving Reading*, the 12th edition of the *Basic Reading Inventory*, and the 5th edition of *Fluency*. He has received numerous awards for his many contributions to literacy, most recently the prestigious William S. Gray Citation of Merit as well as the 2020 Diane Lapp and James Flood Professional Collaborator Award from the International Literacy Association.

Paula Di Domenico is a literacy coach and department chair at Leyden District 212. She is former high school English and reading teacher and currently teaches graduate courses in literacy at Northern Illinois University and Lewis University. Dr. Di Domenico also serves the educational community by working with neighboring school districts to support their literacy and coaching programs, presenting at national and international conferences, and engaging in research to better understand how teachers teach and learners learn. Her work has earned several awards and she has coauthored a book and several articles. She's thankful for the collaborations she has with teachers and all that she learns from her students.

Rachel Lesinski-Roscoe is a literacy coach and Reading Specialist at Grayslake Central High School, District 127. She is especially proud to be a part of their Academic Intervention and Mentoring Program. Dr. Lesinski-Roscoe also has the privilege of teaching graduate courses in literacy at Northern Illinois University and undergraduate courses in English at the College of Lake County. She also serves the educational community as the president of the Secondary Reading League of the Illinois Reading Council, presenting at professional conferences, and engaging in research on any topics that will inform the teaching and learning of all ages of students. She is honored to be a part of her students' lives and feels blessed to be a part of their learning journey. Dr. Lesinski-Roscoe is grateful for the learning and inspiration afforded her in collaborations with teachers, administrators, Dr. Laurie Elish-Piper, Dr. Paula Di Domenico, and, of course, Dr. Jerry Johns.

Preface and Overview

Who Will Use This Book?

As we were writing this book, we imagined various professionals who may find its content useful: middle and high school teachers working directly with students; literacy and instructional coaches; interventionists; and candidates for initial licensure and/or reading specialist endorsements. Because we designed this book to be a practical tool for teachers of math, science, English language arts, and social studies in grades 6-12, it is also ideal for team, school, and district professional development. Professors teaching a content area or disciplinary literacy course will also find it to be a valuable resource.

What's New in This Edition?

The fifth edition has distinct characteristics that set it apart from other strategy books. The primary goal of this text is to provide teachers with tools that will support students' ability to comprehend complex texts independently, and we recognize that middle and high school teachers must provide explicit instruction to students using general literacy strategies. Once this primary goal is achieved, the text will also provide students with discipline-specific literacy strategies that are required for deep, meaningful learning in the disciplines of English language arts, math, science, and history/ social studies.

In order to achieve these goals, we have included research on the specific strategic behaviors that students need to leverage in order to comprehend texts. These behaviors (such as summarizing, brainstorming, inferring, and connecting) are organized into four sections: What the Text Says; What the Text Means; Writing to Unlock Meaning; and Collaborative Discussion around Text. After a brief description of each behavior, we present strategies that will help students enact these behaviors. We also provide specific examples to describe how you may use these strategies in a variety of instructional contexts and within each discipline. When appropriate, templates and examples are provided.

Technology applications for each strategy are included and described on page xvii. You will find a description of the technology tool along with a list of strategies that utilization of the tool would enhance.

What Insights Have Been Provided by Research?

A number of researchers in the field of literacy suggest that teaching students the literacy practices that are unique to each discipline will better prepare them for life beyond high school and help them attain high levels of literacy achievement (Goldman, Britt, Brown, Cribb, George, Greenleaf, Lee, Shanahan, & Project READI, 2016). These researchers have focused not only on the variety of literacy practices specific to each discipline, but also on the ways in which secondary students can engage with these practices in a school setting (Moje, 2008; Shanahan & Shanahan, 2008). Part of this work involves using certain literacy strategies that teach students how to read discipline-specific texts using discipline-specific strategies (Gillis, 2014; Lee & Spratley, 2010; Moje, 2008; Shanahan & Shanahan, 2008). Shanahan and Shanahan (2008) argue that because literacy demands become increasingly specialized when learning disciplinary content, secondary teachers must transition students from the basic, more generalized literacy processes taught in earlier grades to the advanced, complex literacy processes specific to the disciplines. Oftentimes, however, secondary teachers spend a majority of instructional time teaching intermediate literacy strategies (see Figure 1 below) that don't always lead to more complex disciplinary learning. Examples of intermediate literacy strategies, sometimes called general literacy strategies, include activating prior knowledge, clarifying, making predictions, or summarizing.

One goal of this text is to provide examples of how these types of intermediate literacy strategies can serve as a bridge to more discipline-specific literacy instruction. It has been established that there is an important relationship between literacy and learning in the content areas (Gray, 1925; Herber, 1970). Students must internalize the language of specific disciplines in order to think critically about the content. Unfortunately, studies have found that as content becomes more complex, students' engagement with subject area reading declines significantly, most often by eighth grade (Gottfried, 1985). The National Assessment of Educational Progress (NAEP) indicates that students' reading scores continue to decline after eighth grade (2015). Thus, a continued focus on supporting students' disciplinary literacy learning is key to their post-secondary preparedness.

Figure 1. Increasing Specialization of Literacy (adapted from Shanahan & Shanahan, 2008)

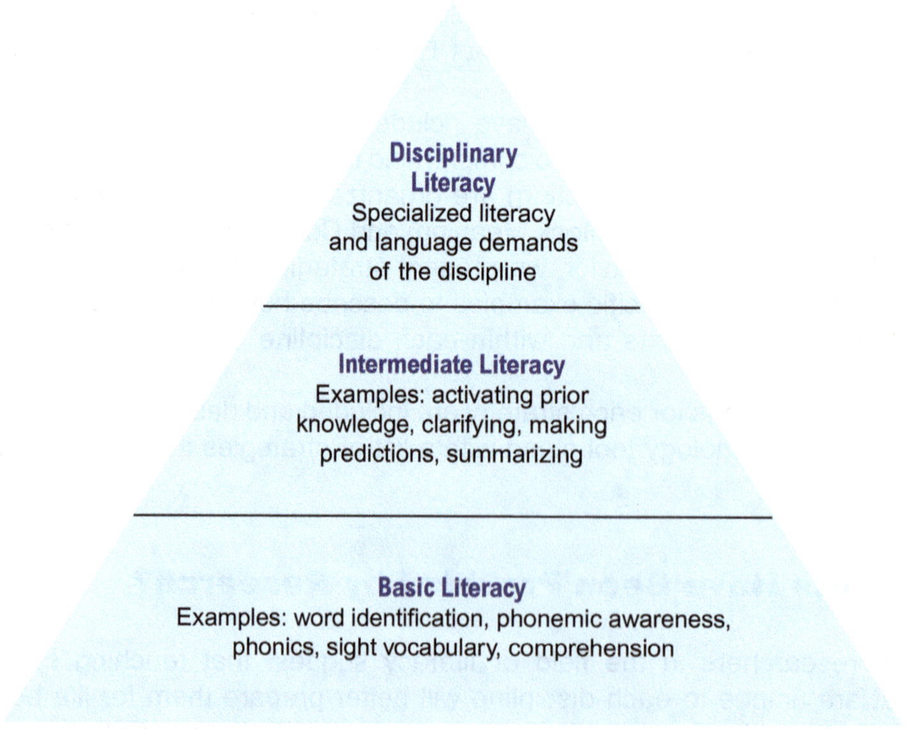

Research on disciplinary literacy analyzes how experts in the disciplines read and suggests that a one-size-fits-all approach is ineffective (Shanahan, Shanahan, & Misischia, 2011). Disciplinary experts use distinct literacy practices. For example, historians pay close attention to authorship and continuously juxtapose sources with one another (Wineburg, 1991). Scientists in the field of physics focus their attention on information they do not already know and information that contradicts what they have previously thought about the topic to deepen their understanding of complex ideas (Bazerman, 1985). Each of these examples demonstrates that in order to read and learn from complex disciplinary texts, students need to engage in the habits of thinking used in these disciplines, which can occur with the use of the strategies and ideas in this book. Some researchers have thus defined disciplinary literacy in the following way:

> Disciplinary literacy involves the use of reading, reasoning, investigating, speaking, and writing required to learn and form complex content knowledge appropriate to a particular discipline. (McConachie & Petrosky, 2010, p. 16)

Consequently, content-area instruction should focus on teaching specific strategies that allow students to engage in the thinking required for deep understanding of a text in a specific discipline.

The strategies in this book target disciplinary-based reading/literacy methods by focusing on the specific behaviors that these strategies target. Examples of disciplinary-based behaviors, according to the Wisconsin Department of Public Instruction (2012), include:

- building prior knowledge
- building specialized vocabulary
- learning to deconstruct complex sentences
- using knowledge of text structures and genres to predict main and subordinate ideas
- mapping graphic and mathematical representation against explanations in the text
- posing discipline-relevant questions
- comparing claims and propositions across texts
- using norms for reasoning within the discipline (i.e., what counts as evidence) to evaluate claims

Content-area literacy strategies can serve as important scaffolds for disciplinary habits in reading, writing, talking, and thinking (Brozo, Moorman, Meyer, & Stewart, 2013). Explicit strategy instruction can provide students opportunities for learning and retaining content knowledge (Stahl & Fairbanks, 1986). Strategy instruction needs to be clearly explained, modeled, scaffolded, and aligned with disciplinary purposes for learning. To move toward a more discipline-specific purpose for reading, students need to be guided to summarize in order to achieve a particular disciplinary objective. In history, for example, the goal may be to connect key events to explain the causes and effects of a larger historical movement. In science, the goal may be to encapsulate critical steps in a scientific process. While it is clear that summarization is an effective strategy for achieving these goals, it is a more intermediate literacy strategy. Therefore, summarization needs deeper emphasis in order to be effective for more complex disciplinary texts and to support students in developing discipline-specific habits of thinking.

The strategies in this text are an initial step toward disciplinary literacy, but your actions as a teacher are key to your students' ability to independently apply these strategies. Consider the following gradual release model, described below and shown in Figure 2 (page xvi), (Buehl, 2014; Pearson & Gallagher, 1983; Wisconsin Department of Public Instruction, 2012).

- Tell students the goals for learning in the discipline.
- Tell students how the strategies promote disciplinary learning.
- Model the habits of reading, writing, talking, and thinking in the discipline.
- Model how the strategies are used to promote those disciplinary habits.
- Think-aloud by describing what goes on in your mind while you are using the strategy.
- Gradually release responsibility to students.
- Provide guided practice so students can learn how the strategy will help them understand the content.
- Reinforce student efforts.
- Develop the strategies over time and remind students to use the strategies as needed.
- Have students reflect on the strategies and how certain strategies help in particular contexts.

Figure 2 is an example of the gradual release of responsibility in the context of disciplinary literacy instruction. The model represents the scaffolding and support needed to engage students in constructing disciplinary knowledge. As guided practices fade, student ownership of both intermediate and disciplinary strategies increases. The goal is for students to use disciplinary literacy strategies to construct meaning. To achieve that end, you can create classroom activities that engage students in direct strategy instruction and instill in them discipline-specific habits of reading, writing, thinking, and speaking through collaborative inquiry. Over time, student meaning-making should become increasingly discipline-specific using disciplinary literacy strategies that are relevant and appropriate.

What Are the Key Features of This Book?

In the introduction to each section, we provide a research-based rationale for the strategies included in the section. We then describe the strategic behaviors the strategies target. The format and organization of this book make it very user-friendly. Each strategy is organized under the following headings:

Description provides an explanation of the strategy along with its practical purpose. For example, the Writer's Notebook is described as a useful strategy traditionally used to hold a writer's ideas for future writing projects, practice playing with words, and engage in writing exercises. It might also serve as a mathematician's notebook that can be used to hold formulas, record conjectures, and reflect on learning processes and problem solving.

How and Why Would I Use This Strategy outlines instructional routines that this strategy would support. For example, in Writer's Notebook, ideas include supporting students' writing skill development and reinforcing their learning process by making connections, summarizing learning, listing questions, and engaging in the inquiry process.

How Do I Teach/Present the Strategy offers step-by-step implementation ideas and instructions for use. These steps will provide you with all the information you need to implement each strategy in your classroom.

Connections to the Disciplines provides key behaviors the strategy supports along with examples for use. For example, in Writer's Notebook, key behaviors presented for a science course include: Evaluate processes; Determine conclusions; Synthesize learning; Conduct experiments and/or labs; Summarize learning about content; and Make connections among ideas. An example about the use of a Writer's Notebook when engaging in lab learning is also included. The key behaviors and examples are provided for English language arts, math, science, and social studies.

Resources provides additional helpful information. This section may include templates, prompts, links to further information, or student examples.

Figure 2. Gradual Release of Responsibility

Activating Disciplinary Knowledge	Scaffolding Disciplinary Knowledge	Constructing Disciplinary Knowledge
Modeling Direct Instruction Teacher Think-Aloud	Examples of Intermediate Strategy Use: Annotation Informational Text Structures GIST List-Group-Label RAFT Synthesis Journal *Guided Practice* Classroom Activities Strategy Instruction Apprenticeship of Learning Collaborative Inquiry	Examples of Disciplinary Strategies: Building prior knowledge Building specialized vocabulary Learning to deconstruct complex sentences Using knowledge of text structures and genres to predict main and subordinate ideas Mapping graphic and mathematical representations against explanations in the text Posing discipline-relevant questions Comparing claims and propositions across texts Using norms for reasoning within the discipline (i.e., what counts as evidence) to evaluate claims
Framing Learning	Meaning Making	Disciplinary Literacy

I Do / You Watch → I Do / You Help → You Do / I Help → You Do / I Watch

Parts of the figure adapted from *Classroom Strategies for Interactive Learning* (4th ed., p. 31) by Buehl (2014) and from the Wisconsin Department of Public Instruction (2012).

Technology Applications

Teachers teaching in face-to-face, hybrid, one-to-one, or fully online courses may consider using the technology applications described in the chart below to support students' engagement with the strategies. The chart contains a link to the application, a brief description of the application, and the strategies that would work well with this technology application.

Strategies	Technology Application/Description
Annotation Strategy SMART Sticky Notes Embedded Questions Chunk N Go	InsertLearning *www.insertlearning.com* allows users to insert links to media, sticky notes with teacher-generated questions, student responses, and questions for students to consider as they read on any web page, including a Google Doc.
Cross off Summary	Diggo *www.diggo.com* is an online annotation tool that allows users to mark up texts online.
Bookmarks GIST Say Something Frayer Model Semantic Mapping STAR RAFT/GRASPS Writer's Notebook Climbing and Diving Marathon Writing Double-Entry Journal Cornell Notes	Google Docs is an online word processor. Links to these online documents can easily be shared, and students can collaborate on documents.
Word Sorts List, Group, Label Scenario Writing Listing	Bubble *www.bubble.us* is a web-based tool that allows users to create graphic organizers and easily move and categorize information.
Vocabulary Continuum List, Group, Label	Padlet *www.padlet.com* is an application that allows users to post on a collaborative digital wall. Videos, images, links, and text can all be added.
Annotation Strategy	Hypothesis *www.web.hypothes.is* is a collaborative annotation tool that allows students to annotate course materials and collaborate to share those annotations.
Word Sorts Sketch to Stretch	Jamboard *www.jamboard.google.com* is a collaborative, smart whiteboard that integrates with Google Apps for Education. Students can collaboratively create whiteboards, sticky notes, and images as well as manipulate text.
Entrance and Exit Slips	GoFormative *www.formative.com* provides a space for students to submit quick assessments of their current understanding. You can provide timely feedback and track students' learning using the application.

Section 1

What the Text Says

Contents for Section 1

Many middle and high school students struggle to deeply comprehend the complex texts they encounter in their courses. This is primarily because the types of texts students encounter in middle and high school not only increase in complexity, they are also the types of texts students encounter less frequently and therefore have less experience with. For example, though students will often encounter narrative texts, they rarely come across first-person historical accounts, scientific lab reports, and complex mathematical models in their daily lives. Compounding the challenge for students is that some content area teachers state that though they believe they should explicitly instruct students in strategies to support their reading of complex texts, they report that they do not make this a regular part of their practice (Popp, Di Domenico, & Makhlouf, 2021).

The foundation of discipline-specific literacy instruction is teaching students how to produce and comprehend the texts of the discipline (Moje, 2007). Though the focus of this approach to literacy instruction is on supporting students as they learn to employ discipline-specific thinking as they read complex texts, you must first ensure that students are able to comprehend the material. When students are presented with content that they are unable to comprehend, discipline-specific strategies are not enough (Faggella-Luby, Graner, Sampson, Deshler, & Drew, 2012). Therefore, it is key to explicitly teach strategies that support students' literal comprehension of the text in addition to engaging in discipline-specific literacy strategies.

When trying to understand how successful readers engaged with texts, cognitive scientists discovered processes that successful readers engage in and less successful readers do not (Castles, Rastle, & Nation, 2018). In this book, we refer to these cognitive processes as strategic behaviors. A way to practice strategic behaviors is through the use of structured activities. Throughout the book, we will connect the structured activities we are sharing (often called strategies) to the strategic behaviors readers will engage in. In the first section of the book, our focus is on supporting students and helping them learn to unpack what the text says.

The strategic behaviors for which we present strategies (structured activities) are defined in the chart below.

Strategic Behavior	Strategies that Support this Behavior
Monitoring Comprehension: When a reader monitors their comprehension, they are more likely to actively engage with the text as they read it. Flagella-Luby and Deshler (2008) found that for adolescents, this is one of the four most impactful strategic behaviors in which students can engage to support their reading comprehension. Students can be explicitly taught to monitor their comprehension by chunking the text and stopping frequently, asking and answering questions, and engaging in self-questioning (Crabtree, Alber-Morgan, & Konrad, 2010).	■ Annotation page 3 ■ Bookmarks page 5 ■ SMART page 8 ■ Sticky Notes page 12 ■ Embedded Questions page 15
Summarizing the Text: When readers summarize text as they are reading, they consider what they already know about the topic presented in the text, make connections among ideas, and organize information as they read. This supports comprehension as it requires readers to think deeply about the text (Lenski, Wham, Johns, & Caskey, 2011).	■ Chunk and Go page 18 ■ Cross-Out Summary page 23 ■ GIST page 28 ■ Say Something page 33
Word Work/Conceptual Learning: There is a strong correlation between students' knowledge of words and their comprehension of text. Focusing on helping students learn more words and learn how to learn words directly supports their comprehension of complex texts (Malatesha, 2005).	■ Frayer Model page 38 ■ List-Group-Label page 48 ■ Semantic Mapping page 48 ■ STAR page 62 ■ Vocabulary Continuum page 68 ■ Word Sorts page 73

Annotation

Description

Text annotation is a reading and writing strategy that encourages students to note important ideas, connections, and examples in the margins of a text (Brown, 2007; Nist & Hogrebe, 1987; Porter-O'Donnell, 2004). Annotation offers opportunities for students to engage deeply with the text, use active reading techniques, and talk to the text (Porter-O'Donnell, 2004). Annotation also supports students' reading of complex texts in specific disciplines. For instance, annotation supports the reading of complex scientific texts because it helps students better visualize and focus on important ideas in the text, which aids comprehension (Zywica & Gomez, 2008). Annotations can take several forms, including Bookmarks, SMART, or Sticky Notes. When you provide a focus, students can also annotate directly on the page. Procedures for each technique are on pages 6–14, along with templates and examples.

When and Why Would I Use This Strategy?

- Annotation can be used with both informational and literary text.
- This strategy works best when students have a specific focus for reading, and the text is challenging for them. If the student doesn't struggle to comprehend the text, annotation may inhibit readers who would otherwise proficiently read the text (Narter, 2013).
- When supporting students' comprehension, annotation can help students make connections, ask questions, note important ideas, see the text structure, analyze ideas, infer, note vocabulary, and otherwise enhance their comprehension.

Disciplinary Focus	Behaviors Targeted by the Strategy	Examples in Context
ELA	Track author's purpose; Note character development; Identify symbolism; Note use of rhetorical devices	An ELA teacher might select annotation as a strategy when students are reading a novel or short story. Teachers might tell students to focus on an author's choice, such as the use of imagery, and prepare for a discussion regarding the impact of the author's use of imagery. To provide additional focus for students, teachers might also provide guiding questions such as, "What can you visualize?" or "What appeals to your senses?" while they are reading and annotating the text.
Math	Unpack the context of a problem; Consider applicable theorems and rules	A math teacher may instruct students to note the context of the problem. They may ask students to consider what is happening in the problem and what the values are. By sketching the content of the text while they read, students can better understand the problem at hand.
Science	Note text structure; Identify the problem; Critique the methods; Summarize solutions; Identify processes; Note important vocabulary	When learning about processes and cycles in science, annotation can help students understand the stages and steps of those cycles. Helping students use headings to identify the components of the cycle may ensure that they capture the essential process.
Social Studies	Determine perspective; Note significance of events; Identify historical figures	When reading about historical events, students can annotate to trace a series of events throughout the text, note important historical figures, and comment on perspective.

The following pages (5–14) offer three specific annotation strategies and templates you can use with your students.

Bookmarks

Description

Bookmarks (Beers, 2003; Daniels & Zemelman, 2004) give students a place to record their thoughts while reading. When students record their thinking on the Bookmarks, they become active readers who make connections, ask questions, and determine important ideas. Students may also use Bookmarks to record key concepts or vocabulary terms that are significant to the reading.

How Do I Teach/Present the Strategy?

1. Duplicate and distribute copies of the Bookmarks on page 6.
2. Assign students a portion of text to read.
3. Read a portion of the text aloud and model the type of thinking you'd like them to capture on the Bookmark. These could range from general comprehension behaviors (e.g., making connections, summarizing, noting important vocabulary) to more discipline-specific thinking (e.g., use of imagery, noting historical significance, summarizing scientific processes). Examples from social studies and science follow on page 7.
4. Invite students to discuss their responses with a partner or in collaborative groups.
5. Encourage whole-group sharing to identify the range and variety of responses students recorded while reading.
6. Students can also use Bookmarks after reading to help them recall their understanding of selected text.

Template for General Bookmarks

Name: ______________________________ Date: ____________

Topic: ______________________	Topic: ______________________
	Vocabulary Word: ______________ Page ______
	Vocabulary Word: ______________ Page ______
	Vocabulary Word: ______________ Page ______
	Vocabulary Word: ______________ Page ______

Example for Science

Name: *Luca*

Date: ______

Topic: *Calvin Cycle*

—*The introduction states that carbon in our bodies was once part of carbon dioxide in the air.*

—*There are three stages of reactions in the Calvin cycle: carbon fixation, reduction, and regeneration of the starting molecule.*

—*The text keeps saying that the reaction occurs without light, but it depends on ATP and NADPH from light reactions. This is confusing.*

Topic: *Calvin Cycle*

Vocabulary Word: *fixed*

Page *47*

Incorporated into atom structures

Vocabulary Word: *stroma*

Page *48*

Location of Calvin cycle reactions; inner space of chloroplasts

Vocabulary Word: ______

Page ______

Example for Social Studies

Name: *Amy*

Date: ______

Topic: *Louisiana Purchase*

—*Robert Livingston and James Monroe negotiated the purchase.*

—*What would have happened if Napoleon decided not to sell the Louisiana Territory?*

—*I think at the time, $15 million was a lot of money for the purchase.*

—*How much land did the U.S. actually acquire?*

Topic: *Louisiana Purchase*

Vocabulary Word: *code*

Page *362*

To grant or give up land

Vocabulary Word: *Louisiana Territory*

Page *362*

Land from the Mississippi River west to the Rocky Mountains

Vocabulary Word: ______

Page ______

Vocabulary Word: ______

Page ______

Self-Monitoring Approach to Reading and Thinking (SMART)

Description

SMART, the Self-Monitoring Approach to Reading and Thinking (Buehl, 2014; Vaughan & Estes, 1986), is a strategy that encourages students to develop an awareness of what they do and do not understand as they read. This self-monitoring strategy helps students think about their reading and be more aware of how it is proceeding. Students use a notation system during reading and a variety of fix-up strategies, such as consulting a glossary or asking for help, for difficult portions of the text. They also evaluate the usefulness of the strategies, thereby enhancing their metacognition (awareness of one's own learning).

How Do I Teach/Present the Strategy?

1. Find a passage consisting of several paragraphs that may be somewhat challenging for students. The passage may need to be enlarged for effective viewing by students as you model the use of the strategy.
2. Read the first few sentences of the passage aloud to model the use of the strategy. If it makes sense to you, place a check mark in the margin and say something like, "This makes sense to me. I feel like I really understand it." If it seems confusing, place a question mark in the margin and say something like, "I'm not sure what this means. Maybe as I read on, I will understand better."
3. Continue modeling the use of the check mark and the question mark and comment on your reasons for using the marking system. You might say, "These marks will help me think about my reading and how well I am understanding what I am reading. Attentive readers know when they aren't understanding something, and they also know when they should try something else when they don't understand."
4. After completing the modeled reading for students, look at each question mark and talk with students about how to make sense of these parts of the text. Sometimes rereading helps the reader understand. If this is the case, change the question mark to a check mark in the margin. For other question-marked sections, talk about the problem. Why is this section difficult to understand? Is it the vocabulary? Is the language confusing? Do you know very little about the topic?
5. Ask students to share their ideas for ways to help the text make sense. List these ideas as students offer them. Suggestions might be to paraphrase the text; to use pictures, charts, or graphs for clues to the text's meaning; to check the glossary or other references for the definition of unknown or difficult words; to look at other parts of the text, such as the summary and review sections; and to ask a teacher or another classmate for help. Take time to discuss how the various strategies may provide clues to help construct meaning.

6. Introduce the passage students will be reading. Tell students to use a pencil to lightly mark the text using check marks and question marks to help them monitor their reading.
7. Make copies of the SMART Strategy Log on page 10. After students have read and marked the passages, have them work with a partner and discuss the sections marked with question marks. Instruct them to use the SMART Strategy Log to record their reading processes. Remind students that if the problem is "something else," there is space provided to write it.
8. After completing the SMART Strategy Log, discuss the strategies that helped the students work through problems with the text. Review or teach what the students need to do when they don't understand what they are reading in subsequent lessons.
9. Have students complete the SMART Strategy Log from time to time to make them more aware of ways to monitor their comprehension. A completed SMART example for mathematics is found on page 11.

SMART Strategy Log

Name: ______________________________ Date: __________

Directions: After reading, find the page and paragraph for each question mark (?) in the margin of your text. Note the locations of each under the *Page/Paragraph* headings. Reread those sections of text. Ask yourself, *What's the Problem?* Circle the relevant problems and/or write in your own. Then try some fix-up strategies. Circle the ones that you tried under the *What I Tried* column. Then think about how each strategy worked. Mark your response in the *How it Worked* column.

Page/Paragraph with "?"	*What's the Problem?*	*What I Tried*	*How It Worked*
____ / ____	Difficult Word Confusing Sentence Don't Know Much About It ____________________ ____________________	Glossary Reread Text Pictures/Graphics Summarize Review Section Diagrams Ask Someone Something Else ____________________	Great! I Get It! It Helped OK Not Much Help
Page/Paragraph with "?"	*What's the Problem?*	*What I Tried*	*How It Worked*
____ / ____	Difficult Word Confusing Sentence Don't Know Much About It ____________________ ____________________	Glossary Reread Text Pictures/Graphics Summarize Review Section Diagrams Ask Someone Something Else ____________________	Great! I Get It! It Helped OK Not Much Help
Page/Paragraph with "?"	*What's the Problem?*	*What I Tried*	*How It Worked*
____ / ____	Difficult Word Confusing Sentence Don't Know Much About It ____________________ ____________________	Glossary Reread Text Pictures/Graphics Summarize Review Section Diagrams Ask Someone Something Else ____________________	Great! I Get It! It Helped OK Not Much Help
Page/Paragraph with "?"	*What's the Problem?*	*What I Tried*	*How It Worked*
____ / ____	Difficult Word Confusing Sentence Don't Know Much About It ____________________ ____________________	Glossary Reread Text Pictures/Graphics Summarize Review Section Diagrams Ask Someone Something Else ____________________	Great! I Get It! It Helped OK Not Much Help

Sample SMART Strategy Log for Mathematics

Directions: After reading, find the page and paragraph for each question mark (?) in the margin of your text. Note the locations of each under the *Page/Paragraph* headings. Reread those sections of text. Ask yourself, *What's the Problem?* Circle the relevant problems and/or write in your own. Then try some fix-up strategies. Circle the ones that you tried under the *What I Tried* column. Then think about how each strategy worked. Mark your response in the *How it Worked* column.

Page/Paragraph with "?"	*What's the Problem?*	*What I Tried*	*How It Worked*
36 / 3	Difficult Word Confusing Sentence Don't Know Much About It ________________ ________________	Glossary Reread Text Pictures/Graphics Summarize Review Section Diagrams Ask Someone Something Else ________________	Great! I Get It! It Helped OK Not Much Help
Page/Paragraph with "?"	*What's the Problem?*	*What I Tried*	*How It Worked*
38 / 1	Difficult Word Confusing Sentence Don't Know Much About It ________________ ________________	Glossary Reread Text Pictures/Graphics Summarize Review Section Diagrams Ask Someone Something Else ________________	Great! I Get It! It Helped OK Not Much Help

Sticky Notes

Description

Sticky Notes (Daniels & Zemelman, 2004; Harvey & Goudvis, 2007; Hoyt, 2009) encourage students to monitor their thinking while reading by jotting down brief notes and sticking them on the pages of the text that prompted their thoughts. Students can jot down brief comments, write questions, make predictions and connections, or mark an interesting phrase or sentence in the text. Teachers may also instruct students to focus on discipline-specific thinking as they read the text. See page 3 (annotation description) for more information about discipline-specific notes students may record. Sticky Notes become a record of students' thinking that can later be used for review, discussion, and assessment.

How Do I Teach/Present the Strategy?

1. Choose a passage from a text to read aloud and provide copies or display it so that students can follow along with you. Explain that you will be stopping while reading to write down your thinking on Sticky Notes.
2. Begin reading the text aloud and stop at a point where you can share a personal connection, ask a question, make a prediction, note the author's use of language, or share a discipline-specific habit of thinking. On a Sticky Note, write down your prediction, read it aloud to students, then place it on the page to mark the spot in the text to show your thinking. Continue reading and stop to share your written thoughts on Sticky Notes.
3. As you continue reading aloud, elicit students' thoughts. Model how to jot down their responses on Sticky Notes using a chart, LCD projector, or interactive whiteboard.
4. After modeling several examples, provide time for students to practice individually by having them silently read and record their thinking on Sticky Notes.
5. Invite students to share their Sticky Notes with a partner or use them in a whole-class discussion. You might ask students to place their Sticky Notes on a chart or use the reproducible template on page 13. Responses can be organized into categories and used to engage students in a discussion. An example of a Sticky Notes Record Sheet for ELA is on page 14.
6. Upon completing the reading, students should have a collection of Sticky Notes that can be stored in a notebook for later discussion and review.

Sticky Notes Record Sheet - General Comprehension

Name: ______________________________ Date: ____________

Title : ____

My Predictions	My Questions
My Connections	My Evaluation
My Summary	

Example of Sticky Notes Record Sheet for ELA

Title : ______________________________

Author's Use of Imagery - What do I see?	Author's Use of Imagery - What do I smell?
Author's Use of Imagery - What do I feel?	Author's Use of Imagery - What do I hear?

Embedded Questions

Description

Embedded Questions (Lenski, Wham, & Johns, 1999; Urquhart & Weir, 2016) serve as a scaffold for teaching students to attend to the text as they are reading. Initially, you would chunk the text (see Chunk and Go pages 18-20) and craft questions to help focus students' attention on the significant points in each chunk. Then, give students the opportunity to discuss the responses to their questions with their peers. After students have successfully read several texts using the Embedded Questions strategy, present them with a whole text and encourage them to use annotations to help monitor meaning. You can craft questions that support student thinking in the disciplines and use those questions to help students attend to important components of each text as they are reading.

When and Why Would I Use this Strategy?

- This strategy is best used with students who do not monitor their comprehension, as the questions encourage them to attend to the text and ensure they are understanding the text as they are reading it.
- This strategy can be used with any type of text, and you can tailor questions to support the thinking and attention you want students to develop as they interact with the texts you give them.

How Do I Teach/Present the Strategy?

1. Once you have selected a text for students to read, chunk the text.
2. Using the Disciplinary Guide for Examples of Embedded Questions found on page 17, insert questions into appropriate chunks of the text. This can be done by writing in the margins or by using the comment feature for computer documents.
3. For the first few times students use this strategy, read the beginning portions of the text to the class. When you get to an Embedded Question, pause and ask the students to discuss the answers to the question in pairs or small groups.
4. Ask students to read the assigned text and record the answers to the questions as they read. Students may be paired in groups to read and answer questions, or they may complete the work independently.
5. If students have read the text independently, ask them to create a pair or join a group to share the responses to their questions.
6. After students have used the strategy successfully several times, encourage them to create their own questions on a text that has not been chunked. They can then begin to annotate the text on their own.

Disciplinary Focus	Behaviors Targeted by the Strategy	Examples in Context
ELA	Attend to setting; Attend to author's choice about character; Attend to author's use of rhetoric; Ask questions	When reading a short story, embed questions in the text that encourage students to attend to the setting and to make predictions at several points throughout the text. Toward the end of the text, embed questions that support students' thinking about how the setting impacted the message of the text.
Math	Consider the information that is presented in a problem, what that information means, and what students know about the information provided; Ask questions	Give students several triangles and ask them to prove whether or not they are congruent. Prompt them with questions about what information they have, what theorems might apply, and how they might apply those theorems.
Science	Consider the information presented in the introduction; Determine the methods; Question the findings; Ask questions	When reading a lab report, embed questions that ask students to attend to the context provided in the introduction, the research question/hypothesis, and the methods.
Social Studies	Focus on the speaker and his/her perspective; Consider the context; Connect to other events happening in that period; Ask questions	Provide students with a primary source document and embed questions that ask them to focus on the source, the context, and the period.

Disciplinary Guide for Examples of Embedded Questions

Name: ______________________________ Date: __________

Discipline	Possible Use of Embedded Questions
ELA	▪ What do you notice about the setting? Where is this set? ▪ Stop and describe the main characters. Who are they, and what are their relationships to other characters? ▪ What do you think will happen next? ▪ How does the author's use of ________ make you feel? ▪ Are there any words that are unfamiliar to you in this section?
Math	▪ What information are you given in this problem? ▪ What do you know about what you see? ▪ What does this information mean? ▪ After solving the problem, does your answer make sense in the context you have been given?
Science	▪ What is the problem as presented in the introduction? ▪ What methods are used? Are they sound? ▪ How does this new information compare to what you already know about the topic? ▪ What are the steps in the _____ process? ▪ How does this differ from what you already know about the topic?
Social Studies	▪ Who is the author? ▪ When and where was the document created? ▪ Why was this document written? ▪ What happened before _____ event? ▪ What happened directly after _____ event?

Chunk and Go

Description

Chunk and Go is a strategy that encourages students to break down text into "chunks" or segments. This strategy allows them to grasp bigger ideas by synthesizing them to create a summary or determine a theme or claim. Students need to be taught how to struggle successfully with a complex text (CCSS, 2010; Fisher, Frey, & Lapp, 2012), so it is valuable to provide them with small, manageable chunks of text to encourage skill development. This strategy provides students with the opportunity to skim and reread, read slowly, underline, take notes, organize information, and discuss (Lenski, Wham, Johns, & Caskey, 2011). In addition, Chunk and Go supports the difficult task of summary writing, a critical skill done prior to the work of synthesizing, corroborating, comparing, and contrasting multiple complex texts.

When and Why Would I Use this Strategy?

- To support students in accessing complex, nonfiction texts
- To develop students' ability to comprehend independently and collect evidence
- To provide a system for organizing students' thinking and for summarizing their ideas

How Do I Teach/Present the Strategy?

1. As you look over the text you will use in the lesson, bracket the text into manageable segments, approximately five sentences long. Students can also be responsible for dividing the text into chunks themselves. Chunking can follow the paragraphing of the text, or you can determine other stopping points depending on the text and your goals for the lesson.
2. After the text is divided into chunks, number each chunk for easy reference. See pages 21–22 for examples of how to chunk and label text.
3. Before students begin to read, provide them with a purpose for reading, possibly in the form of an Essential Question. See Disciplinary Focus for ideas on page 20.
4. Then, for each bracketed chunk, ask students to underline or highlight something important that stands out to them or jot down a note in the margin to highlight big ideas.

5. After reading and marking the text, bring students together as a large group and ask each student to share one important item/note/quote/piece of evidence from the text that they find to be most valuable.
6. Type up what each student explains to you. Make sure that all students can see the class notes, either on an overhead screen or through shared Google Documents. All students need access to these notes and ideas.
7. If multiple students share the same or similar information, bold that information to indicate that other students found it valuable and that students agree with one another.
8. After all comments are in the shared document, organize the information into groups or categories of ideas.
9. Through this process of grouping evidence, topics will begin to develop and a summary will emerge.
10. It is important to note that topics should develop organically during and after the categorizing process. Giving topics to students first can sometimes hinder their ability to categorize. Not all people think in the same way, and providing topics in advance limits the potential of the exercise.
11. Sometimes the topics are simple: beginning, middle, end. Sometimes the topics become more complex: background information, relationships, changes. If the purpose for reading has become clear, topics will reflect the specificity of the goal: e.g., why the character changed, the impact of war, lessons for the future.

Disciplinary Focus	Behaviors Targeted by the Strategy	Examples in Context
ELA	Determine key ideas and details; Comprehend text; Develop a summary; Consider theme; Develop thesis; Understand character motivation	Provide students with a human-interest nonfiction piece and ask them to determine the narrator's motivations and life lessons. Essential Questions could include: ▪ What is the motivation of the narrator? ▪ What is the life lesson that can be taken from this text? In addition, after students have created categories and topic titles for the categories (after step 11), they can generate a theme idea and develop a thesis.
Math	Engage in close reading; Analyze vocabulary; Create a concise explanation	Before students begin to perform analysis of data on space shuttle launches, they can read about the history of space exploration, including the Space Race and what happened to the space shuttle Challenger. Students can be asked to consider the following: ▪ Why is it valuable to be precise when explaining and analyzing in math-based careers? ▪ Why is it important for mathematicians to check their work?
Science	Consider evidence; Develop a hypothesis; Summarize a point of view; Eradicate misconceptions; Create a concise summary; Recognize cause and effect	During a unit on heat and insulation, students can read about a variety of inventions. The goal can be to eradicate misconceptions surrounding heat and insulation and heat conductors. Ask the following: ▪ What surprised you during your reading? ▪ What ideas contrast or contradict what you thought prior to reading?
Social Studies	Understand claim and point of view; Consider evidence; Develop thesis; Recognize cause and effect; Craft a concise summary	When students are reading a complex primary or secondary source, ensure that their chunks are small and manageable. You might also provide the following Essential Questions: ▪ What is the goal of this document? ▪ What language in the text suggests that?

Example of General Chunk and Go with Text Retyped into a Template

Name: ______________________________ Date: __________

Segment of Text excerpted from Manderino, Berglund, & Johns, 2014.	**Margin Summary Ideas and Notes**
1. Consequently, content area instruction should use the primary disciplinary literacy habits of thinking if students are to acquire deep content knowledge. Disciplinary literacy is an approach to building the requisite disciplinary knowledge required by a given domain.	Need to know the content on a deep level and not just memorize for the test
2. We agree that we need to move students toward these disciplinary habits of reading, writing, talking, and thinking, but they may need support through the use of content area strategies. Disciplinary habits... have also been delineated in the Common Core State standards. For the first time, literacy standards have been designed to treat reading, writing, talking, and thinking in the disciplines as distinct practices. As such, it is clear that students will need support to meet these discipline-specific literacy practices.	Content strategies will support development of disciplinary literacy strategies
3. Content area literacy approaches have traditionally focused on more generalized reading processes such as summarization, predicting, questioning, and visualizing. These strategies are consistent with the report of the National Reading Panel that offered several strategies for effective comprehension instruction, including teaching students to summarize what they read.	Generalized practices are good to start and then move closer and closer to discipline-specific thinking

Example of General Chunk and Go Using Text Excerpted from Manderino, Berglund, & Johns, 2014.

Name: ______________________________ Date: __________

> Disciplinary literacy involves the use of reading, reasoning, investigating, speaking, and writing required to learn form complex content knowledge appropriate to a particular discipline. (McConachie & Petrosky, 2010, p. 16)

Consequently, content area instruction should use the primary disciplinary literacy habits of thinking if students are to acquire deep content knowledge. Disciplinary literacy is an approach to building the requisite disciplinary knowledge required by a given domain. Disciplinary literacy entails the habits of practice valued in the disciplines and is comprised of 1) the habits of thinking used to make meaning; 2) a full range of texts and language use that shape thinking and practice; 3) the habits of practice enacted within the disciplines; and 4) the beliefs about knowledge and knowledge production that constitute the disciplines (Fang, 2012; Manderino, 2012; Moje, 2007, 2009; Shanahan & Shanahan, 2008; Wilson, 2011).

We agree that we need to move students toward these disciplinary habits, but they may still need support through the use of content area strategies (Fang & Coatoam, 2013). Students who lack conceptual knowledge and strategies in history, science, English language arts, or math to comprehend complex texts may be considered struggling adolescent readers (Alexander & Fox, 2011). As a result, explicit strategy instruction may be profitable for apprenticing disciplinary literacy instruction (Schoenbach, Greenleaf, & Murphy, 2012).

Disciplinary habits of reading, writing, talking, and thinking have also been delineated in the Common Core State Standards (CCSS) (NGA Center & CCSSO, 2010). The CCSS have been specifically written for the disciplines in grades 6-12. For the first time, literacy standards have been designed to treat reading, writing, talking, and thinking in the disciplines as distinct practices. These standards **"are meant to complement the specific content demands of the disciplines, not replace them"** (NGA Center & CCSSO, 2010, p. 60). As such, it is clear that students will need support to meet these discipline-specific literacy practices (Zygouris-Coe, 2012.)

Content area literacy approaches have traditionally focused on more generalized reading processes such as summarization, predicting, questioning, and visualizing. These strategies are consistent with the report of the National Reading Panel (2000) that offered several strategies for effective comprehension instruction, including teaching students to summarize what they read. According to Cunningham (2001), the comprehension section of the National Reading Panel Report is potentially valuable. The following principles are generally consistent with two other major reviews (Pearson & Fielding, 1991; Tierney & Cunningham, 1984) and a related chapter (Pressley, 2000) of research on teaching comprehension.

1. Teach students to be aware of their own comprehension. This strategy is often referred to as comprehension monitoring or metacognition.
2. Have students work together on their strategies. This is referred to as cooperative learning.
3. Have students construct graphic summaries of what is read through the use of graphic and semantic organizers. Use them as a bridge to student-generated talk or writing.
4. Teach text structure.
5. Help students learn to ask and answer text-based questions.
6. Teach students to summarize what is read.

Cross-Out Summary Strategy

Description

The Cross-Out Summary Strategy allows students to determine the main ideas of text by crossing out words and lines that seem to pertain to details and nonessential information that might be interesting, but not important (Burvall & Ryder, 2019; Kleon, 2010). When students complete their deletions, they are left with main-idea words and concepts that can be constructed into summary sentences.

Opportunities for students to compare their cross outs and summary sentences with others is valuable to learning and self-editing. You may model the strategy using a think-aloud, and you might also consider using focus questions to guide students toward the main ideas of the text.

When and Why Would I Use this Strategy?

- To enhance students' ability to find essential information
- To develop students' critical thinking skills
- To modify how students approach finding main ideas of a text
- To support close reading of a text

How Do I Teach/Present the Strategy?

1. Select a passage or excerpt that is about 1-2 pages in length, depending on the density of information. See pages 26–27 for a template and an example of the strategy being used with a dense, complex text.
2. Ensure that the passage corresponds to the goals for the lesson and contains main ideas as well as details.
3. Provide students with the text and instruct them to look it over to orient themselves with the topic and text structures in place. For an outline of the procedure with verbal cues, see on page 25.
4. Explain to students that they will be crossing off information that does not seem important so that they can ultimately write a brief summary of the text.
5. Students can gauge the importance of the information based on the guiding questions that you have provided for the lesson. See Disciplinary Focus on page 24 for ideas.
6. Remind students that they will need to read slowly and carefully and that they may need to reread the entire text, or portions of the text, in order to determine what they want to cross out. Students should use an electronic document or a pencil so that they can revert to a previous draft if they need to.

7. After they have crossed out portions of the text, instruct the students to make a list of words and phrases remaining. An electronic document will allow them to copy and paste these ideas, which will help move the process along.
8. Once they list words and phrases, they can begin to draft a summary with the goal of answering the guiding questions you have provided.
9. Consider modeling the Cross-Out Summary Strategy on a portion of the text each time you use the strategy.
10. Describe the goals and purposes of the lesson in more detail as you think-aloud and model the crossing-out process.
11. Consider allowing students to provide you feedback on what you choose to cross out based on the guiding questions.
12. Allow students to work in pairs to begin the process on their own segment of text.

Disciplinary Focus	Behaviors Targeted by the Strategy	Examples in Context
ELA	Recognize the use of literary techniques; Notice character traits; Consider the tone of language and the mood of the text	Students can cross out words that are *not* focused on emotion in order to summarize the mood, tone, or character's motivations. A guiding question might be: What word choices has the author made?
Math	Consider misconceptions; Recognize gaps in knowledge	Students can read a text-based overview of a unit and cross off vocabulary and concepts they are familiar with. This will allow students to summarize gaps in knowledge and recognize misconceptions prior to the start of a unit. A guiding question could be: What do I currently understand about this topic?
Science	Cultivate awareness of bias and stance	Students can cross off words and phrases in texts regarding debatable environmental topics. They can then determine the author's stance. The guiding question might read: What does the author want me to understand and believe?
Social Studies	Consider point of view; Analyze various arguments; Recognize leading language	Students can delete words and phrases that do *not* support a given argument in order to eventually determine the author's point of view. The guiding question could be: What words demonstrate bias?

Instructions for the Cross-Out Summary Strategy

Name: ______________________________ Date: ____________

Provide students with the text and instruct them to look it over to orient themselves with the topic and text structures in place. Say, "Students, take a moment and look over this text. Notice the title and consider what you think this text might be about."
Explain to students that they will be crossing out information that does not seem important so that they can ultimately write a brief summary of the text. They can determine importance using the guiding question you provide. Say, "Students, as you read, you will be crossing out information that does not seem important. It may seem like extra information that is not as focused on the main ideas. It is important to determine what is important rather than what is just interesting. We will ultimately be writing a summary of this text."
Articulate the guiding question and post it for students to refer to throughout the lesson. Say, "In order to determine what is important information and what is not, I am giving you a guiding question. This question will help you determine what you need to take away from this text and what you will write a summary about."
Remind students that they will need to read slowly and carefully, and that they may need to reread the entire text or portions of the text in order to determine what they want to cross out. Say, "Read slowly and carefully. Feel free to erase or undo cross-outs, but do not get too caught up in going back. Try to keep moving forward."
After they have crossed out portions of the text, have students make a list of words and phrases remaining. Say, "I have been monitoring your progress. You are at a good place to start to gather up ideas. Find valuable words and phrases that you have NOT crossed out. Write them in the box designated for these words."
Once they have a list of words and phrases, they can begin to draft a summary with the goal of answering the guiding questions you have provided. Say, "Now that you have these main idea words and phrases, draft a brief summary of this text."

Template for Cross-Out Summary Strategy

Name: ____ Date: ____________

Guiding Question: ____ ____
Text: ____ ____ ____ ____ ____ ____ ____ ____ ____ ____
Words and Phrases: ____ ____ ____ ____
Summary: ____ ____ ____ ____

Example Cross-Out Summary Strategy for a General Text

Name: ______________________________ Date: __________

Guiding Questions: In what ways is bridging content area strategies with disciplinary strategies valuable to adolescents?

Examples: word identification, phonemic awareness,
phonics, sight vocabulary, comprehension

Figure 1. Increasing Specialization of Literacy (adapted from Shanahan & Shanahan, 2008)

~~Examples of~~ intermediate literacy strategies ~~include activating prior knowledge, clarifying, making predictions, or summarizing. These~~ strategic behaviors ~~are~~ embedded ~~into what have been termed~~ content area literacy strategies. ~~Examples include the strategies that are provided in this text such as GIST, Possible Sentences, QARs, and Semantic Mapping.~~

~~One~~ goal ~~of this edition is to provide~~ examples ~~of~~ how ~~these types of~~ intermediate literacy strategies ~~can serve as a~~ bridge to moving ~~toward more~~ discipline-specific literacy instruction. ~~It has been established that there is an~~ important relationship ~~between literacy and learning in the content areas (Gray, 1925; Herber, 1970). Students must~~ internalize ~~the~~ language of specific disciplines ~~in order to~~ think critically ~~with subject area reading~~ declines significantly, ~~most often by eight grade (Gottfried, 1985). The National Assessment of Educational Progress (NAEP)~~ scores ~~also~~ indicate ~~a~~ decline ~~in~~ reading performance ~~in~~ eighth grade (Grigg, Donahue, & Dion, 2007). ~~These drops are~~ related to a decrease ~~in content area~~ literacy instruction that encourages metacognition and deep reading (Guthrie & Davis, 2003).

Research on disciplinary literacy (Shanahan, Shanahan, Misischia, 2011) analyzes how experts in the disciplines read and suggests that one-size-fits-all approach is ineffective. Disciplinary experts use distinct literacy practices. For example, historians pay close attention to authorship and continuously juxtapose sources

Words and Phrases: Intermediate literacy strategies, strategic behaviors, embedded, content-area literacy strategies; goal, example, bridge discipline-specific literacy instruction; relationship, internalize language, thinking critically, student engagement, decrease, literacy instruction encourages metacognition and deep reading

Summary: Bridging content area literacy strategies with discipline-specific literacy strategies will allow students to think more deeply and metacognitively about what and how they are reading and engaging with text. Students need to internalize the language and thinking of the text in order to understand the discipline and be successful in college and in their careers.

GIST

Description

GIST (Cunningham, 1982, 2013; Manderino, Berglund, & Johns, 2014) is a strategy that provides a structure for students' summary writing. It is completed during the reading of a text passage. Prior to reading, students chunk the text into smaller parts. While reading, students stop at the end of each chunk and construct a GIST summary. Each time, the prior 20-word summary is brought into the construction of the newest summary, thus facilitating the development of a comprehensive summary of a lengthier text.

In order to facilitate a discipline-specific lens for reading, you can provide a guiding main idea question for each chunk of text. You will want to model the GIST process, begin the process with shorter excerpts of text, and proceed through a gradual release of responsibility model by instructing students to pair and share their summaries with small groups and peer edit to support the construction of summaries less than 20 words.

When and Why Would I Use this Strategy?

- To develop students' ability to concisely summarize a text
- To provide structure when students are asked to find main ideas
- To scaffold student interaction with text so that their overarching understanding of text can be used for future lessons

How Do I Teach/Present the Strategy?

1. Duplicate the GIST reproducible on page 31, or create a two-column organizer for students to GIST.
2. Select a one- to two-page text that is challenging and divide the text into three to five smaller segments. See the Chunk and Go strategy in this section on page 18 if you are unsure about how to divide the text.
3. You may want to provide students with a focus question for each division of the text, depending on the goal of the lesson and on students' comfort with the strategy and topic. Sample discipline-specific guiding questions are offered in Disciplinary Focus on pages 29–30. Also, see the partial example on page 29, which shows how guiding questions can be included in the GIST template. A completed example is on page 32.

Example GIST for **Science**

"Fighting for Clean Water"	Science Text
First Passage: What is the problem? *Indigenous communities in Canada did not have clean water and they were often under a boil water advisory.*	
Second Passage: What actions are being taken? *Indigenous communities in Canada had contaminated water and a girl named Autumn decided to fight to get them clean water.*	

4. Read aloud the first divided segment and model an initial 20-word summary about the first segment of the text. You may want to demonstrate your editing process by thinking aloud. You might say, "Okay, first I am going to pull out big idea words. Now I am going to arrange them into sentences. This is a good draft. Let me count my words. I have too many! Let me rephrase this to cut 5 words. Now I will reread and make sure it still says what I want it to say."
5. After modeling and using a think-aloud, have students read the second segment of text and together, draft and edit a second 20-word summary about both segments of the text.
6. Students can then read the third divided segment of the text and, independently or in pairs, draft and edit a 20-word summary about all three segments of text.
7. The process continues until students have read the entire text and have written a 20-word comprehensive summary of the entire text.
8. Depending on students' needs, GIST may be a strategy that you always do as a class or in small groups with your support. Some students really struggle with summary writing and need a lot of supported practice.

Disciplinary Focus	Behaviors Targeted by the Strategy	Examples in Context
ELA	Recognize character motivation and point of view	Students can construct a GIST summary focused on character motivation and point of view. It can be beneficial for some students to have a prompt to focus their reading. Some examples include: ■ What decisions is the character making in this segment of text? ■ What solutions does the character seek?

Disciplinary Focus	Behaviors Targeted by the Strategy	Examples in Context
Math	Recognize multiple representations; Understand processes; Consider problem and solution relationships	Students can write a GIST summary of a problem-solving process and apply it to a numerical representation. Students can also use GIST to explain their reasoning. Some ideas for guiding questions in each chunk of text might include: ■ What is the problem? ■ What steps do I need to follow? ■ What is my overall approach? Alternatively, students may create a two-column chart to write a GIST next to each numerical step of the problem.
Science	Recognize cause and effect patterns; Develop ideas to create models of processes	Students can use GIST to summarize a problem-solution process. For each chunk of text, guiding questions may include: ■ What happened? ■ What caused it to happen? ■ Why did it happen? ■ What is the effect/result? In addition, you may want to provide students with cause-and-effect transition words and phrases to look for when reading, such as *for, because, since, as a result of,* and/or *due to*.
Social Studies	Develop an argument; Consider a claim; Establish point of view	Students can write a GIST summary of a secondary source in order to use that background knowledge to evaluate a primary source of the same topic. To enhance the compare and contrast that will occur after GIST writing, direct the questions accordingly. For each chunk, you can ask questions such as: ■ What viewpoint, conclusion, or theory is being proposed? ■ What biases are suggested?

Template for General GIST

Name: ______________________________ Date: ____________

First Passage:

____

____

____

Second Passage:

____

____

____

Third Passage:

____

____

____

Fourth Passage:

____

____

____

Final Summary:

____

____

____

Example GIST for Science

Name: *Augustus* Date: ______

Fighting for Clean Water	Science Text
First Passage: What is the problem?	
Indigenous communities in Canada did not have clean water and they were often under a boil water advisory.	
Second Passage: What actions are being taken?	
Indigenous communities in Canada had contaminated water and a girl named Autumn decided to fight to get them clean water.	
Third Passage: What is the solution?	
The water for Canadian Indigenous communities was not regulated by the government and their supply was contaminated until Autumn fought for them.	
Final Summary: What is the argument?	
Everyone deserves clean water so Autumn petitioned the Canadian government and now Indigenous communities have an ongoing clean water supply.	

Say Something

Description

Say Something (Beers, 2003; Short, Harste, & Burke, 1996; Manderino, Berglund, & Johns, 2014) provides structure and opportunity for students to respond to the text during their reading rather than waiting until afterward. This allows students to summarize their thinking while simultaneously making connections. The strategy highlights the social nature of reading and the value of connecting with text by asking students to share their thinking with a partner or partners as their thoughts begin to form. At pre-selected stopping points in the reading, students make connections between the text and their own experiences, which supports the development of active reading, deep reading, and empathetic connection (Wolf, 2018). Proficient readers have a running monologue in their minds as they read; this strategy allows thinking to become transparent and concrete, while also encouraging metacognition (Schoenbach, Greenleaf, & Murphy, 2012).

When & Why Would I Use this Strategy?

- To encourage collaboration and learning from peers of different skill levels
- To promote active reading and engagement with text
- To provide a discipline-specific approach to text

How Do I Teach/Present the Strategy?

1. Select a reading and locate logical stopping points that correspond to the purpose of the lesson.
2. Embed Say Something stems at the stopping points, or provide students with the chart of sample stems and instruct them to choose the stems they want to use. See pages 36 and 37 for sample stems.
3. Determine whether students will be reading aloud to their partners or engaging with the text silently. Determine whether students will say something aloud immediately or silently jot notes in the margins to share at a given time. It is important however, to keep in mind that the social aspect of this strategy is what makes it successful. Therefore, you should encourage students to share their ideas with each other as much as possible.
4. Introduce the strategy by using think-aloud to model how students should be cataloging their ideas.

5. Instruct students to begin the strategy with their partners.
6. Emphasize that all responses are acceptable as long as students can support their position and ideas. If students are struggling with Say Something, encourage them to reread or to listen to others' responses first. You can also provide more descriptive prompts until they get comfortable.
7. After students have completed the reading of the text and shared Say Something ideas with their partners, as a class, work to clarify misunderstandings and reread portions of the text for clarity and evidence to support students' comments.

Disciplinary Focus	Behaviors Targeted by the Strategy	Examples in Context
ELA	Connect text to world and self; Collaborate to engage with text; Comprehend and analyze	When reading a text, choose stopping points that demonstrate the actions and motivations of the main character. You may include Say Something stems such as: ■ The character may have reacted this way because... ■ The character was dealing with a lot, including... ■ I would not have acted like the main character because…
Math	Think through the process; Analyze patterns; Develop vocabulary; Consider multiple representations	When looking at an answer key, learning a process, or reading an explanation of the reasoning behind a solution, instruct students to jot down Say Somethings in the margins. Set a timer so that students know when to share their comments. Some Say Something stems could include: ■ The part of this problem that caused me to stop and think was... ■ I am still unsure about... ■ I think this answer makes sense because...
Science	Observe changes and patterns; Notice similarities and differences; Question what has happened, is happening, or will happen; Wonder about the next steps for action	As students analyze interactive graphs, models, or diagrams, it is helpful to provide time for them to observe and notice before asking them to question and wonder. Use Say Something stems to encourage students to observe and notice. Some ideas include: ■ When looking at this part of the model, I noticed… ■ Did anyone else notice that… ■ When reading the labels on the diagram, I noticed...
Social Studies	Collaborate with peers; Corroborate sources; Critique point of view; Analyze bias	When considering a short, summarized account of a historical or current event, students can form pairs, read aloud to each other, and stop to discuss Say Somethings at particular points you noted in the text. ■ This event reminds me of… ■ I would not have made that decision because… ■ I wonder if the author has a bias about...

Example: Say Something Stems for General Comprehension of Texts

Name: ______________________________ Date: __________

Make a Connection	■ This reminds me of… ■ This situation makes me think of… ■ This character is just like...
Make a Comment	■ This is confusing because… ■ I think that… ■ This is hard because… ■ I like the part where...
Ask a Question	■ Why did … ■ I don't understand… ■ I'm confused about… ■ What if… ■ I am wondering if… ■ What is this section telling us?
Clarify Something You Did Not Understand	■ This makes sense now because… ■ This part seems to be saying… ■ At first I thought… ■ Now I am thinking… ■ This could mean...
Make a Prediction	■ What might happen is… ■ I am assuming that… ■ The last time I heard this, I… ■ Reading this part makes me think this will happen next...
Identify Arguments	■ It is also important to think about… ■ One side of the argument seems to be… ■ I hear this side of the argument… ■ Others may think... ■ This word makes me think...

Example: Say Something Stems for Texts in the Disciplines

Name: ______________________________ Date: __________

Disciplinary Focus	Say Something Stems
ELA	Maybe this character did this because… The character seems to realize that… I understand the character's actions because...
Math	If I put this in my own words, I would say… This part of the process is hard for me because… If I said this equation out loud, I would say…
Science	These words slowed me down because... Could this mean… I think this evidence suggests… The impact of this on our world could be…
Social Studies	It is also important to think about… The author seems to believe that… I feel differently because… This text shares the experiences of...but not...
Metacognition	I started to think about… In my experience… I need to reread this part because… These words made me slow down because...

Frayer Model and Math Rule of Four

Description

The Frayer Model (Frayer, Frederick, & Klausmeier, 1969; Manderino, Berglund, & Johns, 2014) is a categorization activity that helps students develop a thorough understanding of important concepts. It also provides a visual organizer to distinguish ideas that help define the concept from those that are merely associated with it. In fact, providing a definition is not "adequate for vocabulary attainment," and instead students need to be exposed to examples and nonexamples, as well as concrete, visual, and verbal representations and applications (Archer & Hughes, 2011, p. 70), which can be accomplished using the Frayer Model.

This strategy is especially critical to disciplinary learning. In order to build disciplinary knowledge, students need to be able to develop deep conceptual understandings of discipline-specific, complex concepts and vocabulary. For mathematical disciplines, the Frayer Model can also be used to support the Math Rule of Four, which encourages a graphical, numeric, textual (written or spoken), and symbolic representation of equations, concepts, and operations (Huntley, Marcus, Kahan, & Miller, 2007).

When and Why Would I Use This Strategy?

- To clarify students' understanding of words and concepts that are easily confused with others, those that are somewhat abstract, and those that are valuable to anchor a lesson or unit or discipline-specific understanding
- To develop a thorough understanding of vocabulary and concepts
- To demonstrate a variety of ways that information can be represented and communicated

How Do I Teach/Present the Strategy?

1. Select a key word or concept from the lesson, for example, Ecosystem. For a math problem that is conceptual, an example might involve a cell phone data plan. Determine the headings in each of the squares. When using the traditional Frayer Model, your headings could include Essential Characteristics, Nonessential Characteristics, Examples, and Nonexamples. When using the Math Rule of Four, the headings could include Graphical Representation, Numeric Representation, Textual Representation, and Symbolic Representation. See pages 43–47 for examples and templates.

2. Generate a list of key characteristics about the concept. Key characteristics for Ecosystem might include relationships, interactions, surroundings, living things, and non-living things. For math, generate a list of what each representation could look like. For example, Textual Representation could be an explanation of the process or a close, annotated reading of the original word problem about cell phone plans.
3. Introduce the concept (e.g., Ecosystem) to students and show them your list of key characteristics. For math, introduce the problem to be solved (e.g., which phone plan is a better deal) and explain what students should develop for each of the representations. Provide students access to the necessary template and example, which can be found in Resources on pages 43–47.
4. In small, cooperative groups, students can complete the boxes in the organizer. If the focus is on the concept of Ecosystems, students can fill in *forests, cities, deserts,* and *oceans* in the Examples box. Students may write glaciers, insects, buildings, and birds in the Nonessential Characteristics section. Students can then put concepts and ideas like automobiles, solutions, and electricity in Nonexamples. An example follows.

Example Frayer Model for **Science**

Examples	**Essential Characteristics**
Forests *Cities* *Deserts* *Oceans*	*Water cycle* *Climate* *Flora and fauna* *Community*
Nonexamples	**Nonessential Characteristics**
Automobiles *Electricity*	*Glaciers* *Insects* *Buildings* *Birds*

ECOSYSTEMS

5. If students are struggling to understand how to accomplish one of the four representations in math, it may help to provide more examples. Another idea is for you to develop two of the four representations and ask that students develop the other two. You could provide the word problem and a graph that visually compares the three phone plans while they develop the equations to solve as well as a table of plotted points.

Example Math Rule of Four

Words

There is a relationship between the input of 1 to 10 as is seen in the five points.

Equation

$y = 10x$

TOPIC/ CONCEPT

Table of Plotted Points

Input (x)	Output (y)
0	0
1	10
2	20
3	30
4	40

Graph it on the Number Line

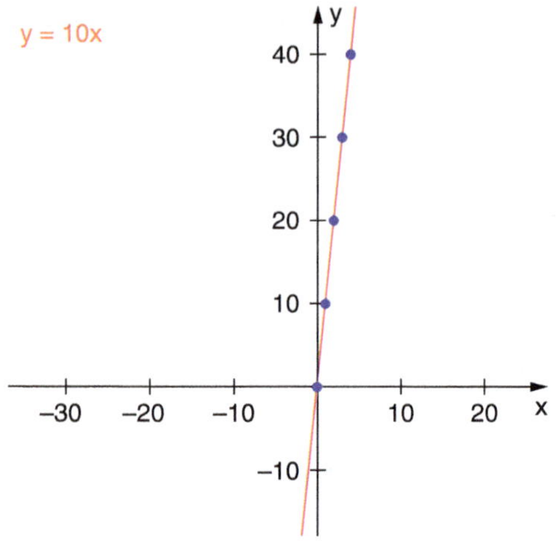

6. Encourage students to add, change, and modify their responses as they continue reading, discussing, and researching the concept. In fact, some responses may need to be moved into a different category on the Frayer Model as they learn more. For Math Rule of Four, emphasize to students that you welcome and appreciate different ways of solving and representing. Encourage students to explain their thinking.
7. After gaining an in-depth understanding of the concept, word, or equation/problem have students compare and contrast their ideas, generate a retelling or a description of the concept or key word, or use the organizer when studying for an assessment or when demonstrating their knowledge on an assessment. An example is shown above.

Disciplinary Focus	Behaviors Targeted by the Discipline	Examples in Context
ELA	Working with words often found in complex texts; Recognize denotation and connotation; Understand synonyms and antonyms; Use words in context	Consider using the *Academic Word List* (Coxhead, 2000) as it offers high-utility, tier-two (Beck, McKeown, & Kucan, 2013) words that students need to understand deeply in order to succeed in English language arts. Consider labeling the four boxes using these headings: ■ What it Is/Definition ■ What it Is Not/Antonyms ■ Alternate Contexts for Use ■ Drawing and Sentence The drawing should represent the meaning of the word and the sentence should use the word correctly and explain the meaning of the drawing.
Math	Recognize and work with multiple representations; Use and develop SAT vocabulary	If using the Frayer Model, consider using some math vocabulary found in the SAT (SAT, 2016) when choosing what words to teach. The squares on the organizer can be labeled with the following: ■ Definition ■ Picture ■ Example ■ Other Vocabulary or Additional Meanings (other than math) However, when applicable, work with students through the Rule of Four especially when working with functions and linear equations. Some ideas are shown in Resources on pages 46–47.
Science	Determine key characteristics; Notice nuances in scientific terms; Categorize; Compare and contrast	When students have gained some familiarity with a concept like Ecosystems, it might be helpful to have students work through the strategy using the topics of: ■ Essential Characteristics ■ Nonessential Characteristics ■ Diagram of Process ■ Examples In this case, you would need to provide a bank of words or some resources for students to draw from.

Disciplinary Focus	Behaviors Targeted by the Discipline	Examples in Context
Social Studies	Interpret a visual; Compare and contrast; Construct a retelling; Cause and effect; Determine key elements and figures	The Four Square/Frayer Model strategy can be used when students are analyzing a key historical concept or event. Possible topics for the squares can include: ■ Key Figures ■ Documents ■ Places ■ Events Another idea is to complete the model *for* students using terms and vocabulary that students will need to know for the unit. Then challenge students to use the terms to render a retelling of an event or to determine cause and effect. Topics for the squares can include: ■ Key Figures ■ Actions ■ Results ■ Changes and Developments

Template for General Frayer Model

Name: ______________________________ Date: ____________

Essential Characteristics	Nonessential Characteristics
Examples	**Nonexamples**

A word that means about the same as the key term is ______________________.

A word that is more general than the key term is ______________________.

A word that is more specific than the key term is ______________________.

Example Frayer Model in Biology

PROTIST

Essential Characteristics	Nonessential Characteristics
Have organized nuclei *Flagella or cilia* *Unicellular* *Microscopic* *Live in water or damp places*	*Contain chlorophyll* *Sexual* *Asexual* *Capture food*
Examples	**Nonexamples**
Euglena *Diatoms* *Protozoa* *Slime molds* *Paramecia*	*Animals* *Fungi* *Plants* *Monerans*

A word that means about the same as protist is *protista*.

A word that is more general than protist is *organism*.

A word that is more specific than protist is *protozoa*.

Example Frayer Model Template in Math

INTEGER

Essential Characteristics	Nonessential Characteristics
Natural elements, their opposites, and zero *Is a number* *Has no fraction part* *Has no decimal part*	*The "+" sign* *May be positive* *May be negative* *May be zero*
Examples	**Nonexamples**
5 100 –73 2 0 325	$\frac{-15}{2}$ 1.25 0.5 $\sqrt{2}$

A word that means about the same as integer is *number*.

A word that is more general than integer is *rational number*.

A word that is more specific than integer is *whole number*.

Template for ELA Vocabulary Frayer Model

Name: ______________________________ Date: ____________

<table>
<tr><td colspan="2" rowspan="1">Definitions</td><td rowspan="3">Synonyms (same meaning)/What it is like</td></tr>
<tr><td>Dictionary</td><td>Teacher/Class Notes</td></tr>
<tr><td>Connotations</td><td>Denotations</td></tr>
<tr><td colspan="3">WORD + Forms/Prefixes/Suffixes/Part of Speech</td></tr>
<tr><td colspan="2">Picture</td><td>Antonym (opposite meaning)/
What it is not like</td></tr>
<tr><td colspan="2"></td><td></td></tr>
<tr><td colspan="3">Sentence Describe the picture above. Use the word in the sentence.</td></tr>
<tr><td colspan="3"></td></tr>
</table>

Template One for Math Rule of Four

Name: ______________________________ Date: ____________

Algebraically

1. Write the function in...
   a. slope-intercept form
   b. point-slope form

2. What is the equation of the inverse of the function?

Numerically

x	y
–4	–6
0	2
2	6

1. Add two more ordered pairs to the table above.

Verbally

1. Is the function increasing at a constant rate? Explain. If yes, what is that rate?

2. What is another name for the value you found above?

Graphically

1. Graph the function and find each of the following:

   x-intercept(s): ____________

   y-intercept(s): ____________

   Domain: ____________

   Range: ____________

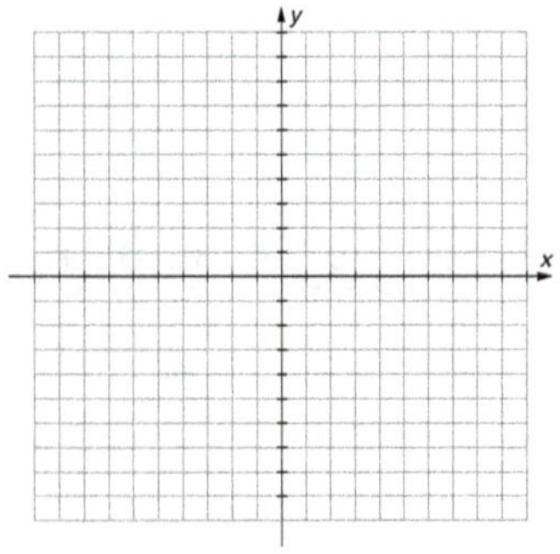

Template Two for Math Rule of Four

Name: ______________________ Date: __________

One-Variable Inequalities What does your variable represent?	
Words	Inequality
Numbers that are Solutions	Graph it on the Number Line

Template Three for Math Rule of Four

Name: ______________________ Date: __________

Given the equation for a linear function, graph the function using the y-intercept and slope.	
Algebraic Representation: Solve this equation or inequality.	Numerical Representation: Create a Table/ Data Set.
Textual/Verbal Representation: Explain the steps of how you solved the equation.	Graphical Representation: Graph the equation on a coordinate plane.

List-Group-Label and Semantic Mapping

Description

List-Group-Label, also known as Semantic Mapping when represented in graphic organizer form (Heimlich & Pittelman, 1986; Johnson & Pearson, 1984; Pearson & Johnson, 1978; Taba, 1967), is a powerful strategy that provides students an understanding of how words relate to other words and then to larger concepts and categories. Through the organization and categorization processes, students become active in their learning, enhancing their ability to remember new vocabulary and information. Students do need to know the definitions of the words on the list. However, if using this strategy early in a unit, you can provide definitions and students can go back later in the lesson or unit to rearrange their groups and labels based on new realizations or information.

The initial step is to create a list of words within a major concept or topic. Students can create their own lists by previewing a text or researching a topic or concept and writing down all of the relevant vocabulary. Or, students can brainstorm all of the vocabulary that they have been using for the unit and you can fill in the missing words. Naturally, you can also create the list.

When and Why Would I Use This Strategy?

- To solidify prior knowledge
- To connect new learning to previous learning to prepare students for higher-level thinking processes
- To categorize and communicate information in multiple ways
- To provide students with a discipline-specific focus for understanding information

How Do I Teach/Present the Strategy?

1. Determine the Essential Question for your unit and determine which concepts will be featured in the word list.
2. Ask students to generate a list from the text(s) or from the learning they have already engaged in. Alternatively, you can generate the list.
3. Try to keep the list to approximately 20-25 words. See page 52 for an example.
4. When the words have been listed, read them aloud and provide definitions or make sure that students know the meanings of the words.
5. Ask students to cluster the terms into smaller groups based on shared relationships or characteristics. This can be done in list form or in graphic form. See List-Group-Label template on page 51 and a Semantic Mapping template on page 54.

6. Ask students to label their word groupings or clusters, or provide them with titles to indicate what the terms have in common. You may wish to have students complete this step in small cooperative groups. It is often possible for some of the words on the list to become category headings.
7. Have students share their reasoning for the groupings and the category labels. This step is just as important as the grouping process itself.
8. Students can then write a summary of the information or respond to the Essential Question.

Disciplinary Focus	Behaviors Targeted by the Discipline	Examples in Context
ELA	Analyze theme; Develop thesis; Analyze character; Compare fiction and nonfiction	When students are reading historical fiction, it may be beneficial to also share a nonfiction account of the situation. Then, create a word list that encourages students to be specific when communicating the argument or author's craft. Essential Questions include: ▪ What are the discrepancies between the fiction and the nonfiction account of a similar event? ▪ How does the author develop their argument? For fiction texts, Essential Questions include: ▪ What motivated this character to act the way they did? ▪ How does the setting contribute to mood?
Math	Determine lacking information; Ask questions; Build specialized vocabulary	As students learn more and more vocabulary in a given unit, take time to solidify their learning. Generate a list of terms and ask students to group the terms and develop labels based on essential questions: ▪ What are the characteristics to identify a geometric shape? ▪ In what ways can these processes be used? ▪ What data-based vocabulary can be used to summarize this process? ▪ Which of these categories are central to the explanation of a certain concept or process?

Disciplinary Focus	Behaviors Targeted by the Discipline	Examples in Context
Science	Develop an argument; Classify and categorize information; Analyze the parts of a whole; Build specialized vocabulary	As students are learning major concepts in science, they can act like scientists by categorizing and classifying information through this strategy. You may choose to have students categorize the properties of elements, systems of the body, natural phenomenon, or electrical forces, fields, and circuits. Some essential questions may include: ■ Why is the nervous system the most valuable system of the body? ■ Which groups of minerals are most beneficial? ■ In what ways have electrical forces, fields, and circuits changed society?
Social Studies	Focus on a claim and organize evidence; Develop an argument; Build specialized vocabulary	As students are reading a variety of documents to better understand a historical event, they can begin to analyze, synthesize and/or describe some components of each or some of the arguments presented. Possible Essential Questions could include: ■ What seems to have the strongest impact on the longevity of a civilization? ■ What was the most influential cause for a specific historic event? ■ In what ways does the government benefit our lives? ■ How does author bias and point of view change our perception of this event?

Template for General List-Group-Label

Name: ______________________________ Date: ____________

____
(topic)

1. Brainstorm a list of words related to the topic given to you by your teacher. Write the topic on the line above and list the words that are related to it in the space below.

2. Now consider how some of the words listed above might be related. Think of ways they might be grouped together by their meanings. Write the title of the categories or headings on each line below. (You may have a greater or lesser number of words and groupings than the number of lines below.) Then list the words under the appropriate headings. Use the back of this paper for additional words and clusters if you need it.

______________________ (cluster heading)	______________________ (cluster heading)
1. ____________________	1. ____________________
2. ____________________	2. ____________________
3. ____________________	3. ____________________
4. ____________________	4. ____________________
5. ____________________	5. ____________________

______________________ (cluster heading)	______________________ (cluster heading)
1. ____________________	1. ____________________
2. ____________________	2. ____________________
3. ____________________	3. ____________________
4. ____________________	4. ____________________
5. ____________________	5. ____________________

Example List-Group-Label for ELA

Name: *Milo* Date: ______

Essential Questions: How does the setting contribute to the mood?

Word Bank: Below is a bank of mood words. Group them into categories with a setting as a label. Try for at least three setting categories and four words per category. Be prepared to explain your reasoning.

cheerful	lighthearted
reflective	hopeful
gloomy	melancholy
humorous	idyllic
tense	whimsical
mysterious	romantic
ominous	angry
calm	fearful

Setting Category 1: *The House*	Setting Category 2: *The Pond*	Setting Category 3: *The School*
cheerful	*reflective*	*gloomy*
humorous	*idyllic*	*ominous*
hopeful	*calm*	*tense*
lighthearted	*romantic*	*mysterious*

Example List-Group-Label for Science

Name: *Olivia* Date: ____________

Nervous System
(topic)

1. Brainstorm a list of words related to the topic given to you by your teacher. Write the topic on the line above and list the words that are related to it in the space below.

brain	*brain stem*	*autonomic*
somatic	*sympathetic*	*reflexes*
cerebellum	*spinal cord*	*parasympathetic*
cerebrum	*meninges*	*nerves*

2. Now consider how some of the words listed above might be related. Think of ways they might be grouped together by their meanings. Write the title of the categories or headings on each line below. (You may have a greater or lesser number of words and groupings than the number of lines below.) Then list the words under the appropriate headings. Use the back of this paper for additional words and clusters if you need it.

Central Nervous System (cluster heading)	*Peripheral Nervous System* (cluster heading)
1. *brain*	1. *autonomic*
2. *spinal cord*	2. *somatic*
3. *cerebellum*	3. *sympathetic*
4. *cerebrum*	4. *parasympathetic*
5. *brain stem*	5. *reflexes*
6. *meninges*	6. *nerves*

Template for General Semantic Map

Name: ____ Date: ____________

____
(topic)

Directions: Think of ways the ideas from your lesson might be clustered together. Below is one way you might begin to cluster them into categories. You may add to the map below or create a map of your own on the back of this page.

Summary:

Example Semantic Map for Science

Name: *Vivian* Date: ____________

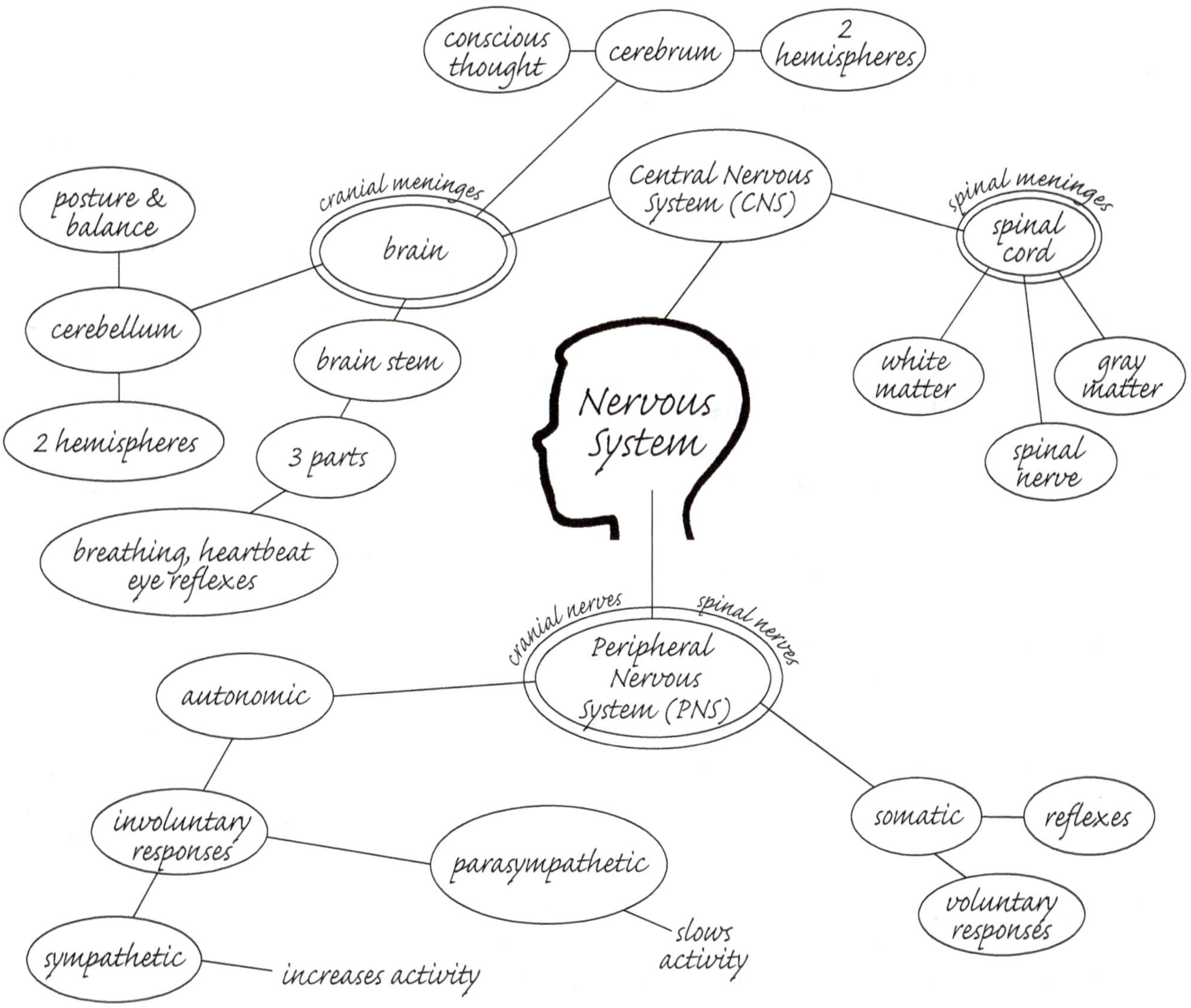

Summary: *The brain is one part of the central nervous system. Surrounded by cranial meninges, the brain has three parts: the cerebellum, the cerebrum, and the brain stem. The cerebellum has two hemispheres and controls posture and balance. The cerebrum has two hemispheres and controls conscious thought. The brain stem has three parts and controls breathing, heartbeat, and eye reflexes.*

Scenario Writing

Description

Scenario Writing is a vocabulary strategy that encourages students to understand words in context and to recognize that different forms of words within the same word family can take on different meanings. Students often begin to struggle with discipline-specific text comprehension when familiar words are used in unfamiliar ways (Schoenbach, Greenleaf, & Murphy, 2012). Students need practice in recognizing situations when words do not make sense in a particular context, and this strategy allows you to provide such opportunities.

Prior to using this strategy, take some time to look over the vocabulary for a unit in order to determine which words might be confusing for students in a discipline-specific context. Consider words such as *food, carbohydrate, protein, and fat.* These are words that students may be familiar with but not have a true grasp of when faced with a unit on digestion. Similarly, in an English language arts classroom, students may be familiar with the term *justice,* but they may not understand when a character tries to *justify* their actions (Schoenbach, Greenleaf, & Murphy, 2012).

When and Why Would I Use This Strategy?

- To eradicate students' misconceptions
- To clarify the meaning of words in discipline-specific contexts
- To use context to support students' in applying words
- To explore words and language to add to students' lexicon

How Do I Teach/Present the Strategy?

1. Determine words that students need to know that will be useful in comprehending a text, discussing a situation, or for other discipline-specific purposes (e.g., writing a lab report). See pages 59–61 for examples and templates of the different ways this strategy can be used.
2. Define the terms in the word bank, if necessary, so that students are able to practice using the words correctly. This will enable them to learn more about the words rather than be confused by them.
3. Decide whether you or the students will create the scenarios based on the goals of the lesson. An example of a teacher-created science scenario and a student-written ELA scenario can be found on page 61.
4. You and the students can work together to construct a few scenarios so that you can model how the strategy is used. In addition, it might be important to practice the strategy using words that are not related to the lesson, but rather words that will gain student interest and allow them to practice the strategy.

5. Students can also develop scenarios with a partner and share their scenarios with other teams.
6. It might be helpful to encourage students to talk to each other using the words identified for the strategy. You can then gently correct any misuse of the words by saying the words aloud back to the student in the correct form and context.
7. The goal of this strategy is for students to have the opportunity to play with words and language, to further develop their lexicon, to understand words in context, to develop content knowledge, and to create personal connections with words and content.

Disciplinary Focus	Behaviors Targeted by the Discipline	Examples in Context
ELA	Understand words in context; Recognize denotation and connotation; Evaluate the ways that different word forms take on different meanings	In order to encourage diverse vocabulary when discussing and writing about a text, it is valuable to present students with opportunities to play with language and enjoy working with words that they can then use with a text. See page 61 for ELA examples that showcase the language students can use when discussing characters in a novel.
Math	Understand math in context; Use math vocabulary; Explain and solve; Define characteristics; Establish logical process	Consider the language that students need to solve word problems accurately and to explain their processes. Provide students with the preselected terms and ask them to develop a word problem scenario using the vocabulary. For example, division words may include: per, a, out of, ratio of, quotient of, percent (divide by 100), equal pieces, split, average
Science	Attend to and reduce misconceptions; Differentiate between how words are used in the discipline and common use	In this discipline more than others, discipline-specific words take on different meanings in everyday speech. In fact, science words are often used incorrectly in common language. Therefore, side-by-side scenarios using the same words in context is helpful. Words such as *mass* and *weight*, or other words that confuse students, are important in this strategy. In one scenario, the words can be used in a science-specific context, and in the other, the word can be used in a commonly used context. Students can analyze and discuss how the word is used differently and how the meaning changes based on the context and the discipline.

Disciplinary Focus	Behaviors Targeted by the Discipline	Examples in Context
Social Studies	Develop argument; Recognize point of view; Use discipline-specific vocabulary in context	When using this strategy in social studies, you can ask students to develop a scenario that portrays what might have happened if one event had changed during a historical moment. Alternatively, students can reconstruct a scenario from various points of view. Students should have access to a word bank, and possibly definitions, to ensure that they are using the words correctly. Some words can be easily confused. One example of this would be the concept seceded, which can easily be misread as succeeded. Therefore, you should consider reading the word aloud and providing a clear definition so that students do not form a misunderstanding and use words incorrectly in their writing.

Template for Scenario Writing in ELA

Name: ______________________________ Date: ____________

Find an image and create a scenario using the words in the word bank.
Word Bank:
INSERT IMAGE HERE
Type Scenario Here: ______________________________ ______________________________ ______________________________ ______________________________ ______________________________

Template for Scenario Writing for Science

Name: ______________________ Date: __________

Scenario One: Common Use	Compare and Contrast Explanation	Scenario Two: Scientifically Accurate Usage

Example of Scenario Writing for Science

Name: *Dan* Date: __________

Scenario One: Common Use	Compare and Contrast Student Explanation	Scenario Two: Scientifically Accurate Usage
I have this theory that my parents only make me stay home on weekends when they have nothing to do. I must be their only entertainment. It is totally my amazing idea, and I can prove it by telling you all about what we do when my parents make me stay home.	*In the common-use scenario, "theory" is used to show an idea that someone has. However, in the accurate scenario, "theory" is used to show an idea that has been tested by many people under scientific laws and rules of experimentation. The definition of "proof" seems to be different as well. In the common-use scenario, the word "prove" seems to indicate reasoning or some kind of evidence. But in the accurate scenario, proof seems elusive. It seems like "proven" means that support for the theory may change depending on the data or the argument.*	*After experimenting and observing using the same controls as Scientist Amazing, I also suggest the theory that global warming is occurring because of a specific set of factors. While most things cannot be proven, this model will help demonstrate why it is a supported and viable theory.*

Example for Scenario Writing for ELA

Name: ______________________ Date: __________

You put your popcorn bag into the microwave and accidentally hit an extra zero. The popcorn catches fire because you cooked it for 30 minutes instead of three minutes. The popcorn fire burns your most prized possession.
Choose one word defined below and explain. Would you: A. feel *animosity* towards the popcorn? (strong dislike) B. *abhor* the popcorn? (deep hatred) C. feel *virulent* towards the popcorn and want revenge? (spite) D. remain *amicable* toward the popcorn? (forgiving and peaceful)
I would feel ______________ toward the popcorn because

Example of Scenario Writing for ELA

Name: Paul Date: __________

Find an image and create a scenario using the words in the word bank. These words will prepare you to read and discuss the chapter from The Girl Who Fell from the Sky.
Word Bank: benevolent feasible adversary malevolent fortitude
INSERT IMAGE HERE
Type Scenario Here: In Rachel's situation, there are benevolent people who try to help her. One person is Drew, who helps Rachel escape and deal with her malevolent past. However, in the situation with Anthony Miller, things are different. What advice would you give Rachel? Should she push through her experiences with Anthony Miller with fortitude even though he is an adversary? If she talks to someone about what has happened, she may stop it from happening again. It is definitely feasible that it could happen again to someone else.

Select Three and Reflect (STAR)

Description

Select Three and Reflect (STAR) is a strategy (Hoyt, 2009; Johns & Berglund, 2011; Manderino, Berglund, & Johns, 2014) that encourages students to develop a personal relationship with vocabulary in a text. This strategy gives students the freedom of self-assessing their prior knowledge and choosing the vocabulary words that will make the lesson meaningful to them.

After choosing three words from the text, ask students to write an explanation for their choices, which will bring a metacognitive, reflective element to their learning. You can also establish additional parameters depending on the needs of the students and the goals of the lesson. For example, you can ask students to focus their word choices on a particular topic or category.

This strategy is a great way to formatively assess students' prior knowledge of a topic and the extent of their vocabulary knowledge. In addition, students can self-assess their own comfort with the topic and with discipline-specific vocabulary. If students are struggling to share academic choices and explanations of choices, this strategy is a low-risk, manageable approach to encourage collaborative discourse using academic vocabulary.

When and Why Would I Use This Strategy?

- To assess, formatively, students' prior knowledge
- To encourage students to self-assess
- To support use of discipline-specific vocabulary
- To provide students with choices
- To develop vocabulary knowledge

How Do I Teach/Present the Strategy?

1. Once you have selected a text, determine if you will use the STAR strategy before reading, in order to preview the text; during reading, in order to encourage close reading around an established purpose; or after reading, to support a retelling or metacognitive reflection.
2. Ask students to review a selection or passage.
3. Ask students to identify three words or phrases from the reading that relate to the prompt or to the purpose for the lesson. When using this strategy during or after reading, students may need to reread the passage or parts of the passage.

4. If the prompt is more open-ended, discuss with students the wide variety of reasons why we might choose particular words. Explain that sometimes words elicit a personal connection or remind us of another topic we have learned. Other times, they are words that we recognize and want to learn more about or words that are confusing and need clarification in order to understand them.
5. After students have chosen their words and phrases, instruct them to complete the bottom half of the organizer to explain their reasoning. See page 65 for a blank template of the organizer. Examples for ELA and math are on pages 66–67.
6. If the prompt is more specific, you may guide students to write about why and how they feel the words they have chosen respond to the prompt of the lesson.
7. Encourage a diverse interpretation of the prompt, as this strategy is intended to promote choice, personal connections, and vocabulary awareness. To accomplish this, encourage and reinforce both the variety of words chosen and the students' reasons for choosing them.

Disciplinary Focus	Behaviors Targeted by the Discipline	Examples in Context
ELA	Recognize nuances in language; Consider diction when writing; Understand characters' motivations	During Reading: When students are analyzing an exemplar essay, ask them to identify transition words and explain the purpose. During and After Reading: When tracking a character's development, students can identify the words used to describe the character.
Math	Analyze a scenario or word problem; Develop an understanding of key factors of a concept; Use language for accurate explanation	Before and During Reading: Ask students to break down the language of a word problem. See Resource on page 67 for an example. After Reading: Students can break down the concepts they will need in order to solve a problem. Students can also identify language associated with a given concept. Before Reading: Another idea is to provide students with a list of words they can use to accurately explain a process. Students can identify three of the words from the list and then develop an explanation using the chosen words.

Disciplinary Focus	Behaviors Targeted by the Discipline	Examples in Context
Science	Analyze bias; Develop an understanding of key factors of a concept; Identify text structures based on transition words; Use language to develop an accurate explanation or to label a model	During Reading: Science texts often rely on certain informational structures (Shanahan, Fisher, & Frey, 2012) such as cause and effect, causation, order and sequence, enumeration, and generalization, to name a few. Students can use STAR to identify transition words and phrases and then identify the text structure. If students are better able to recognize and identify key transition words, they will be better able to identify text structures and thus have a stronger grasp of complex science texts.
Social Studies	Recognize difficult vocabulary in a primary source; Rewrite a historical event; Explain the relationships among words and concepts; Develop point of view; Recognize author's point of view	Before Reading: When given a primary source document, students can first scan the document and identify three words that seem difficult. After learning the meaning of the words, students can write a prediction of the author's bias, point of view, or claim. During Reading: Students can also be asked to identify words that support an argument or oppose an argument. After Reading: Students can look back to determine if their findings and predictions were accurate.

Template for Select Three and Reflect (STAR)

Name: ______________________________ Date: __________

Directions: Choose three words from the selection and explain why you chose them. You can also explain how they relate to your reading or your life.

Title: ____

Word 1	Word 2	Word 3

Why Words Were Chosen

____

____

____

____

____

____

____

____

____

Example Select Three and Reflect (STAR) for ELA

Name: *Georgia* Date: ________

Directions: Choose three words from the selection and explain why you chose them. You can also explain how they relate to your reading or your life.

Title: *The Poet X by Elizabeth Acevado*

Word 1	Word 2	Word 3
peaceful	*power*	*understand*

Why Words Were Chosen

Xiomara is trying to find peace within herself. She has so much strength and power, but does not know how to use it to make herself what she wants to become. She is hoping and looking for someone to understand her, but first she must understand herself and her own power to find peace.

Example Select Three and Reflect (STAR) for Math

Name: ______________________________ Date: ____________

Directions: Choose three words from the selection and explain why you chose them in relation to the prompt provided.
Prompt: Prior to responding to the following questions in class discussion, consider the vocabulary within each.
If a limit is a finite y-value, how is it possible for a function to have a limit at infinity if x will never actually reach infinity? Explain the differences in closure among the intervals of continuity that meet at the different types of discontinuities. Use the concept of continuity to explain how the IVT can be used to guarantee that an equation has a solution.

Word One	**Word Two**	**Word Three**

Why Words Were Chosen:

Vocabulary Continuum

Description

Language and vocabulary acquisition and development are not linear, scaffolded processes. Rather, they are dynamic and flexible (IRA/NCTE, 2010). The Vocabulary Continuum strategy, also termed Linear Array (Johns, Lenski, & Berglund, 2006), encourages students to engage with language, concepts, and vocabulary in dynamic and flexible ways. Throughout this strategy, students must explain their reasoning, categorize, compare and contrast, and make personal connections (Marzano, Pickering, & Pollock, 2001). The success of the strategy really hinges on ensuring that the words and concepts chosen are interesting to students and have a purpose outside of a single lesson.

Students will have access to a list of words within a certain category or under a certain topic heading. When needed, the students can also access the definitions. Within collaborative groupings, students will strive to place each word at a different place on a continuum.

Depending on the purpose of the lesson, the ends of the continuum can be labeled in a variety of ways including: *most impactful* to *least impactful; most valuable* to *least valuable; most specific* to *least specific;* and *most intense* to *least intense.* Students will then defend their choices and a larger discussion can ensue about when and how to use such terms in context.

When and Why Would I Use This Strategy?

- To develop vocabulary so that students can understand content, discuss a topic, or articulate their ideas
- To fill in word gaps and develop students' understand of concepts
- To work on decision making and grouping skills

How Do I Teach/Present the Strategy?

1. To prepare to use the strategy, you must first determine the language that students will need in order to learn and engage fully in a particular unit or lesson. Then, develop a list of words within a singular category. In the student example on page 72, the teacher generates a list of verbs that authors use when conveying their ideas in a text. A blank template can be found on page 71.
2. Some situations may require that students engage with words prior to the lesson so that they become familiar with the definitions. However, in other situations, you may want to provide definitions to eliminate the potential for students to solidify misunderstandings. See the student example on page 72.

3. Once you have created a word bank, you can determine what you want to label each of the ends of the continuum. The labels should be broad enough to celebrate and encourage students' personal interpretations while still supporting the goals of the lesson. In the student example found on page 72, the teacher chose three labels: *Least Opinionated, More Opinionated,* and *Most Opinionated.* The goal of this lesson was for students to recognize author bias.
4. To begin the strategy with the students, place them in pairs or collaborative groupings. Students should have the opportunity to collaborate in order to determine where the words should be placed on the continuum. Encourage students to develop an explanation and remind them that their group will need to share and defend their choices with the class at some point during the lesson.
5. In some cases, there may not be a correct answer and you may want to have students explain their choices based on their personal connections to words, on the way they have seen the word used in context, or on the conclusions they made after some additional work on Dictionary.com.
6. In other cases, students may have determined a response based on word connotations or discipline-specific uses. Because there is a broad range of possibilities, it is important that you are specific with students about what you are looking for. It might help if you model your decision-making processes and define your expectations.
7. After students use the vocabulary continuum, you should then familiarize them with the words in context and ask them to reflect back on their continuum.

Disciplinary Focus	Behaviors Targeted by the Discipline	Examples in Context
ELA	Assess bias; Write precisely; Label mood and tone; Attend to imagery; Understand character motivation; Attend to detail	When describing an author's argument in nonfiction or discussing a character's motivation in fiction, students need to develop specific language. Therefore, before asking students to describe or discuss, consider using the vocabulary continuum. You can provide students with "jealousy" words or "anger" words. The continuum can be labeled from *Admiration* to *Resentful* or from *Peaceful* to *Enraged.* Draw students' attention to the value of specificity when explaining and describing.
Math	Write precisely; Categorize; Seek patterns; Group similar concepts; Develop predictions; Consider prefixes and suffixes	A critical skill in the discipline of mathematics is the ability to be precise with language. Students can place unit vocabulary on a continuum that reflects their level of understanding, from *I understand everything about this word* to *I am still hesitant about my understanding of this word.* Mathematicians recognize that there are multiple approaches to solving any given problem. Students can leverage this strategy to determine which approach is the most efficient. Students can either work through multiple avenues to solve a problem or receive examples of varied approaches to analyze. You can then ask them to place each approach on a continuum from *Most Efficient* to *Least Efficient.*
Science	Assess bias; Analyze results; Attend to details; Recognize arguments; Critique processes and methods	When reading a text, students can place value on the content that is presented. They can gather a group of words or concepts from the text and place them on a continuum from *Most Important* to *Least Important* in terms of solutions presented, information shared, or environmental concerns impacting society.
Social Studies	Consider point of view; Assess bias; Sequence information; Determine cause and effect; Engage with discipline-specific language	The continuum can be used for students to better understand certain concepts. For example, if working with a prompt like, *What changes affected these peoples?,* students can be instructed to: *Place the following concepts on a continuum from Most Impactful to Least Impactful: population, technology, religion, transportation, environment, economic, and political.* In addition, to draw students' attention to bias, argument, and/or conflict, encourage them to use this strategy to place words along a continuum from *This author is trying to deceive me* to *This approach is attempting to be objective*, to name one example.

Template for General Vocabulary Continuum

Name: ______________________________ Date: __________

Continuum Organizer: Work with your group to place each word in a category from *Least Opinionated* to *Most Opinionated.* Provide your reasoning. **Word Bank:**

Words on Continuum	Reasoning for Placement
Label	
Label	
Label	

Example Vocabulary Continuum in ELA

Name: *Archer* Date: ____________

Using Words that Convey an Author's Ideas and Perspectives		
Continuum Organizer: Work with your group to place each word in a category from *Least Opinionated* to *Most Opinionated.* Provide your reasoning. Word Bank:		
Observe – to see, watch, or notice	Reveal – to make known, disclose or make obvious	Emphasize – to lay stress upon; to show importance
Claim – to maintain a fact; to demand; to assert and demand recognition	Criticize – to discuss pros and cons; to find fault	Express – to put a thought into words; to set forth opinions or feelings
Believe – to have confidence or faith in a truth or a stance	Discuss – to explore solutions; to debate; to consider fully	Assert – to state with confidence; to defend oneself

Words on Continuum	Reasoning for Placement
Least Opinionated/ Commentary	
observe	*This word does not seem emotional*
reveal	*People want you to know the truth but not in a judgy way, like when an author reveals something about a character*
suggest	*A suggestion is just an idea unless the person keeps saying it a lot and it gets pushy*
More Opinionated/ Stronger Push	
express	*This word sounds like it would be someone venting about how they feel*
emphasize	*It seems like the person would not let an idea go, and they would keep making it obvious*
Most Opinionated/ Strongly taking a Stand	
believe	*When people have beliefs, they are usually strong because they are a part of your identity*
assert	*It would feel like someone wanted me to change my mind*

Word Sorts

Description

A Word Sort (Manderino, Berglund, & Johns, 2014; Templeton, Johnston, Bear, & Invernizzi, 2010) is an activity that engages students in classifying words into categories that make sense to them. The strategy is derived from Taba's (1967) List-Group-Label strategy (also in this text on page 48) and is based on the concept that placing words into categories helps students organize and remember vocabulary and concepts. There are two types of Word Sorts, Closed and Open, and both involve classifying words into categories.

A Closed Word Sort, which is usually easier, involves moving words into predetermined categories that students receive at the outset. In an Open Word Sort, students are invited to consider the characteristics and meanings of the words and then cluster them into categories that they determine. The same Word Sort can be used before and after reading to encourage reflection and metacognition.

Unlike with List-Group-Label, students do not need to know the words and sort them correctly (Daniels & Zemelman, 2004). This strategy, especially when used in conjunction with a text, primes students to encounter vocabulary and to notice if their predictions and categories make sense. Students are actively able to correct misconceptions and set a purpose for reading.

When and Why Would I Use This Strategy?

- To develop connections between concepts and information
- To support vocabulary development and application
- To demonstrate the value of vocabulary and word choice in meaning-making
- To encourage students to slow down and attend to vocabulary in the text

How Do I Teach/Present the Strategy?

1. Select 15-20 vocabulary words or concepts that are important for understanding a lesson or unit. Be sure to include some familiar words along with the new words that students will encounter. Decide if you will ask students to do a Closed Word Sort or an Open Word Sort. In a Closed Word Sort, the categories and words will be provided by you. In an Open Word Sort, you will provide the words, but students create their own categories while sorting the words. See Resources on pages 76–77 for templates.

2. Write the words and concepts on note cards or on sticky notes in a Jamboard. The strategy is much more effective if students are able to physically maneuver or drag and drop the cards into different groups or categories. Ensure that each small group has access to their own "deck" of cards, and provide students with a template for their Sort. See Resources on pages 76-77 for templates.
3. Create groups of three or four students, and give each group a set of the cards with the words on them.
4. Explain to students that they will be organizing the words and concepts into categories in order to increase their understanding of the ideas in the upcoming unit. Share with students that our brains have a natural desire to categorize and sort information, and thus, they will enjoy engaging in this activity because it makes learning more active and more natural.
5. If it is a Closed Word Sort, provide the categories students should use when grouping the words. If it is an Open Word Sort, ask students to read and discuss the words and then arrange them into groupings that make sense to them. Then, ask students to label their categories and provide reasoning.
6. Students will need about 10-15 minutes to complete the sort. If students take longer, monitor for signs of frustration and possibly provide more direction.
7. After they have completed their Sort, students can move around the room to see how other groups categorized their words.
8. Ask students to share their reasoning behind their groupings.
9. During or after the unit, you can ask students to return to their Word Sorts and reflect on their choices, making changes where they deem necessary based on new learning.

Disciplinary Focus	Behaviors Targeted by the Discipline	Examples in Context
ELA	Make inferences; Analyze and synthesize information; Generate an understanding of the meaning of prefixes and suffixes; Analyze literary devices	Students can attempt to categorize and define unknown words using prefixes, suffixes, and word patterns. They can also categorize figures of speech, examples of literary terms, parts of speech, and transition words. Alternatively, categories can be established pertaining to the parts of an essay or to compare and contrast character attributes across texts.
Math	Analyze characteristics of data; Analyze mathematical terminology; Develop vocabulary	Since math relies on progressive learning, students can tend to forget the differences among related concepts. For that reason, having students work with categories that are related, seemingly related, or often confused will support understanding. Some ideas include: ▪ equation, inequality, and problem solving ▪ factor, factoring, factor pairs, and factor tree ▪ least common multiple, least common denominator, and greatest common factor
Science	Apply prior knowledge; Recognize cause and effect relationships; Establish process and product relationships	In Earth science, have students sort names of rocks into categories based on how the rocks are formed and other defining characteristics and qualities.
Social Studies	Understand similarities and differences among concepts; Compare and contrast language and vocabulary	The concepts of social studies are vast and complex. This discipline has a lot of information; thus, using a sort can help students see the characteristics and non-characteristics of particular concepts. Sorts can include categories such as: ▪ geography, religion, politics, economics, and social structure ▪ social, political, economic ▪ isolationism, urbanization, industrialization

Template for a General Closed Word Sort

Name: ______________________________ Date: __________

Closed Word Sort: The categories have already been determined. Make sure to fill them in as your teacher instructs. Then, arrange each of the words and concepts into one of the categories provided based on their characteristics and meanings.
Topic:
Word Bank:

Category One:	Category Two:	Category Three:

Template for a General Open Word Sort

Name: ______________________________ Date: ____________

Open Word Sort: Arrange the words and concepts into groups based on their characteristics and meanings. It is your job to label the categories based on the reasons why you grouped the words together.			
Topic:			
Word Bank			
Category One:	**Category Two:**	**Category Three:**	**Category Four:**

Section 2

What the Text Means

Contents for Section 2

What the Text Means

Strategies

Reading text with a discipline-specific purpose can help students engage with the text, and the information found in the text, on a deeper level. The depth of understanding is critical so that students become aware of how members in the discipline create and communicate information. After working with single texts, students can then learn to synthesize what they have learned across multiple texts and form a complex understanding of a disciplinary idea. You can support this process by creating, adapting, or adopting literacy strategies that support a discipline-specific stance (Elish-Piper, L'Allier, Manderino, & Di Domenico, 2016).

Discipline-specific literacy instruction allows students to consume texts in a manner that invites them to think more deeply about what they are studying through inquiry, reflection, and critical thinking practices (Hamilton & Stowe, 2016). You can provide opportunities for students to engage in the respective habits of thinking in the disciplines through explicit instruction and through the use of strategies that foster the type of thinking valued in the disciplines (Di Domenico, 2016). Overall, the goal is to apprentice students into the disciplines so that they can contribute to the development and communication of knowledge in the post-secondary world.

As mentioned in Section One, this book will connect the structured activities, or strategies, we are sharing to the strategic behaviors that students will engage in. In this section of the book, our focus is on supporting student engagement with complex texts in order to develop a more nuanced, specific, disciplinary lens when working with information in the discipline.

In the chart on the next page, we have connected the strategy to the dominant strategic behavior that is developed, when the strategy is used in the ways suggested.

Strategic Behavior	Strategies that Support this Behavior
Synthesizing Ideas: Students synthesize information when they collect ideas from multiple sources and merge it with their own understanding (Keene & Zimmermann, 1997). Because students are asked to engage deeply with the ideas presented in the text, they are creating a new and deeper understanding of complex topics in the disciplines.	■ I-Chart page 89 ■ Intra-Act page 115 ■ Synthesis Journal page 122
Making Inferences: An inference is an educated conclusion that readers develop by building on information they have been gathering and moments they have experienced (Hall & Barnes, 2017). The ability to make inferences is at the heart of other critical thinking skills that are valued by multiple disciplines. This includes making and testing hypotheses, making and supporting claims, and crafting and testing conjectures. Being able to make accurate inferences is a foundational skill of learning in the disciplines.	■ Observation-Inference Chart page 81 ■ They Say, I Say, and So page 106

Observation-Inference Chart

Description

The Observation-Inference Chart (Manderino, Berglund, & Johns, 2014; Nokes, 2008) is an organizational scaffold for distinguishing between observations and corresponding inferences. In addition, it will enhance students' ability to use textual evidence to support an inference or to reveal an implicit meaning in the text.

While this strategy is intended mainly for nonprint texts (e.g., photographs, cartoons, videos, or lab demonstrations), it can be applied to print texts as well. Just like nonprint text, there is implicit meaning embedded in traditional, print texts.

Constructing meaning involves recognizing and observing various components of a text that can be found both within the text and within the context of the text (Buehl, 2011). In addition, many texts synthesize print and nonprint forms of communication, which can add another element of difficulty. Thus, constructing meaning can be frustrating for students who assume a more straightforward, surface-level interpretation of text. Therefore, it is important that you provide scaffolded opportunities for students to analyze and construct meaning from all forms of text, which can be done through the use of this strategy (Shanahan, 2012).

When and Why Would I Use This Strategy?

- To closely read the non-print and print features of text
- To demonstrate the ways in which a variety of text structures and genres influence meaning
- To navigate a variety of discipline-specific text structures and text types
- To promote students' recognition of the need to comprehend the whole text

How Do I Teach/Present the Strategy?

1. Select a nonprint source for students to analyze. Examples might include a photograph, artwork, political cartoon, figure, diagram, or a dynamic text like a lab demonstration or video. If you are choosing a print text instead, please note the additional ideas presented in step 16.
2. Provide students access to the Observation-Inference Chart found on page 87. You can provide access by sharing a Google document template or through a printed copy.
3. Be sure to model the process for students; you can use a photograph of student sit-ins in the 1960s, like the one below.

© Bettmann/Corbis

4. Talk students through your ideas while completing the Observation-Inference Chart on page 87.
5. You can make the following observations:
    a. First observation: African American students are sitting at a lunch counter without food in front of them. (Document that observation on the chart and ensure that the chart and your notes are visible to students so that they can see your progress.)
    b. Second observation: There are only African American people sitting along the entire lunch counter. (Again, document your response on the chart so that it is visible to students.)
    c. Third observation: They are all young men and women. Some are smiling. (Again, document your response on the chart so that it is visible to students.)
6. After recording these observations, you can verbally think through the inferences that can be drawn, saying, "I know that this was during the Civil Rights Movement. Thus, I can infer that the restaurant refused service to African American individuals. Also, since there are no white people with them, I can infer that the sit-in was planned by

African American men and women. The people appear to be younger based on their style of dress and physical appearance. I am also thinking that this was a scary time and even though they are smiling, they may be masking their fear rather than showing happiness."

7. Encourage students to draw arrows from observation to inference in order to solidify the observation and inference connection and ensure the rational development of ideas drawn from the text and other knowledge.
8. Then, model for students how to put the ideas together into cohesive statements, saying "Based on the observations I pulled from the text, combined with my research and knowledge of this time period, I am going to infer that the restaurant was refusing to serve African American people. I am also going to infer that the young African American men and women planned this sit-in as a protest. However, I can also observe that they are smiling, which is confusing. Knowing this time period, I am going to infer that they are not happy, but rather trying to remain calm and positive despite their worry and possible fear."
9. You may want to provide sentence stems when you ask students to develop summaries and conclusions. Observation-Inference Chart summary statement sentence stems can be found at the bottom of page 88. A completed example is at the top of the page.
10. After direct instruction, provide students with a similar photo and have them practice the process in small groups. You may want to keep the time period consistent so that they have concrete knowledge to draw from.
11. While in small groups, ask students to gather observations and then develop inferences from those observations. Instruct students to draw arrows connecting the observations and the inferences.
12. Circulate among student groups and monitor their progress. Guide them towards valid observations and inferences. Be sure to provide students with time and give them opportunities to process and practice the procedure before providing a photo that might be very different.
13. Provide sentence stems when students are ready to connect their observations and inferences in a more cohesive way. Observation-Inference Chart summary statement sentence stems can be found on page 88.
14. If students are struggling to come up with rational and logical inferences, provide additional research and scaffolding of the knowledge and information they will need in order to be successful at this step. Be liberal with your modeling and provide many examples. Provide a series of pictures that are similar. Try not to move on until students are ready. Analysis of a nonprint text is difficult for many and might be a new skill.
15. When students have arrived at logical inferences, instruct them to share ideas with and ask questions of one another. Make sure you clarify and add additional details to student statements in order to model a thorough response.

16. When using a print text, instruct students to pull quoted textual material, make observations about that material, and then develop an inference. For example, in the novel *Of Mice and Men* (Steinbeck, 1993), there is a section that describes how Lenny is walking "dragging his feet a little" as he comments, "I thought you was mad at me, George."
    - ✓ Students can explain, as an observation, that Lenny is walking slumped over and slow.
    - ✓ The inference can be that he is worried or sad or feeling defeated.
    - ✓ Students' inference statement can read: "Based on the quote and what I know so far in this story, the way Lenny is walking directly relates to how defeated he feels and how much George's opinion of him matters. I can infer that Lenny cannot live without George's support and reassurance."
17. Additional ideas for use of this scaffolding tool are available in Examples in Context on pages 85–86.

Disciplinary Focus	Behaviors Targeted by the Strategy	Examples in Context
ELA	Consider author's craft and use of literary devices; Gather evidence; Support a claim; Consider figurative, deeper meaning; Trace character motivations; Visualize the story; Provide textual evidence	When teaching a literary text, you can use the Observation-Inference Chart to support students in active reading. Students can be asked to track the author's use of literary devices. They can then make inferences about why the author would make those literary moves and how they contribute to the overall meaning of the text. Another idea is to collect observations of a character's actions in order to infer about motivation. For nonprint text, using this strategy with panels from a graphic novel or graphic memoir like *Stitches,* by David Small (2010), would be beneficial. Students can track how images convey emotion.
Math	Organize and apply data and information; Seek out patterns; Analyze graphs or tables	In statistics, students can be asked to analyze random samples and make observations about the data in order to develop inferences. Students can analyze population data reporting on family size, family needs in a home, or preferred size of yard. Then, students can begin to make observations about the patterns they see in the data and engage in research about the topics that emerge. Ultimately, inferences can be made about construction and development, what families need in a new home, and what decisions should be made when planning a housing development. Students can also be asked to use the Observation-Inference Chart to analyze their textbook. It is important to note that students can struggle to read mathematical texts because they are often based on the assumption that students have mastered all previous concepts (Buehl, 2011). The text is usually dense and packed with information. Students can make observations of the upcoming topics while also making inferences regarding the concepts that they will need to revisit in order to be successful.

Disciplinary Focus	Behaviors Targeted by the Strategy	Examples in Context
Science	Collect observable data; Develop inferences; Draw conclusions; Provide textual evidence; Closely analyze nonprint, dynamic texts; Take an inquiry approach to learning	Texts in science may often consist of demonstrations and diagrams, and these complex and dynamic texts can feel unmanageable to students. An Observation-Inference Chart is a tool to help students make sense of what they are seeing before asking them to try to piece it all together and construct meaning. It is also important for students to understand that in science, scientists are constantly revising their inferences based on new data that is being discovered and made available. Simulations offer students a glimpse of this scenario. The Observation-Inference Chart can be completed when students are looking at a simulation. Students can mark time and complete the Observation-Inference Chart at multiple predesignated time markers and then consider all aspects of the data across time.
Social Studies	Determine point of view; Consider bias; Access nonprint, complex text; Read with a critical lens; Analyze details and synthesize into a conclusion	History texts are often nonprint and can include maps, political cartoons, visual primary sources, and photographs.The Observation-Inference Chart provides a scaffolded, concrete way for students to approach a variety of texts. Historians often engage in the practice of making inferences about the past using maps, photographs, and other nonprint materials. Students, however, must first have time to look at these materials carefully and make observations, as well as have time to research and fill in any gaps in their understanding. History is a deeply complex discipline in this regard. A political cartoon, for example, not only relies on political understanding, but also humor, values, bias, and an understanding of the context of the situation. Students will need time and guidance when making observations and in knowing to merge their observations with prior knowledge and research in order to come up with inferences.

Template for Observation-Inference Chart for Print-Based Text

Name: ______________________________ Date: ____________

Text : ______________________________

Text Evidence	Observation	Inference

Summary:

Template for Observation-Inference Chart for Nonprint Sources

Name: ______________________________ Date: ____________

Text : ______________________________

Observation	Inference

Summary:

Example of Observation-Inference Chart for Social Studies

Name: Beverly Date: ______

Text : Image at Lunch Counter

Observation	Inference
African American students are sitting at a lunch counter without food in front of them. African American people sitting along the entire lunch counter. They are all young men and women. Some are smiling.	Because it is during the Civil Rights Movement, we can infer that the restaurant refused service to African American people. Since there are no white people with them, we can infer that the sit-in was planned by African American men and women who appear to be younger people. We can also infer that even though they are smiling, they may be masking their fear rather than showing happiness. We know this was a time of violence and oppression, so they are probably not happy.

Summary: Based on the observations and combined with my research and knowledge of this time period, I am going to infer that the restaurant was refusing service to African American people. I am also going to infer that these are young African American men and women who planned this sit-in as a protest. However, I can also observe that they are smiling, which is confusing. Knowing this time period, I am going to infer that they are not happy, but rather trying to remain calm and positive despite their worry and fear.

Observation-Inference Chart Summary Statement Sentence Stems

Observation-Inference Chart Summary Statement Sentence Stems
■ Based on (this) observation and my knowledge about (this), I can infer that…
■ (This) observation leads me to believe that…
■ Since I understand that at this point in the text (this) is happening, I can infer that…
■ Typically, when (this) is happening, I would expect (this) outcome, but because I have prior knowledge about (this idea), I know my observation more likely means…

From Jerry L. Johns, Paula Di Domenico, and Rachel Lesinski-Roscoe, *Content Area Literacy: Toolkit of Disciplinary Strategies for Middle and High School* (5th ed.). Copyright © 2023 by Kendall Hunt Publishing Company (1-800-247-3458 ext. 5). May be reproduced for noncommercial educational purposes. Website: www.kendallhunt.com

I-Chart

Description

The Inquiry Chart or I-Chart (Assaf, Ash, Saunders, & Johnson, 2011; Hoffman, 1992; Manderino, Berglund, & Johns, 2014) is an organizational scaffold for synthesizing information across multiple texts to address a larger inquiry question. Its purpose is to support students in developing and organizing subquestions related to an overall inquiry question. It provides a visual for students to determine additional information they may need and background knowledge that they can apply.

Inquiry is a critical habit of thinking found in every discipline. Because inquiry brainstorming can feel disorganized and involve a variety of texts and resources, I-Chart is a great tool for organizing that thinking and categorizing those texts and resources. Students need organizational systems as they continue to build their research, questioning, and synthesis skills.

When and Why Would I Use This Strategy?

- To show how to compare claims across multiple texts
- To support students in developing discipline-relevant questions
- To demonstrate formats for organizing ideas and linking ideas to research
- To showcase ways to integrate and evaluate content presented in diverse formats

How Do I Teach/Present the Strategy?

1. Select an overarching question to investigate related to a topic in your curriculum. Examples might include: "Is the American Dream attainable?"; "What causes cell division?"; and "Should the United States have dropped the Atomic Bomb?" See Examples in Context on pages 92–93 for additional ideas.
2. Provide multiple sources for students on the topic or have students search and locate sources for their topic. The National Children's Book and Literacy Alliance www.thencbla.org has some suggestions for age-appropriate reference sites.
3. Distribute the I-Chart reproducible that can be found in Resources on page 94. Because students will be continuously modifying their work throughout the process, an electronic document will make it easier for them to edit and modify their ideas and share with peers.

4. On the I-Chart, you can provide students with a predetermined set of subquestions or have students generate their own subquestions as you move through each text.
    a. To support students in developing their own subquestions, it is helpful to begin by making sure they have actively comprehended the texts and resources being used.
    b. Students will need to possess strong background knowledge on the topic in order to create subquestions; therefore, you may want to dedicate a previous class session to reading, annotating, and comprehending the texts and developing subquestions.
    c. In addition, you may want to consider using the I-Chart Student References Organizer, found in Resources on page 96.
5. If you have provided subquestions, you can move on to explain why there is a larger inquiry question alongside subquestions, as featured in the example below and in the completed charts in Resources on page 95. Explain that the process of inquiry involves breaking down larger ideas into smaller avenues of thinking so that researchers are able to truly understand and deeply research a topic.
6. Show a chart to students that is blank except for your Inquiry Question and Sub-Questions. Make sure that all students can see it and that they will be able to see clearly what you are typing or writing on the chart.
7. Read aloud one of the texts you have gathered. Make sure you have previewed this text and know what parts of the text you will be discussing with the class as you fill in the chart with them.
8. Use think-aloud to demonstrate how information in the text can provide responses to the subquestions. Use phrasing such as: *This sentence comments on the idea of subquestion two. Let me read that question again. Okay, I think this text is saying (this) about (that idea).* Also, in your think-aloud, model the process for selecting relevant details to include in each response. Use phrasing such as: *At first, I thought this section of the text was relevant to subquestion three, but as I reread the subquestion alongside the information, I think it's a stretch. This information is interesting, but not relevant.*
9. Work through as many texts or text excerpts as necessary for students to internalize the process. If students are struggling, you could find more accessible texts or consider streamlining the amount of subquestions you have.
10. After students are somewhat comfortable with the process, they can continue to read, review, mark and discuss the texts, and respond to the subquestions in small groups of three or in pairs. Consider instructing the students to use comment bubbles to record their thinking if they are working electronically.
11. As students are closely reading the texts within their small groups, they may develop additional subquestions. They can document these ideas under the Additional Subquestions column in the I-Chart. These may be ideas students use later in the unit or as part of their research and inquiry process.
12. You may also choose to extend the inquiry process by allowing students to find their own sources for one or more of the subquestions. The direction you choose depends on your goals and parameters for the lesson.

13. Ultimately, have students share their responses with classmates by projecting their work or sharing their documents electronically, view-only, with peers. Ask students to support their responses by referencing specific passages in the texts.
14. Students can then use their I-Chart to develop a summary response for each subquestion.
15. Ultimately, students can further develop their ideas into a presentation, research paper, or public service video.

Disciplinary Focus	Behaviors Targeted by the Strategy	Examples in Context
ELA	Synthesize multiple sources; Use text to support conclusions; Develop a comprehensive understanding of a topic	For ELA, some of the resources students use to investigate a line of inquiry may be fiction. If you have been using text sets to explore a theme, I-Chart is a good way to organize that exploration. Question: What does it mean to overcome struggle? Suggested Text Set for Book Clubs: Club One: Nonfiction articles or short stories of situations in which people have or have not been able to overcome struggle. Consider *Look Both Ways* by Jason Reynolds (2019). Club Two: *Sorry for Your Loss,* a novel by Jessie Ann Foley (2019). Club Three: *We Speak in Storms,* a novel by Natalie Lund (2019). Club Four: *Long Way Down,* the novel in verse (2017) and the graphic novel, are valuable choices by Jason Reynolds, with art by Danica Novgorodoff (2020). The subquestions can be: ▪ What are the many definitions of *struggle*? ▪ What aspects of society intensify and promote struggle? ▪ What prevents people from overcoming struggle? ▪ Are there proposed solutions to the problems and struggles people face? ▪ Why do some solutions work while others do not?
Math	Analyze graphics; Synthesize statistics; Investigate multiple solutions; Ask questions about data	In math, you may need to navigate this strategy differently by considering ways to inquire about process. For example: Inquiry Question: How many different ways can we approach this situation? Depending on the problem or equation, students can be divided into three groups. Each of these groups would be in charge of responding to a subquestion. The subquestions can be: ▪ How many more examples can you find, and what are they? ▪ Which procedures can be applied to this situation? ▪ Determine a variety of generalizations that can be drawn from this situation.

Disciplinary Focus	Behaviors Targeted by the Strategy	Examples in Context
		The research and text that encompass and support student responses can be in any mathematical form: written, oral, symbolic, or visual. Another possibility is to use a "favorite mistakes" approach and pull multiple incorrect responses that students have submitted. Students can learn a lot by looking at each others' mistakes and figuring out what went wrong in order to reach the correct response.
Science	Collect data; Draw conclusions; Synthesize evidence; Determine gaps in understanding	In science, you can use this strategy to help students consider multiple problem and solution scenarios. **Question:** To what extent does use of compost on farms reduce pollution in stormwater runoff? The subquestions can be: ■ What pollutants from farming typically appear in stormwater runoff? ■ How does the use of compost reduce pollution? ■ How is pollution measured and how is reduction in pollution measured? ■ Are there any farmers currently using compost to reduce pollution and what is the result? Additional support can be found at Western Washington University Libraries self-paced online tutorials www.libarytutorials.wwu.edu.
Social Studies	Consider multiple sources; Synthesize ideas; Interpret evidence; Recognize multiple narratives; Develop a stance and argument	Approaching history as an ongoing narrative can support students in recognizing the role that point of view and bias play in how a situation is reported and argued. **Question:** Should the United States have dropped the atomic bomb? The subquestions can be: ■ What were the negative effects of the bombs? ■ What were the reasons given for dropping the bombs? ■ What were the alternatives to dropping the bombs? ■ What was the reaction of citizens around the world to the dropping of the bombs including Japanese and American citizens?

Template for General I-Chart

Name: ______________________________ Date: ____________

Inquiry Question					
	Subquestion 1	Subquestion 2	Subquestion 3	Other Important Evidence	Additional Questions
What I Already Know: Connections to Self, World, Other Texts					
Source 1					
Source 2					
Summary					

Example of I-Chart for Social Studies

Name: Gus Date: ____________

Inquiry Question To what extent should people be criminally penalized for selling or renting violent video games to minors?					
	Subquestion 1 Are Video Games violent?	**Subquestion 2** Do video games cause violence?	**Subquestion 3** Are minors targeted in video game sales?	**Other Important Evidence**	**Additional Subquestions**
What I Already Know: Connections to Self, World, Other Texts	The games I play are violent	The games I play are sometimes violent but I am not violent	I have to have my parents buy some of the games for me	Some observational studies have found that teenagers rely on video games to make friends.	What laws protect minors from buying violent video games?
Source 1 Deliberating in a Democracy	Study from Kent State University found video game violence to be disturbingly high	There is "less data" on the effects	80% of sales are video game sales 50% of youth favor violent games		How much control should the government have?
Source 2 NPR Article: "Video Game Release Suspended"	Grand Theft Auto is considered violent as there are several acts of violence within that game	No evidence is provided	Grand Theft Auto did receive an adult rating		How many adults purchase these games compared to teens?

Template for I-Chart Student References Organizer

Name: ______________________________ Date: ____________

Directions: Consider your inquiry question and three subquestions. Determine the stance of each source that you have. Does the source agree/support, disagree, or fall somewhere in between? And ultimately, what is your informed opinion?						
Inquiry Question ____________________						
Document 1 ____________	**Subquestion 1** ____________			**Subquestion 2** ____________		
Document 2 ____________	**Yes**	**No**	**Maybe**	**Yes**	**No**	**Maybe**
Document 3 ____________	**Yes**	**No**	**Maybe**	**Yes**	**No**	**Maybe**
Document 4 ____________	**Yes**	**No**	**Maybe**	**Yes**	**No**	**Maybe**
Document 5 ____________	**Yes**	**No**	**Maybe**	**Yes**	**No**	**Maybe**
Your Opinion	**Yes**	**No**	**Maybe**	**Yes**	**No**	**Maybe**

Example I-Chart Student References Organizer for ELA

Name: *Archie* Date: ______

Directions: Consider your inquiry question and three subquestions. Determine the stance of each source that you have. Does the source agree/support, disagree, or fall somewhere in between? And ultimately, what is your informed opinion?

Inquiry Question
To what extent does the chase for the American Dream take over the realities of life?

Text Source/Title	Subquestion 1	Subquestion 2	Subquestion 3
Text Source/Title *The Great Gatsby*	**Subquestion 1** *Is the American Dream attainable?*	**Subquestion 2** *Is sacrifice part of the American Dream?*	**Subquestion 3** *Is it valuable to change the dream if there is prolonged failure?*
Document 1 *Novel excerpts*	**Yes No Maybe**	**Yes No Maybe**	**Yes No Maybe**
Document 2 *Infographic on income levels for Americans*	**Yes No Maybe**	**Yes No Maybe**	**Yes No Maybe**
Document 3 *Interview transcript with an entrepreneur*	**Yes No Maybe**	**Yes No Maybe**	**Yes No Maybe**
Document 4 *Article about happiness levels in American*	**Yes No Maybe**	**Yes No Maybe**	**Yes No Maybe**
Your Opinion	**Yes No Maybe**	**Yes No Maybe**	**Yes No Maybe**

Comprehension, Analysis, Synthesis Strategy (CASS)

Description

The Comprehension, Analysis, Synthesis Strategy (CASS) is useful when students are asked to use multiple texts in order to develop an evidence-based argument. This strategy guides students efficiently and effectively through comprehension, analysis, and synthesis. When using CASS, students will first take the time to comprehend what each text is communicating before they begin to analyze what the text means. From analysis, students will move to synthesis and consider how the texts work together to convey and support an argument.

As students work through the stages of CASS, they are learning how to deepen their engagement with text while strengthening their ability to pull relevant research and use that research to support their argument. At the culmination of the strategy, students will have the workings of an outline that can be used for a verbal or written product.

When and Why Would I Use This Strategy?

- To scaffold engagement with multiple texts simultaneously, including images, graphs, quotations, and text
- To encourage students to find connections among various texts and develop an argument
- To support the skill of comparing and contrasting how various texts approach the same topic
- To develop student autonomy from comprehension, to analysis, to synthesis, to the development of an evidence-based argument
- To enhance ability to find accurate and relevant evidence to develop an argument

How Do I Teach/Present the Strategy?

1. Determine the Essential Question or theme that will guide this lesson. You may have a theme like "Adolescent Depression," "Bullying," or, for math, "Integers." However, you may use an Essential Question such as: "What is teen depression and what can we do about it?" or "Why is it critical to seek help if you think you are the victim of bullying?" or "In what ways can mathematical information be represented?"
2. Choose a variety of research and nonfiction documents that will teach students about different aspects of the topic. Pull brief, but valuable excerpts from these documents, keeping in mind the need for variety in terms of difficulty, perspective, format, subcategories, and subtopics.
   a. Some of the texts that you choose may be images, graphs, quotations, statistics, excerpted sentences, or even video clips.
   b. For example, you may have a quotation from a teen suffering from depression; a statistic about teen depression; an excerpt from J. D. Salinger's (1979) novel *The Catcher in the Rye*; a two-minute video about teen depression coping skills; an image of a teenager talking to a trusted adult; and an excerpt from *Trigger,* a novel by Susan Vaught (2006).
3. For ease of use and distribution, it is helpful to position each text on its own Google slide or on its own document within the same folder. Then, label each one with some identifying mark like a letter, number, or abbreviated title. See page 104 for an example.
4. Students will receive the text excerpts only, not the entire document, so it is crucial that the excerpts can stand alone in terms of message, meaning, and point of view.
5. Before beginning the CASS lesson, engage students with the Essential Question or theme. Let them know that they will be exploring a variety of documents to better understand the topics and themes of the lesson.
6. You will then share the Google folder you have compiled that is filled with excerpts; you are also welcome to provide students with a physical folder with physical copies of the excerpts. However, ensure that each student has their own copies. If you are working with Google, make sure to prompt students to make their own copy.
7. Support students in navigating their folder of documents. Point out the label on each as well as the document type, and read aloud any documents that students may struggle with. Remind students of the topic, theme, or Essential Question of the lesson to support their focus. This topic, theme, or Essential Question should be visible throughout the process for students to easily reference.
8. Explain to students that they will be following a series of steps in order to categorize the documents and come up with labels for their categories.
9. Provide the following instructions verbally and in writing. See Resources on page 103 for instructions and page 104 for a student example, either of which you can share with students.

10. Prompt students:
    a. First, read through each document. After reading each document, take a minute to jot down some summary words or phrases. Ask yourself: *What is this document about? What is it communicating?* You may then jot down notes such as "scary emotions," "struggles with friends," or "good ideas for coping."
    b. Second, begin to analyze the documents. Ask yourself: *Do any of these documents seem to go together? How would I group these documents?* You may conclude: *These two documents go together because one has statistics and the other gives an example of what that looks like in real life.* Or, *these documents go together because they are all suggesting solutions.*
    c. Third, finish grouping the documents based on the similarities you have identified. Your goal is for 2-3 documents per grouping. You may have one document that does not seem to fit into any group, and that is okay.
    d. Fourth, synthesize your ideas by labeling each group with a word or a phrase that articulates your reason for grouping them, such as "struggle," "teenagers," or "frustrations."
    e. Some of you may provide more generalized labels, such as "effects," "treatments," "emotions," "reasons," "specifics," or "general ideas."
    f. Some of you may provide more specific labels, such as "statistics suggest depression is common," or "side effects of meds," or "teens vs. adults."
11. Make sure to check in with students throughout, but especially when they have finished labeling their document groupings. If you realize that students have grouped documents or labeled groupings in ways that you did not expect, encourage students to share their rationale and ensure that their explanation is valid. If students are really struggling, you may want to provide them with labels and have them categorize the documents with the provided labels.
12. At this point, you can take students' work in a variety of directions. You can:
    a. Have students share their work in small groups and explain their reasoning.
    b. Use their grouping labels to draft topic sentences and write paragraphs using the documents as evidence.
    c. Draft a thesis or claim based on their work.
    d. Share responses to the Essential Question by referencing their groupings and the documents within.
13. Through CASS, students have now arrived at a stage where they can develop a stance on the theme, topic, or Essential Question. From here, you can wrap up the lesson or ask students to engage in more research to further explore one of their groupings.

Disciplinary Focus	Behaviors Targeted by the Strategy	Examples in Context
ELA	Find and apply relevant evidence; Synthesize evidence; Develop an argument; Analyze multiple texts on a topic; Establish a purpose for reading; Consider author's argument	A large research paper is approaching. Students need time to explore topics and develop their skills analyzing and synthesizing ideas from multiple texts. Students are reading *We are Called to Rise* by Laura McBride (2014). Students can group quotations and excerpts from the novel with quotations and excerpts from research. Topics such as poverty, PTSD, and immigration can be explored. Students can present or write about their findings.
Math	Make connections among algebraic, numerical, graphic, and verbal representations; Synthesize multiple representations; Use examples and nonexamples; Make connections; Analyze information	When students are learning proofs, CASS will support them in comprehending how the algebraic representation of the equation fits with the verbal and textual representation of the information. This idea can be extended to various mathematical concepts such as theorems, postulates, and properties.
Science	Analyze and interpret information; Work with difficult vocabulary; Engage in an argument from evidence; Obtain, evaluate, and communicate information	When learning about global warming and, more specifically, heat islands, students can read and view a variety of texts from multiple perspectives including: ▪ What are heat islands? ▪ Why do they occur? ▪ How can they be prevented? ▪ What is the overall impact? Data sets, graphs, excerpts from environmental protection websites, and segments of research studies can be used.

Disciplinary Focus	Behaviors Targeted by the Strategy	Examples in Context
Social Studies	Corroborate sources; Recognize point of view; Analyze author's perspective; Synthesize primary and secondary sources; Develop an argument	When students are reading about different types of government structures, they can use CASS to: ■ gain a deeper understanding of each structure ■ form opinions about which structure seems to be the most beneficial. Text excerpts can include: ■ primary sources that articulate the governing rules ■ secondary sources outlining the similarities and differences in government structures Ultimately, students can create what they believe to be an ideal government. CASS will also be helpful when considering disaster relief projects. Students can read excerpts about the ways in which government and nonprofit organizations work to provide disaster relief and then develop a call to action.

CASS Instructions for Students

Instructions
First, read through each document. After reading each document, take a minute to jot down some summary words or phrases. Ask yourself: *What is this document about? What is it communicating?* You may then jot down notes such as "scary emotions;" "struggles with friends;" "good ideas for coping."   Second, begin to analyze the documents. Ask yourself, *Do any of these documents seem to go together? How would I group these documents?* You may conclude: *These two documents go together because one has statistics and the other gives an example of what that looks like in real life.* Or, *these documents go together because they are all suggesting solutions.*   Third, finish grouping the documents based on the similarities you have identified. Your goal is for 2-3 documents per grouping. You may have one document that does not seem to fit into any group, and that is okay.   Fourth, synthesize your ideas by labeling each group with a word or a phrase that articulates your reason for grouping them such as, "struggle," "teenagers," "frustrations."   Some of you may provide more generalized labels, such as, "effects," "treatments," "emotions," "reasons," "specifics," or "general ideas."   Some of you may provide more specific labels such as, "statistics suggest depression is common," or "side effects of meds," or "teens vs. adults."

Example CASS for ELA

Name: *Isabel* Date: ____________

Essential Question: **What is teen depression and what can we do about it?**	
Overview of Documents ■ **Document A: Quotation from a teenager struggling with depression** ■ **Document B: Statistics about teen depression** ■ **Document C: PSA about teen depression** ■ **Document D: Excerpt from a psychology journal** ■ **Document E: Image of a teen talking to a trusted adult** ■ **Document F: Quotation from a novel**	
Doc A: **Quotation from a teenager struggling with depression**	Student Notes on Doc A: *Sounds positive* *Has dreams for future*
Doc B: **Statistics about teen depression**	Student Notes on Doc B: *More common than thought*
Doc C: **PSA about teen depression**	Student Notes on Doc C: *Can be an emotion and clinical diagnosis*
Doc D: **Excerpt from a psychology journal**	Student Notes on Doc D: *Certain behaviors are characteristic*
Doc E: **Image of a teen talking to a trusted adult**	Student Notes on Doc E: *Important to talk about it*
Doc F: **Quotation from a novel**	Student Notes on Doc F: *Character copes in many ways some good and some bad*

Name of Category	The Text Excerpts	Explanation: Why are these grouped together?
Coping	*Documents A & E*	*Show positive moments and ways of coping*
Understanding	*Documents C & D*	*Behaviors that can help diagnose or provide better understanding*
Recognizing	*Documents B & F*	*Everyone's journey is different*

Template for General CASS

Name: ______________________________ Date: __________

Name of the Category	The Text Excerpts (include the Title/Label)	Explanation: Why are these grouped together?

They Say, I Say, and So

Description

They Say, I Say, and So is a strategy that scaffolds the thinking processes students need in order to develop text-based inferences (Beers, 2003). They Say, I Say, and So is an organizer for ideas as well as a linear way of thinking that allows students to closely consider the text while also seeing the connections between the author's ideas and their own (Lenski, Wham, Johns, & Caskey, 2011).

Through the use of this strategy, students will strengthen their ability to closely read text and develop interpretations and conclusions about text. They will be able to monitor their own thinking and recognize the relationship between their thinking and what is presented in the text. Overall, students will develop the skill of procuring relevant prior knowledge and experiences to make logical inferences about text (Beers, 2003).

This strategy is not limited to print-based text, and it can be equally impactful when used to consider a speaker's words during a presentation, speech, or discussion.

When and Why Would I Use This Strategy?

- To support students in recognizing the connection between the messages within a text and their own interpretations
- To encourage the use of text-based evidence to develop an argument or evaluation
- To strengthen students' ability to develop inferences and connect relevant personal experiences and prior knowledge with the text
- To develop students' ability to find accurate and relevant evidence to support a conclusion or evaluation

How Do I Teach/Present the Strategy?

1. Explain what it means to make inferences and provide students with some examples. You might say, "In order to make solid, valid inferences, you, as the reader, will need to reason beyond the text and the information provided. The inferences that each of you make will be different because you are all different people with different knowledge and experiences. The trick is to ensure that all of your inferences are grounded in and supported by what the text says. Thus, all inferences will be developed using information from the text as well as your own knowledge and experiences."
2. Choose the template that best suits your goals, your students, and your ideas for the lesson. A template can be found on page 110, and several examples can be found on pages 111–114 in various content areas.

3. Prior to copying and distributing the template, fill in the headings and the first row of your template so that students have a sample response and you have a concrete way to show your expectations for the lesson.
4. Modify the headings in your template to honor the habits of thinking in your discipline. For social studies, the headings may read "They Say," "I Say," and "So." For math, however, you may need to modify the headings to read "Clues from the Text," "My Prior Knowledge," and "My Inference."
5. After distributing the materials, provide students with their focus for reading the text. Examples can be found in Examples in Context on pages 108–109. This is a critical step as students need to know their purpose for reading.
6. Next, provide students with a text. As they read, they should be underlining passages that stand out to them and that give them insight into the purpose for reading that you have established. That purpose might be "What is motivating the main character?" or "What difficulties do scientists face when trying to investigate the ocean floor?"
7. Once students are done reading, instruct them to share the parts of the text that they have marked. You can decide which passages will be included in the first column of the *They Say* column. Students will write the chosen passages in the *They Say* column.
8. Then, it is your students' turn to react to the text. They will record their reactions in the *I Say* column. They can react by sharing personal experiences about the ideas, by sharing an opinion about the ideas, or by asking questions to try and clarify the ideas presented. Students may need to do research or engage in class discussion to learn some additional information about the ideas from the text before they are able to move forward with developing an inference.
9. Finally, in the *And So* column, students will share an inference, an interpretation, or a conclusion that they developed by bringing together the ideas from the *They Say* column and the *I Say* column.
10. The strategy does not end here, however. Students must then return to the text and ensure that their inferences, interpretations, and conclusions are actually supported by the text.
11. In addition, if students are struggling to make concrete, text-based inferences, you may need to provide additional examples or help students rework their inferences so that they make sense. Another way to support students in generating and focusing their ideas is to provide transition words like "therefore," or stems like "The text says (this) and I say (this). Therefore…".

Connections to the Disciplines	Behaviors Targeted by the Strategy	Examples in Context
ELA	Read closely to determine author's message; Develop inferences; Support ideas with textual evidence; Draw conclusions; Share interpretations	This strategy can be helpful in understanding the relationships in a text. In *The Book of Unknown Americans* by Cristina Henríquez (2004), the relationship between Maribel and Mayor can be better understood using the question: "What motivates the main character?" Columns in the chart can be labeled: ■ They Say: Situation in the Text ■ I Say: My Experiences ■ And So: Overall Interpretation The purpose for reading is to understand why Mayor's father does not want Mayor to have a relationship with Maribel. Students can draw from their relationships with their guardians and the relationships they have with friends. Additional themes include trauma, poverty, family dynamics, and immigration.
Math	Connect mathematical ideas; Draw conclusions; Make inferences; Read closely	For high school statistics and probability, the Common Core State Standards (NGA & CCSSO, 2010) suggests understanding statistics as a "process for making inferences... based on a random sample." Students can distribute a survey and try to draw additional conclusions from the responses they receive. The purpose of the survey can involve asking their classmates about the ways that they learn best. Inferences can be based on the responses received and students' own knowledge of peer groups and high school education. Students can look to respond to the question: "What makes schools successful?" Columns in the chart can be labeled: ■ They Say: Student Survey Results ■ I Say: My Reactions ■ And So: Solutions We Have

Connections to the Disciplines	Behaviors Targeted by the Strategy	Examples in Context
Science	Analyze and interpret information; Gather text evidence; Draw conclusions; Make inferences; Determine author's bias	Scientists must gather evidence in order to draw conclusions and make inferences about impact, the need for future investigations, and the result of conservation efforts. However, scientists must investigate things that they cannot observe directly. In fact, the ocean floor is one topic that scientists continue to find ways to investigate. Students can access online resources like Google Maps and National Geographic sites to learn more about the ocean and view simulations of the ocean floor. They can gather evidence to respond to the question, "What difficulties do scientists face when trying to investigate the ocean floor?" Columns in the chart can be labeled: ■ They Say: Evidence Collected ■ I Say: Conclusions I Made ■ And So: Why It Matters The *And So: Why It Matters* column is where students can make inferences and hypothetically direct future scientific investigations and conservation efforts.
Social Studies	Analyze an author's perspective; Develop an inference based on evidence; Draw conclusions; Share interpretations; Determine need for additional research	Historians must corroborate various perspectives and facts in order to develop an understanding of an event and the causes behind it. Therefore, an interesting application of this strategy is to ask students to read the letters from one President of the United States to another. Letters can be found in the November, 2020 issue of *The Atlantic* (Kalman, 2020). Students can develop some prior knowledge about each President's term in office and then read insightfully to try and make inferences about the underlying messages that each seems to be sharing. Students can look to respond to: "What advice did the Presidents' give to each other and why?" Columns in the chart can be labeled: ■ They Say ■ I Say ■ And So

Template for General They Say, I Say, and So

Name: ______________________________ Date: ____________

They Say… The Text Says…	I Say...	And So...

Example They Say, I Say, and So for ELA

Name: ______________________________ Date: __________

They Say	I Say	And So
Situation in the Text	**My Experiences**	**My Interpretation of this Moment**
Teacher Example: "I felt more American than anything, but even that was up for debate according to the kids at school who'd taunted me over the years. The truth was that I didn't know which I was." Mayor in The Book of Unknown Americans (Henríquez, 2014).	*Teacher Example: I have moved someplace new, and it is hard to do because everything is new. I have also met a lot of people who did not grow up in the United States. It is hard for Mayor, who did not grow up in the United States, to feel like he belongs. The kids at school are mean to him because he is different and does not speak English very well.*	*Teacher Example: Mayor is trying to make his parents happy but he is also trying to fit into his new world that his parents do not understand. It is hard for a teenager to have to keep things from their parents and pretend to be happy.*

Example of They Say, I Say, and So for Math

Name: ______________________________ Date: ____________

They Say	I Say	And So
Student Survey Results	My Reactions	Solutions We Have
Teacher Example: The survey results suggest that 70% of students learn best when they are not tired.	*Teacher Example: I have read some studies about teenagers needing to sleep more in the morning because they tend to stay up very late.*	*Teacher Example: It would help if the school day started a little later than it does now. A later start is healthier for teens.*

Example of They Say, I Say, and So for Science

Name: ______________________________ Date: ____________

They Say	I Say	And So
Evidence Collected	**My Conclusions**	**Why It Matters**
Teacher Example: In the deepest ocean, light doesn't reach the seafloor, and therefore photosynthesis is impossible.	*Teacher Example: I know that photosynthesis happens with energy from light. If it is too dark then that means that photosynthesis cannot happen.*	*Teacher Example: We need to better understand life on the ocean floor and how that life exists. Where do energy and food come from? More investigation needs to happen on this topic.*

Example of They Say, I Say, and So for Social Studies

Name: ______________________________ Date: __________

They Say	I Say	And So
Teacher Example: "Your 'friends' will disappoint you." Letter from George W. Bush to Barack Obama, as printed in The Atlantic (Kalman, 2020).	*Teacher Example: When people are in leadership positions they cannot make everyone happy.*	*Teacher Example: Bush is encouraging Obama to make good decisions and be patient with people.*

Intra-Act

Description

The Intra-Act strategy (Hoffman, 1979; Manderino, Berglund, & Johns, 2014) supports students in synthesizing ideas from multiple texts in order to formulate their own stance on particular issues. In four steps, students move from formulating opinions based solely on one text to synthesizing and developing opinions using multiple texts.

There are four main steps: students construct meaning from a text selection; students make connections based on information in the first text and other texts they find on the topic; students share their own reactions on the topic and the insights or values those reactions convey; and, finally, students reflect on their newly formed insights or values.

In order to think critically and eradicate misconceptions, students need practice approaching issues from multiple perspectives and using a variety of resources and texts in order to determine their personal stance. In addition, students need to be able to listen to peers' ideas and explanations and to respectfully navigate situations in which others do not share their values and beliefs.

When and Why Would I Use This Strategy?

- To determine the need to consider claims across multiple sources and texts
- To support navigation of multiple perspectives and to determine personal values
- To understand how to analyze and synthesize a variety of diverse sources and texts
- To scaffold the process of evaluating point of view and argument

How Do I Teach/Present the Strategy?

1. Explain to students the difference between topics that are explanatory, such as how a bill becomes a law, and topics that are subject to opinion, such as whether or not the U.S. should try and broker peace among other countries.
2. To create an Intra-Act organizer, choose a topic that lends itself to differing opinions that can all be supported by research. Also, when selecting a topic, make sure you can find accessible resources for your students to use.
3. Using a few critical sources that you find, develop four different claim statements about the topic. If your class has enough prior knowledge, you may want to brainstorm claim statements with them and then choose four to put into the organizer. Ideas for topics and claim statements can be found in Examples in Context on pages 118–119.

4. It should be possible to answer the claim statements with either yes or no, such as in the example below. This example can also be found on page 121.

Example of Intra-Act for **Social Studies**

Topic Engaging in Conflicts in Other Countries	**Claim 1** The U.S. has an obligation to enforce justice and world peace.	**Claim 2** We had no business being across the world in someone else's fight.	**Claim 3** We (the U.S) were the best candidates to eliminate Saddam Hussein.	**Claim 4** We should have put all the money that was spent on the Iraq War into our public schools instead.
Group Member 1 Georgia	yes	no	yes	yes
Group Member 2 Vivian	yes	yes	no	no
Group Member 3 Archer	no	no	yes	no
Group Member 4 Augustus	yes	no	yes	no

5. Distribute the template you have made (see page 120) and instruct each student to put their own name in the *Group Member 1* position. Read the claim statements to preview the topic and the texts with your students.
6. Read aloud the first text on the topic. This should be a text that you have previewed and provided copies for the students. Make sure you have read the text closely and marked areas that you want to highlight and discuss with students. It may be a longer text that addresses multiple claims, or a shorter text or excerpt that addresses only one or perhaps two of the claims.
7. After reading the text aloud with students, ask them to consider their stance. They will need to write *yes* or *no* in the organizer under the claim statement.
8. Then go back into the text with students to model how they can pull textual evidence to back up their stance.
9. Reread portions of the text and ask students to highlight them. Think-aloud the stance that portion would support. Talk through your thinking, saying phrases like "This paragraph means (this) and therefore, I see that it supports the stance of (this) because (reason)." Ask students to highlight all of the text segments that you discuss during your think-aloud and to take notes in the margins to capture ideas and thoughts. It might be useful for students to use comment bubbles if the text is an electronic version.
10. After rereading the text, give students time to think through all you have explained and then have them choose the textual evidence they would like to use for their claim responses. Ask them to star the evidence in the text and make a note of which claim it supports.

11. Following the initial text, if you see that students are ready, assign another text that addresses one or more of the claim statements. Ask students to read this text independently and mark the text before writing their yes or no stance in the organizer. Make sure students are: writing *yes* or *no* along their row of the organizer only, that they are marking up the text, and that they are prepared to show the textual evidence they used in their decision-making process. If students are not ready to work independently, you can do some guided practice or allow them to work on the second text in groups. Progress through the four texts in the way that works for your students. You may need to guide them throughout and that is okay.
12. After the four readings have been completed, after students have taken a stance on all claims, and after students have marked textual evidence to support those claims, put students into groups of three or four. When they join their groups, ask them to write in their group members' names in the organizer in the left column.
13. Let students know that the readings and discussions that follow will challenge their ideas and perspectives, and that it is okay to change their stance on a claim if necessary.
14. For each claim, students should share their stance and their evidence with group members. The other group members will listen and write the speaker's stance for each claim by marking *yes* or *no* along the speaker's row. When the speaker shares their text evidence, all group members should find that evidence and mark it with the speaker's initials.
15. After all group members have shared their stance for each of the claims, students are to revisit one of the claims. This might be the claim with a divided stance or it may be a claim that group members want to research further in order to solidify their united stance.
16. Together, students can research this claim and come up with a final, united stance along with additional research to support their decision.
17. Another approach is to see if students want to change their stance on any of the claims. Alternatively, you can regroup students according to their stance if you want them to debate.
18. Finally, have students write out a closing statement expressing their perspective and synthesizing others' perspectives and ideas.

Connections to the Disciplines	Behaviors Targeted by the Strategy	Examples in Context
ELA	Develop a stance; Use text to support ideas; Collaborate with peers; Consider multiple viewpoints	Asking students to research young activists may enlighten them to the ways in which they can make a difference, no matter their age. Topic: Youth Activism Claim statements can read: ▪ Malala was right to speak out against her government even though she knew that her life was at risk because of it. ▪ Teenagers should not get involved in social justice movements because there might be risks involved. ▪ Teenagers can try to join environmental protests, but no one will listen.
Math	Provide explanations; Solve problems in multiple ways; Use math to draft an argument	Encouraging your students to think through some mind-bending and controversial math problems is a great way to use Intra-Act. For each controversial problem, have students try and predict their response before solving or looking up the information. Students can then explain why they answered how they did and discuss any misconceptions they may have held. The 12 most controversial facts in mathematics can be accessed by searching "controversial topics in math" and in Walt Hickey's (2013) article in *Business Insider* magazine. Topic: Controversial Math Problems Statements can read: ▪ There are as many even numbers as natural numbers. ▪ The number "1" appears as the first digit 30% of the time in real-world numbers. ▪ You work in an office of 23 people. What is the probability that two people in your office have the same birthday?

Connections to the Disciplines	Behaviors Targeted by the Strategy	Examples in Context
Science	Eradicate misconceptions; Analyze bias; Consider multiple viewpoints; Rethink previous beliefs; Analyze text	Have students read multiple texts related to a scientific phenomenon and use Intra-Act to support students' causal explanations of that phenomenon. Topic: The Shower Curtain Effect Statements can showcase the different explanations that have been tested over the years: ■ The Bernoulli Principle ■ The Buoyancy Theory ■ The Schmidt Experiment In addition, the Next Generation Science Standards (2010) NGSS phenomena website (McKenna & Zieminski, 2020) has a variety of videos that can serve as the focus for the lesson. Access the videos at www.ngssphenomena.com
Social Studies	Develop a stance; Recognize bias; Consider multiple viewpoints; Use multiple texts	There are so many controversial topics in social studies. The Intra-Act strategy will push students to consider their stance and to do additional research. Topic: The Iraq War Statements can read: ■ The U.S. has an obligation to enforce justice and world peace. ■ The U.S. had no business being across the world in someone else's fight.

Template for General Intra-Act

Name: ______________________________ Date: ____________

Intra-Act

Topic	**Claim 1**	**Claim 2**	**Claim 3**	**Claim 4**
Group Member 1 ________________				
Group Member 2 ________________				
Group Member 3 ________________				
Group Member 4 ________________				

Example of Intra-Act for Social Studies

Name: ______________________ Date: __________

Intra-Act

Topic Engaging in Conflicts in Other Countries	**Claim 1** The U.S. has an obligation to enforce justice and world peace.	**Claim 2** We had no business being across the world in someone else's fight.	**Claim 3** We (the U.S) were the best candidates to eliminate Saddam Hussein.	**Claim 4** We should have put all the money that was spent on the Iraq War into our public schools instead.
Group Member 1 Georgia	yes	no	yes	yes
Group Member 2 Vivian	yes	yes	no	no
Group Member 3 Archer	no	no	yes	no
Group Member 4 Augustus	yes	no	yes	no

Synthesis Journal

Description

The Synthesis Journal is a graphic organizer designed to scaffold student thinking across multiple sources or across multiple text segments within the same source (Manderino, Berglund, & Johns, 2014). The Journal is divided into separate sections to create space for students to record notes and ideas from each source or text segment. One interesting aspect of this strategy is that there can be a space for a voice of "authority," which can be you (the teacher), the author of the text, or even a student, depending on the context of the lesson and the situation (Burrell & McAlexander, 1998).

This strategy is effective in that it supports the use of multiple sources of information. Deep disciplinary learning requires that students use multiple sources of information or different segments of a single text to generate their own knowledge. Research shows that students struggle to synthesize across multiple sources or text segments without scaffolding (e.g., Hynd-Shanahan, Holschuh, & Hubbard, 2004). Thus, the Synthesis Journal can be used to scaffold multiple-text synthesis and comparative analysis, as well as to record assertions, main ideas, details, or relevant evidence identified in each source. The format of the Synthesis Journal supports students in addressing an inquiry question using texts that may be contradictory, complimentary, or unique.

When and Why Would I Use This Strategy?

- To scaffold the comparison of claims across multiple texts or text segments
- To develop students' ability to synthesize sources based on deep conceptual understanding
- To show students ways to organize ideas and draw conclusions
- To take time to explore a question of inquiry with students

How Do I Teach/Present the Strategy?

1. Choose two or more texts or text segments that you would like to use to facilitate student learning. You should consider texts or text segments that present different perspectives or that emphasize different aspects of the topic. Also, recall that "text" is any product that communicates a message: "texts" can be ideas from lectures, mini lessons, notes from class, video clips, articles, images, and websites.
2. Distribute or share one of the Synthesis Journal templates found in Resources on pages 127, 128, and 130.

3. Instruct students to write the topic or inquiry question in the space provided on the organizer. There are multiple areas on the organizer where students can record information, so it is important to label what information students should include in each area. One Synthesis Journal style is inserted below; for additional ideas see Examples in Context on pages 124–126 and Resources on pages 127–131.

Example Multiple-Ideas Synthesis for Science

Inquiry Question: *What causes erosion?*

Text 1: *The textbook says erosion is the wearing away of land or a lake bed. There is surface water erosion and ground water erosion.*

I say: *Erosion is something that naturally happens over time.*

Synthesis: *Erosion has multiple causes including air, water, ice, and human activity. Erosion is mainly caused by water—ground and surface water.*

Text 2: *Erosion causes the formation of valleys. The author defines erosion as a fluid flow. Fluids include wind, water, and ice. The author says water is the most common cause of erosion.*

My teacher says: *Erosion is a process by which rock and soil are removed from the earth. She says erosion is a natural process but humans contribute as well.*

4. Introduce the first text or text segment. Instruct students to summarize or record key ideas, assertions, claims, or evidence for that text in the corresponding area. You might begin by modeling your own thinking with a portion of the text. Point out the key claims or assertions made by the author.
5. Introduce the second text or text segment. Have students record key ideas, assertions, claims, or evidence for the text in the corresponding area. They can also include a summary to keep track of what each text is about.
6. If you choose to have an area for *Teacher Says*, provide direct instruction on the topic. Have students summarize or record key ideas or claims from your instruction in the corresponding area marked *Teacher Says*.
7. If you include an area for *My Classmates Say*, make sure that as the class discussion takes place, you take notes for all students to view. This will help to ensure that students' ideas are accurately represented in their classmates' journals.
8. After completing all sections, ask students to summarize their position or understanding on the topic in the remaining area.
9. Finally, instruct students to synthesize their response to the inquiry question by taking into consideration all other feedback and information they have noted.
10. There are variations to this method, which can be seen in Examples in Context on pages 124–126 and in the completed Synthesis Journal examples in Resources on pages 129 and 131. Ensure that students have enough room to respond by allowing them to use separate sheets of paper or numbered Google slides.

Connections to the Disciplines	Behaviors Targeted by the Strategy	Examples in Context
ELA	Synthesize multiple sources; Use text to support conclusions; Develop deep thematic understanding; Support text to world connections; Summarize multiple viewpoints	Synthesis Journal is powerful, even within one text. Your perspective, the author's perspective, and students' perspectives can be considered. For example, the inquiry question when teaching the novel *Frankenstein* (Shelly, 1994) can be: "Why do humans place so much emphasis on physical similarity or dissimilarity?" The Synthesis Journal can be broken down to include seven or eight areas, each with their own guiding question: ■ Area 1-First Thoughts: Write down your thoughts about the monster. ■ Area 2-Gathering Evidence: Quote one of Victor's lines and explain its significance. ■ Area 3-Analyzing/Closely Reading: Pick a passage that is important to the way you understand or experience the monster's reality. ■ Area 4-Believing/Doubting: Agree with Victor about the monster. What are you agreeing to? Disagree with Victor. Why do you think Victor is wrong? ■ Area 5-Making Inferences: Why do you think the author chose to describe the monster's first days of life in such detail? What do the details suggest about the monster? Provide a quotation from Chapter 11. ■ Area 6-Summarizing: As the monster's narrative develops, we hear about his impressions of language. What do I say, as your teacher, about this topic? ■ Area 7-Synthesis: What is the author trying to communicate about physical appearance? ■ Area 8-Evaluate: What is your response to the inquiry question?

Connections to the Disciplines	Behaviors Targeted by the Strategy	Examples in Context
Math	Navigate mathematical texts; Construct viable arguments; Use proof and reasoning; Analyze graphics and images; Synthesize statistics	When learning about jump discontinuities in math analysis, you can assign each area to a different explanation, such as: ▪ Area 1-The Teacher's Explanation ▪ Area 2-My Classmates' Explanations ▪ Area 3-My Explanation ▪ Area 4-The Textbook Explanation Or, each area can involve a different representation of one jump discontinuity: ▪ Area 1-Visual or Graphic Representation ▪ Area 2-Word Problem for Jump Discontinuity ▪ Area 3-Equation ▪ Area 4-Explanation Another idea is to draw from aspects of math that are not investigated enough, such as the equal sign. Some studies suggest that students have difficulty transitioning from middle school to high school math because they are lacking an operational and relational understanding of the equal sign. ▪ Area 1-Multiple Meanings of the Equal Sign ▪ Area 2-Equation Types Using the Equal Sign ▪ Area 3-Structural Conventions Involving the Equal Sign ▪ Area 4-Situations Without an Equal Sign and Considerations as to Why Note: Mathematical text can be in any mathematical form: text-based, oral, symbolic, or visual.

Connections to the Disciplines	Behaviors Targeted by the Strategy	Examples in Context
Science	Engage in comparative analysis; Collect data; Draw conclusions; Synthesize viewpoints; Determine gaps in understanding; Eradicate misunderstandings	In science, the textbook can be difficult to navigate. There are often graphs, charts, diagrams, and other visuals that need to be comprehended alongside traditional text. The Synthesis Journal can be used to address the multiple representations of information in the textbook. Each area in the Journal can be a place for students to summarize each text segment. Alternatively, the Synthesis Journal can be used across texts. ▪ The Inquiry question can be about a concept like: What is erosion? ▪ Or about a more controversial topic like: Stem Cells and Cloning See Resources on page 129 for a completed sample.
Social Studies	Compare claims across texts; Evaluate claims; Determine valid forms of evidence; Consider multiple sources; Synthesize ideas; Interpret evidence	Provide students with competing sources on the same topic and have students record claims and evidence put forth by each source. Some ideas for topics include exploring the pros and cons of: ▪ Economics: Scarcity ▪ Geography: Fracking ▪ Psychology: Animal Research Sources can include interviews, images/photographs, lecture notes, group discussion notes, and articles.

Template for General Synthesis Journal

Name: ______________________________ Date: ____________

My Teacher Says	Synthesis
Text 1	
Text 2	
My Partner Says	

Template for Multiple-Ideas Synthesis Journal

Name: ______________________________ Date: ____________

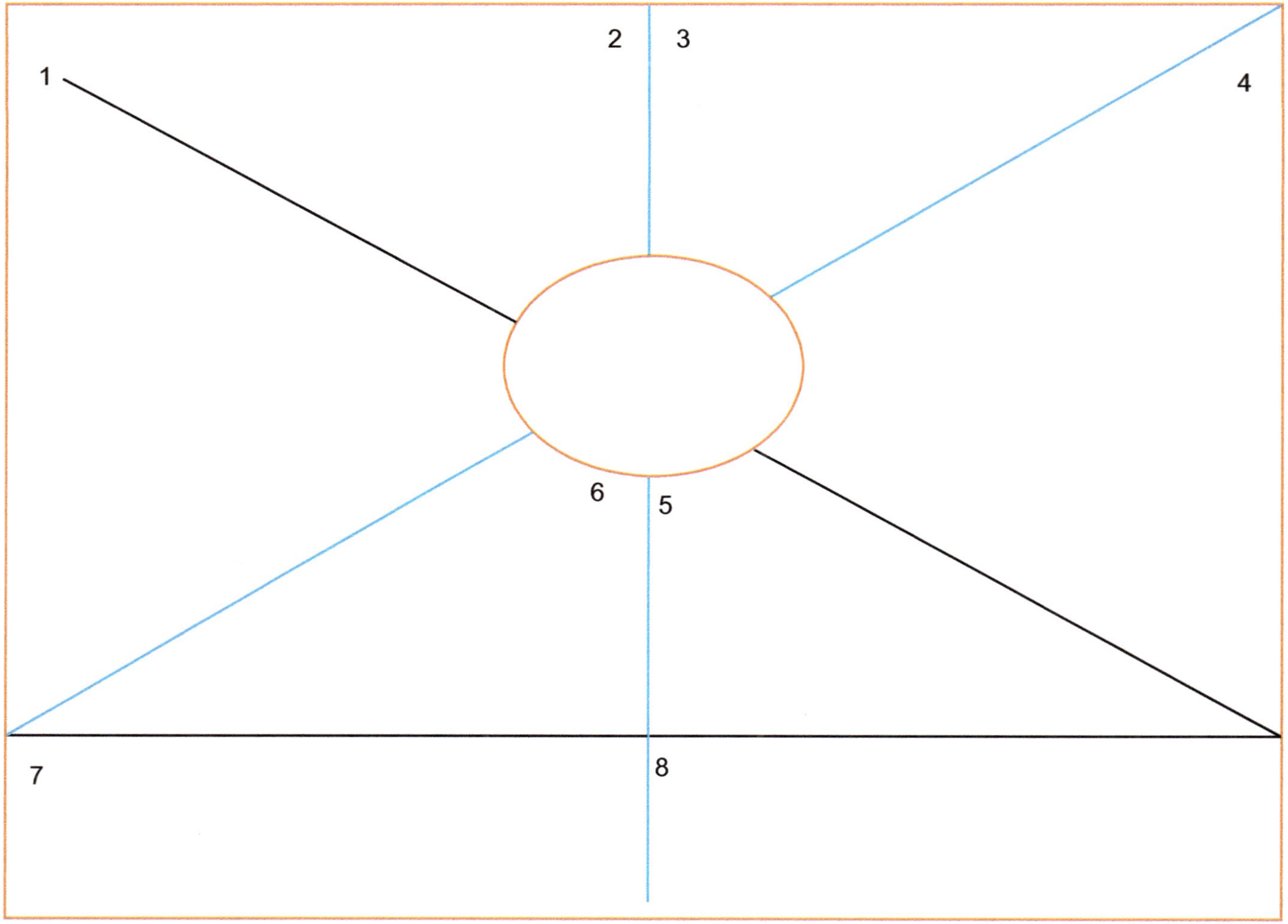

Example of Multiple-Ideas Synthesis Journal for ELA

Name: ______________________ Text: *Frankenstein* ______________________ Date: __________

Why do Humans place so much emphasis on physical similarity or dissimilarity?

1 Area 1: **First Thoughts:** Write down your thoughts about the monster.

2 Area 2: **Gather Evidence:** Quote one of Victor's lines and explain its significance.

3 Area 3: **Analyzing/Close Reading:** Pick a passage that is important to the way you understand or experience the monster's reality.

4 Area 4: **Believing/Doubting:** Agree with Victor about the monster. What are you agreeing to? Disagree with Victor. Why do you think Victor is wrong?

5 Area 5: **Making Inferences:** Why do you think the author chose to describe the monster's first days of life in such detail? What do the details suggest about the monster? Provide a quotation from Chapter 11.

6 Area 6: **Summarizing:** As the monster's narrative develops, we hear about his impressions of language. What does your teacher say about this?

7 Area 7: **Synthesis:** What is the author trying to communicate about physical appearance?

8 Area 8: **Evaluate:** What is your response to the inquiry question?

Template for Two-Text Synthesis Journal

Name: ______________________________ Date: __________

Inquiry Question: ______________________________

Text 1:

I say:

Synthesis:

Text 2:

My teacher says:

Example of Two-Text Synthesis Journal for Science

Name: ______________________ Date: __________

Inquiry Question: *What causes erosion?*

Text 1: *The textbook says erosion is the wearing away of land or a lake bed. There is surface water erosion and ground water erosion.*

I say: *Erosion is something that naturally happens over time.*

Synthesis: *Erosion has multiple causes including air, water, ice, and human activity. Erosion is mainly caused by water—ground and surface water.*

Text 2: *Erosion causes the formation of valleys. The author defines erosion as a fluid flow. Fluids include wind, water, and ice. The author says water is the most common cause of erosion.*

My teacher says: *Erosion is a process by which rock and soil are removed from the earth. She says erosion is a natural process but humans contribute as well.*

Section 3

Writing to Unlock Meaning

Contents for Section 3

Writing-to-learn activities are short, informal, low-stakes writing exercises designed to help students refine their thinking about topics of study in the discipline and/or help them brainstorm ideas for more formal writing processes. Arnold, Umanath, Thio, Reilly, McDaniel, and Marsh (2017) further delineated writing-to-learn activities into two possible categories: elaboration and organization. Elaboration occurs when the writer is making connections to ideas and adding new information to known information. Organization occurs when the writer is involved in organizational processes such as list-making, note-taking, and brainstorming.

When leveraging writing-to-learn strategies, students can deepen their understanding of complex ideas and reflect on their learning. You can help students engage in the strategic behaviors of reflecting, summarizing, making connections, brainstorming, and expanding on ideas in writing. Furthermore, the Writing Across Curriculum Clearinghouse website posits that you can learn to support students' development of thinking by exploring their thought processes through writing (Colorado State University, 2021).

As mentioned in earlier sections, in this edition, we will connect the structured activities we are sharing (often called strategies) to the strategic behaviors that students can develop in order to gain a deep understanding of the disciplines. We have outlined the connections in the chart on the following page, and while there is some overlap, we wanted to provide as much clarity as possible by connecting the strategy to the dominant strategic behavior that is developed.

Overall, our focus is on helping students deepen their understanding about complex disciplinary concepts via writing.

Strategic Behavior	Strategies that Support this Behavior
Summarizing the Text: When readers summarize text as they read, they consider what they already know about the topic presented in the text, make connections among ideas, and organize information as they are reading it. This supports readers' comprehension of text as it requires them to think deeply about the messages with the text (Lenski, Wham, Johns, & Caskey, 2011).	■ Entrance and Exit Slips page 166 ■ Multiple-Text Gist page 175 ■ Cornell Notes page 193
Brainstorming: Brainstorming techniques promote creative thinking and idea-generation (Al-Samarraie & Hj Hurmuzan, 2017). When connected to content in the disciplines, students can expand on their thinking and deepen their understanding of complex concepts and processes.	■ Listing page 162 ■ Climbing and Diving page 171 ■ Marathon Writing page 179
Expanding and Making Connections Among Ideas: When students are able to connect the new information they are gathering to what they already know, they are expanding their knowledge and mastery of topics. When students make connections and reflect on their learning, it deepens their understanding and increases their ability to think critically and from multiple viewpoints (Connor-Greene, 2000).	■ Sketch the Visual page 135 ■ GRASPS page 144 ■ Writer's Notebook page 158 ■ Double-Entry Journal page 183

Sketch the Visual

Description

Sketch the Visual is a strategy that is critical to comprehension and higher-order thinking (Beers & Probst, 2016; Bell, 2007). It requires students to visualize, in detail, what is being described in text and then further develop that image by creating a labeled sketch. While the initial sketch will be created during reading, the strategy extends to include processes for checking, revising, and collaborating during and after reading.

Whether students are asked to sketch or choose an image to represent what they have read in a text, or use a graphic organizer to better understand the relationship of ideas within a text, they are bringing together the two different coding systems of the reading brain. The two coding systems are the symbol-driven coding system and the image-driven coding system (Paivio, 2006). The symbol-driven system allows the brain to decode the letters and know the words; the image-driven coding system makes mental movies, creates color-filled images, and drives the understanding of what the words mean as a whole text (Bell, 2007; Sadoski, 1992). When the two systems work together, students are better able to engage in higher-order thinking processes such as articulating main idea, drawing conclusions, making inferences, predicting, and evaluating (Bell, 2007) and to anchor new ideas in their permanent memory (Marzano, 2004).

How and Why Would I Use This Strategy?

- To enhance students' ability to visualize complicated or technical text
- To support students' in grasping a concept explained in a text
- To teach students how to directly apply textual evidence to their comprehension processes
- To encourage students to reread text and use peer collaboration to modify their understandings

How Do I Teach/Present the Strategy?

1. As you are prereading the materials that you will use in the lesson, consider if there are points in the text that involve a technical or detailed description, a step-by-step process, a timeline, or just a description that might create confusion for students. These are the moments when Sketch the Visual will be appropriate as a reading strategy. See the example in Resources on page 143 for a better idea or example of what this might look like.
2. To begin using Sketch the Visual, you will model the process. First read aloud the entire portion of the text that you will be sketching. Ask students just to listen and try to visualize what you are reading. When you are first using this strategy, try to limit the text segment that you read to five sentences or less. Over time, you can add length and complexity to the text segments that you read aloud. See the Aurora Borealis article example on page 141.
3. After reading the entire portion, break down the text. Reread the first sentence. Ask students, *What does [this] make you picture?* Collect students' responses and write them where all students can see. If students are struggling, you can provide a response since you have pre-read the text and have chosen this text with intention. Your responses should begin with the phrase, *Because of [this] language in the text, I can picture…*
4. Continue with that process through all five sentences, reading one to two sentences at a time. As you continue through the process, you can treat it more like a think-aloud and contribute your ideas to teach students how to visualize as they read. Your responses should begin with the phrase, *Because of [this] language in the text, I can picture…*
5. As you continue through the process, you can continue to collect ideas from students and take notes or mark up the text. As students share their ideas, feel free to add detail to students' responses by offering choices such as, *Do you picture the country opening their borders to immigrants or having armed guards at the border? Let's refer back to the text. What would make you picture that?* Or, *Do you picture the characters in the novel to be standing close together or farther apart? Are they in a circle formation or do you picture something else?*
6. After collecting students' responses, create the sketch based on all of their ideas. Explain aloud as you sketch and reread and reference the text and the notes as much as possible. *Because of [this] language in the text, I can picture… Therefore, I am going to draw [this] here. Is there anything in the text that would indicate this image needs to be changed? Does anyone visualize it differently?*
7. The goal isn't for the sketch to be artistic, but rather one that is detailed. If students are struggling to add detail, send them back into the text. Point out key terms and talk through what you visualize allowing the student to add ideas when they can.
8. After or during sketching, label the sketch with text-specific language as much as possible. The Aurora Borealis article and sketch on pages 141–143 will provide an indication of the value of labels to support understanding and to recognize various aspects of a sketch.
9. The power of this strategy is partially in the visual and partially in the concrete representation of how text becomes visual. Therefore, when it is completed, you can explain the sketch verbally using the words from the text.

10. Now it is the students' turn. Continue to support the process carefully. Make sure they have all of the supplies that they will need to complete the sketch. Depending on your goals there are a variety of options for sketching online, but paper and pencil works well, too.
11. Continue to support the process carefully by repeating steps 2-9 with the students. They can take notes or you can continue to gather their ideas. Prompt students for additional details using the questions below as well as the questions and stems provided on page 140.
    a. *What does [this] make you picture?*
    b. *Because of [this] language in the text, what do you picture?*
    c. *Do you picture [this] or [this]? Let's refer back to the text. What would make you picture that?*
    d. *Because of [this] language in the text, I pictured [this]. What did you picture? What did you draw? Is there anything in the text that would indicate your sketch needs to be modified? Did anyone visualize it and sketch it differently?*
12. Other options are to have students work in pairs to compare sketches and explain sketches or to develop the sketches together. It is helpful to have one student checking the text and the other student sketching.
13. Ensure that students are being as specific as they can with their sketches and labeling them with text-specific language as much as possible. If the text itself is just too confusing to comprehend, take a step back and work with students to complete a close-read of the text, defining difficult language and even providing some images to prompt students' thinking and understanding. The Aurora Borealis article and subsequent sketch can be used with students to model the process of Sketch the Visual. Closely reading the text, marking it, underlining key moments, and clarifying unknown words are critical components of developing a good sketch.

Connections to the Discipline	Behaviors Targeted by the Strategy	Examples in Context
ELA	Visualize text; Draw conclusions; Elaborate on ideas; Use textual evidence to develop ideas; Draw conclusions based on text	Oftentimes when reading novels, the setting is described in such detail that it is difficult to visualize without a sketch to assist. Commonly, the island in *Lord of the Flies* (Golding, 2011) is sketched. Another idea is to ask students to sketch the setting as well as the action in the final scenes of *To Kill a Mockingbird* (Lee, 2006), when Scout and Jem are being chased through the woods on their way home. Contemporary novels would also work well for Sketch the Visual, including a sketch of the jail and jail cell in *Punching the Air* (Zoboi, Salaam, & Pasha (2020); the elevator in *Long Way Down* (Reynolds, 2019); or the landscape in *The Maze Runner* (Dashner, 2010). Another idea is to sketch the characters to make them feel truly real, such as the characters encountered on each floor of *Long Way Down* (Reynolds, 2019), or the character of the Scythe in the novel *Scythe* (Shusterman, 2017).

Connections to the Discipline	Behaviors Targeted by the Strategy	Examples in Context
Math	Develop a visual representation of information; Form concrete associations; Interpret vocabulary; Apply concepts	Mathematicians constantly generate images to understand mathematical ideas and concepts. such as when working with fractions, setting up equations, outlining word problems, and when they are thinking about graphic representations of textualized material. For this strategy, students have found success sketching vocabulary for a variety of reasons: ▪ Oftentimes students learn the nontechnical definitions of discipline-specific words and need practice shifting their understanding to a more precise, mathematical definition (Sammons, 2011; Thompson & Rubenstein, 2000). This is often the case with words like *volume, plane, factor, similar,* and *divide*. ▪ Other mathematical vocabulary only applies to mathematics, such as *hypotenuse, integer,* and *octagon*. ▪ Some mathematical vocabulary is easily confused with other terms and concepts like *factoring, factor, factor pair, factor tree,* and *greatest common factor.* ▪ Some words are used differently depending on the discipline, like *solution* or *radical*. Sketch the Visual can be beneficial in all of these instances, especially when students are able to sketch the concept within the context of the lesson and also sketch application examples.
Science	Evaluate processes; Determine conclusions; Collaborate with peers; Visualize concepts and processes; Use text to drive understanding; Articulate ideas	The most common science unit involves the ideas of cellular respiration and photosynthesis. While common, this unit is extremely complex and involves various scientific processes coming together. In addition, the amount of discipline-specific vocabulary is vast and yet it must be mastered for students to truly understand this concept. Sketch the Visual can support students in grasping the processes of cellular respiration and photosynthesis. When students label the sketch, they will be applying vocabulary and committing it to memory. You can also monitor and fix misconceptions by simply viewing the sketch, by asking students to explain their sketch, or by asking students to compare sketches to determine any differences or inconsistencies.

Connections to the Discipline	Behaviors Targeted by the Strategy	Examples in Context
Social Studies	Corroborate sources; Visualize events; Use text to drive understanding; Evaluate cause and effect relationships; Interpret point of view; Analyze change	Social studies texts often provide visuals as part of the communication of information. These visuals include illustrations, timelines, political cartoons, charts, graphs, and tables. The use of visuals to communicate information demonstrates how valuable Sketch the Visual is to social studies. Taking students through the process of using text to create their own visual solidifies for them the process that historians use to communicate information through images. One skill in history is to analyze what has changed and what has stayed the same. Drawing a before and after of major cities during the Industrial Revolution, for example, is a powerful moment for students to take into account how much the landscape of cities changed during this time period. When reading timelines of events, students can develop more detailed visuals of certain points on the timeline. One example is the timeline of Reconstruction. Students can draft sketches illustrating the changing borders or the advancement of soldiers to analyze the progress and the lack of progress that occurred. In addition, drawing examples of how laws and amendments have been interpreted over the years can become a powerful way to compare and contrast. The 14th Amendment is one that can be considered from a variety of angles.

Example Prompts

Name: ______________________ Date: __________

Prompts
What does [this] make you picture?
Because of [this] language in the text, what do you picture?
Do you picture [this] or [this]?
Let's refer back to the text.
What would make you picture [that]?
Because of [this] language in the text, I pictured [this].
What did you picture?
What did you draw?
Is there anything in the text that would indicate your sketch is missing something?
Is there anything in the text that would indicate your sketch needs to change?
Did anyone visualize it and sketch it differently?
Are there any additional labels we can use?
What words do we need definitions for?

Example Aurora Borealis article

Name: Olivia Date: ____________

Original Article: Weisberger, M. (2020). An aurora that lit up the sky over the Titanic might explain why it sank. *Live Science.* https://www.livescience.com/titanic-sunk-by-aurora.html

Article of the Week

Link to Listen. Start by Clicking Here
1. Mark your confusion: *Unfamiliar Words & Ideas that You Don't Understand*
2. Show evidence of comprehension in the margin: *Write Big Ideas*
3. Reflect: *Complete the Prompt*

An aurora that lit up the sky over the Titanic might explain why it sank	*My Notes:*
Live Science | | Sept. 28, 2020 The sinking of the Titanic is one of the most famous sea disasters ever. More than 1,500 passengers died when the giant ship hit an iceberg and sank on April 15, 1912. But what made it so deadly? The glowing auroras that shimmered in the skies over the northern Atlantic Ocean that fateful night might give a clue. It might have meant that there were disruptions to the ship's navigation and communication systems. And those disruptions may have fueled the disaster, said Mila Zinkova, an independent weather researcher.	Overall, this paragraph is about the Titanic sinking and people died because there were disruptions to the ship's navigation and communication systems.
Part 2 Zinkova published her study online on August 4 in the journal Weather. Eyewitnesses described auroras in the sky as the Titanic went down. Auroras are also called northern lights or aurora borealis in the northern hemisphere. One observer testified that "the northern lights were very strong that night." Auroras are displays of light that take place high in the atmosphere. The reason we see these colored light displays is due to solar storms, which are disturbances on the sun. And solar storms can affect Earth. The sun is mostly made of plasma, which is a superhot mix of charged particles. When charged particles move, they create magnetic fields. These fields can tangle and cross, which can cause an explosion of energy called a solar flare. The charged particles released by solar flares can be detected in our atmosphere.	Overall, this paragraph is about auroras in the sky the night the Titanic went down and those are a superhot mix of charged particles, magnetic fields, and explosions.

Example Aurora Borealis article, continued...

An aurora that lit up the sky over the Titanic might explain why it sank	*My Notes:*
Part 3: Sometimes a powerful solar flare is accompanied by a coronal mass ejection. <u>This is a sudden and violent release of bubbles of plasma and magnetic fields.</u> A solar storm occurs when major eruptions like solar flares or coronal mass ejections happen in the solar atmosphere. They can send a <u>high-speed stream of charged particles and magnetic fields hurtling toward</u> us. But Earth also has a <u>magnetic field, which shields us from most of the sun's energy and particles</u>. When this solar matter <u>collides with our atmosphere</u>, the surrounding magnetic field deflects it toward the north and south poles. There, it interacts with gases in the atmosphere, which then can glow green, red, purple, and blue. This creates the beautiful auroras that we see in the sky. But this solar matter can also <u>interfere with electrical and magnetic signals on Earth. Another name for a solar storm is a geomagnetic storm.</u>	*Overall, this paragraph is about a geomagnetic storm which is when solar matter interferes with electrical and magnetic signals on Earth.*
Part 4: <u>Northern Lights Were Strong When Titanic Sank</u> The Titanic navigated through the water using a compass, <u>where the compass needle responded to Earth's magnetic field</u>. It is a <u>magnet that makes a compass point north</u>. A solar storm powerful enough to produce an aurora would have <u>affected compasses and radio communication on the Titanic</u>. It would have affected nearby ships trying to come to her aid. Even a small disruption might have been enough to <u>doom the vessel</u>, Zinkova said in the study. And the Northern lights were highly visible when the Titanic sank. - Sample ends here -	*Overall, this paragraph is about the Northern lights and the Titanic and how the Earth's magnetic field affected communication that night causing it to take longer for people to get rescued, and it also impacted the compass.*

Remember to use your margin notes to respond below.
Prompt: If a friend asked you, "What did you just read about in this article?", what would you say?

This article uses the science surrounding Earth's magnetic field to explain why the Titanic's navigation system did not react to the iceberg.

Sketch for Aurora Borealis article

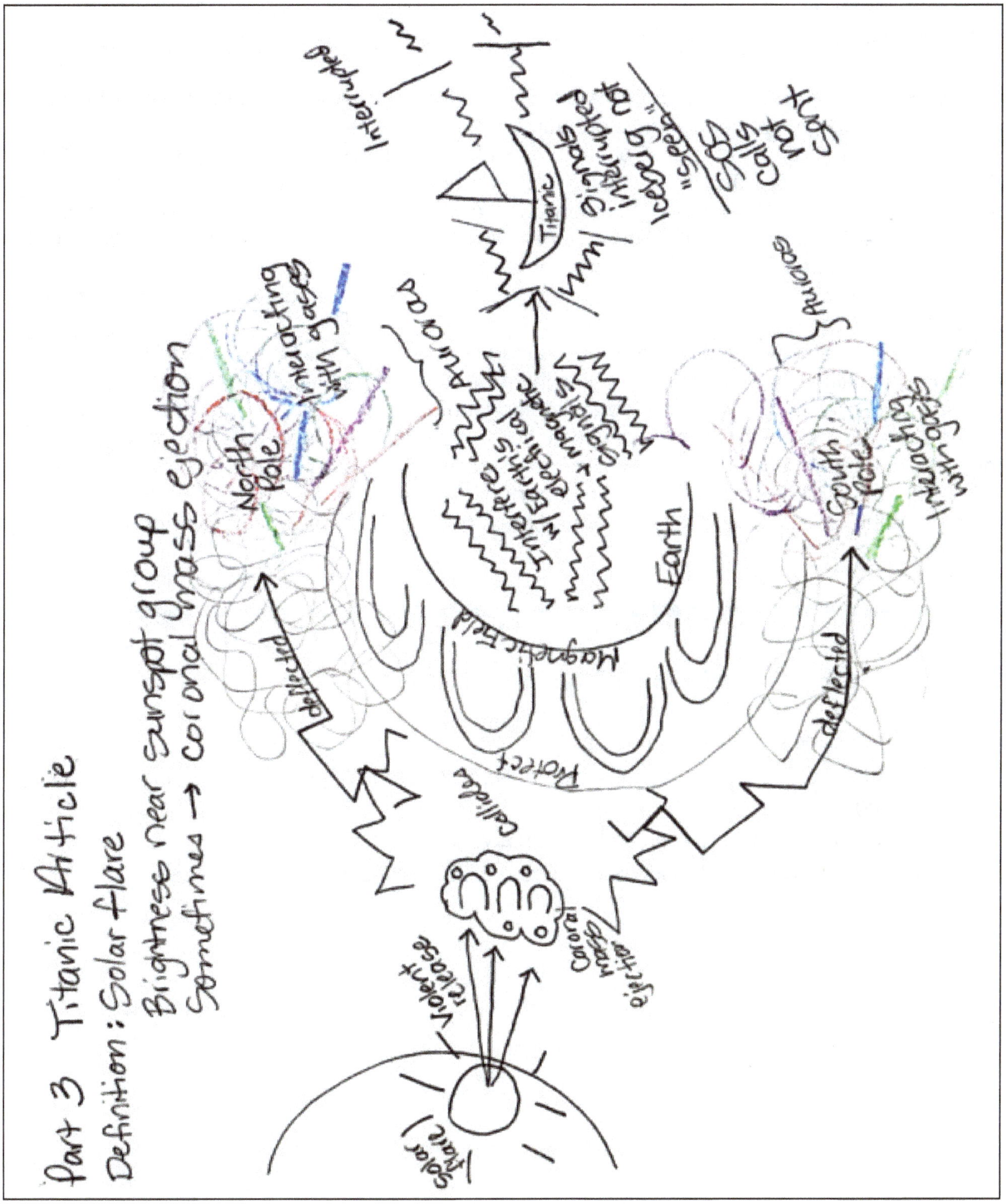

GRASPS

Description

GRASPS (Wiggins & McTighe, 2008) is a writing-to-learn strategy that can be used to support students in thinking more deeply and more authentically during their learning experience. GRASPS is an acronym that stands for Goal, Role, Audience, Situation, Product/Performance, and Standards for Success. Traditionally, GRASPS has been used as a performance task in which students are able to showcase their knowledge and understanding in an authentic form. For example, after learning about the Revolutionary War, students can take on the role of a colonist who is giving a speech to the king to stop unfair taxation. The goal is for students to shift their perspective in order to persuade an authentic audience rather than just report about the topic of Revolutionary War.

GRASPS is a powerful strategy that is also versatile. Each aspect of GRASPS (e.g., role, audience, situation, etc.) pushes students to integrate knowledge and skills, to provide evidence of genuine understanding, and to develop and demonstrate discipline-specific literacy practices.

As students engage in the thinking necessary to respond to each of the elements of GRASPS, they take on an empathetic, active, first-person stance, which is a powerful approach to learning (Riess, 2018). GRASPS also provides an opportunity for flexibility and choice, both for you and for your students. GRASPS works best when aligned with discipline-specific behaviors and literacy practices.

How and Why Would I Use This Strategy?

- To encourage synthesis of material
- To support students in taking an empathetic, first-person approach to learning and reading
- To motivate students to think and write in a variety of modalities
- To develop students' ability to demonstrate their learning in a variety of ways

How Do I Teach/Present the Strategy?

1. First, consider your standards, goals, and intended outcomes for the lesson. Ensure that an authentic task can be created by students in order to integrate and extend their understanding.
2. Also, consider the major concepts or processes that you want students to learn and use in a given unit of study. See Examples in Context on pages 146–148 for ideas.
3. Once your instructional goal has been clarified, determine choices for each element. Define possible roles, audiences, situations, products or performances, as well as criterion for success. Decide how much choice to give students based on their understanding of GRASPS and each individual element. Use the template for teacher planning on page 149 to support your thinking and creation of a GRASPS task.
4. Now that your assignment is complete and you have thought through all components of your unit, introduce GRASPS to your students.
5. Explain to students how all writers have to consider various aspects of writing, including:
   a. The Goal: Why am I doing this?
   b. The Role: Who am I as part of this process?
   c. The Audience: Who am I doing this for?
   d. The Situation: What is going on and what is involved?
   e. The Product or Performance: What should I do/create to best communicate my message?
   f. The Standards or Criteria for Success: What are my parameters? What will make this successful?
6. Provide students with the completed GRASPS brainstorming example on page 152 as you discuss each aspect above in Step 5.
7. At this point, you can use the template for brainstorming with students on page 151 in order to develop your assignment.
8. Once students are clear about what the strategy entails, provide students with a blank template, such as the example on page 154. Together, brainstorm additional topics, roles, formats, audiences, and products that might be beneficial for a GRASPS task based on the learning within your unit. Use the list of ideas in Resources on page 156 to guide students' work. This step will provide students with an opportunity to unlock meaning by positioning their ideas within the various elements of GRASPS (i.e., role, audience, situation).
9. Support students in talking through how and why certain GRASPS choices will support their communication efforts, while others will detract from their goals (e.g., using a brochure to present information to a large group of people in a darkened convention center is not the best choice). While students' brainstormed ideas may not be included in the final GRASPS assignment, the goal is for students to think through each of the elements of GRASPS in relation to the unit of study.

10. Put students into small groups. Distribute the assignment you have created as well as the template for student planning on page 154. Ask students to choose one role and then brainstorm possible information, emotions, and situations that might be shared. Ask them to consider the best product to communicate these ideas. While the writing is brief, it will support students in integrating their knowledge and ideas about the unit.
11. When students have gained enough knowledge and understanding to begin to think more deeply about the topics and have a firm understanding of GRASPS and each element (i.e., role, audience, product), introduce your GRASPS assignment as a whole. Again, depending on students' exposure and use of GRASPS, you will have to decide how many choices students will have for each element. When first using this strategy, you may opt not to provide a choice or to limit choices to 2-3 options or choices just in one element (e.g., choose one audience from these three options). See Resources on page 156 for ideas.
12. Because GRASPS assignments vary a great deal, it is helpful to share a rubric at the onset that is linked to the standards and criteria for success. See Resources on page 157 for ideas.

Connections to the Disciplines	Behaviors Targeted by the Strategy	Examples in Context
ELA	Adopt alternate perspectives and viewpoints; Draw conclusions; Cultivate empathy; Develop and apply inferences; Synthesize evidence	Goal: To determine the main character's motivations behind their actions and recommend a course of treatment Role: Therapist Audience: Parents and Teachers of the Main Character Situation: The main character of the novel is making poor choices that will negatively impact their future, and their parents have sent them to therapy to try and work through their struggles. You will need to present your findings to the parents and the school after working with the main character for three months. Product/Performance: A meeting in which you report your findings and present a brochure outlining the diagnosis you think is most feasible Standards for Success: I can synthesize research and textual evidence to draw conclusions. I can present my findings in multiple formats including a brochure and brief verbal explanation (see the rubric for additional parameters).

Connections to the Disciplines	Behaviors Targeted by the Strategy	Examples in Context
Math	Articulate processes; Solve problems; Synthesize multiple forms of communication; Use visual representations; Synthesize data from multiple sources; Draw conclusions	Goal: To offer advice to an investor about which tech company they should invest in Role: Financial Advisor Audience: A potential investor who knows that technology is a good business to invest in, but they know nothing about investing or about apps Situation: Your client is an investor and they want to invest in a tech startup company but are unsure of which one to choose. You will need to look at each company's business plan and consider the financials and potential earnings of each company and advise your client. Also, since both companies are designing apps for a teenage crowd, you will need to collect data from a teenage focus group to conclude which app has the potential for more earnings. Product/Performance: A graphic representation demonstrating potential for earnings, risks, information from the focus group, the investor's potential earnings, and potential losses. Standards for Success: I can use a variety of modes to communicate information. I can draw data from a variety of sources and synthesize it to draw conclusions.
Science	Develop procedures; Evaluate processes; Collaborate with peers; Solve problems	Goal: To design the procedure for an experiment Role: Environmental Scientist Audience: Teachers who need experiments for their freshmen students to use in class Situation: You are a scientist who sells your ideas to teachers for use in the classroom. You have discovered that different types of materials hold heat at different rates. Now, you need to create the procedure for high school students to follow in order to make this same discovery. Product/Performance: An organized procedure including materials, preparation, and step-by-step instructions for how to carry out the experiment. Standards for Success: I can think through a process from beginning to end without missing any steps. I can explain my ideas clearly and accurately.

Connections to the Disciplines	Behaviors Targeted by the Strategy	Examples in Context
Social Studies	Corroborate sources; Consider and explore multiple viewpoints; Examine bias; Integrate knowledge	Goal: To make a judgment Role: Lawyer Audience: The community, school board, medical advisors, students, and other invested parties and stakeholders Situation: Two businesses want to buy land in the town and build a business there. One wants to open a clinic to provide people better access to doctors and the other wants to open a school so that students do not need to travel over an hour to school. The problem is that you need to listen to multiple perspectives and determine who the town should sell the land to. Product/Performance: A legal forum in which both sides will deliver their arguments and you will come to a ruling using data, financial considerations, and anecdotal accounts from all invested parties. Standards for Success: I can develop an argument that addresses multiple audiences at one time. I can use a variety of forms of evidence to support my stance.

Template for Teacher Planning of GRASPS

Name: ______________________________ Date: __________

In order for GRASPS to work, you will need to carefully think through your unit. Consider each aspect below and ensure that you are prepared to talk through each one clearly with students. Also make sure that your unit lends itself to a lot of different ideas.

Performance Assessment Acronym GRASPS		
Goal	What is the instructional goal of using GRASPS? What do you hope will be the outcome? What will students learn, and how will GRASPS allow them to deepen their learning? What is the problem or challenge that is within the unit? What is the context of that problem? Do students have a strong understanding of the content so that they are able to work with the information in creative ways?	
Role	What are some of the real-life personas that students will be able to adopt? How will you explain to students that they will be taking on a different perspective and point of view in order to deepen their knowledge and understanding of a situation? Do you want to assign students roles, provide a limited list of choices, or allow students to work freely?	
Audience	What is the content-based scenario that students are working with? Who, then, would be a target audience? Are you going to brainstorm ideas with students, provide them with a list to choose from, or give all students the same audience? Remember, the audience is the hypothetical, or potentially real, group of people who will listen, critique, and make decisions.	
Situation	What is the real-world connection? What is the context of the scenario that students will be focusing on? What are the parameters? How can you build the background knowledge?	

Template for Teacher Planning of GRASPS, continued...

Performance Assessment Acronym GRASPS		
Performance or Product	What is the student expected to create? What makes sense within your time constraints and your ability to access materials and supports? Will students have enough time to revise their performance or product? Will you be video recording or will performances be live? Do you have a rubric ready so that students have a clear view of what is expected? Have you given students enough flexibility in options that they are able to truly express themselves and show what they know and are able to do?	
Success Criteria	In what ways will students struggle? How can you modify the assignment to support all learners? Are your goals and purposes clear? Have you considered the principles of multiple intelligences and learning styles? Do students have enough structure to support their progress, but not so much so that it inhibits their creativity? How will you formatively assess students along the way?	

Adapted From Wiggins, Grant and Jay McTighe. Understanding by Design Professional Development Workbook. Alexandria, VA: Association for Supervision and Curriculum Development. 2004. http://nvsd44curriculumhub.ca/wp-content/uploads/2017/09/GRASPS-Instructions.pdf

Template for Brainstorming GRASPS With Students

Name: ______________________________ Date: ____________

Consider the unit we have been studying. Look through the lists of possible roles, audience, and products. What ideas do you have for the following elements Take into account our unit, the position you would like to take, and possible hypothetical audiences.

Unit of Study: ______________________________

Topics/Lessons: ______________________________

Role Who am I as a part of this process?	**Audience** Who am I doing this for?	**Situation** What is going on and what is involved?	**Product/Performance** What should I do/create to best communicate my message?

Look at your ideas above. Choose one of the roles. Navigate through the following questions and determine if this role is right for you.

Role Chosen: ______________________________

1. Describe me.	
2. What feelings do I have?	
3. What information do I need to convey?	
4. What words or ideas might I include to get my point across?	
5. What do I know about my audience? What type of information or persuasion might they need?	
6. What do I already know about the format? How might it look?	

Example of Brainstorming GRASPS With Students

Name: *Lucy* Date: ____________

Consider the unit we have been studying. Look through the lists of possible roles, audience, and products. What ideas do you have for the following GRASPS? Take into account our unit, the position you would like to take, and possible hypothetical audiences.

Unit of Study: Revolutionary War

Topics/Lessons:

- The Stamp Act (March 1765)
- The Townshend Acts (June-July 1767)
- The Boston Massacre (March 1770)
- The Boston Tea Party (December 1773)
- The Coercive Acts (March-June 1774)
- Paul Revere's Ride (April 1775)
- British attacks on coastal towns (October 1775-January 1776)

Role Who am I as a part of this process?	**Audience** Who am I doing this for?	**Situation** What is going on and what is involved?	**Product/Performance** What should I do/create to best communicate my message?
Young Colonist	*Sons of Liberty*	*Colonists and Sons did not appreciate each other. Sons just dumped all of the goods in the water and ruined them. We lost a lot of money. This needs to stop.*	*Create propaganda*
Paul Revere's Horse	*Other War Horses*	*Alerted the American colonial militia that British forces were approaching and carried men into battle*	*Song of hope and strength; saddle blanket decorated to represent certain ideas; a flag with symbols that your rider can wave to communicate ideas*
Patriot Soldier	*Your Family*	*Rebelled against authority*	*Needs to be secret, so a coded letter or a picture with a specific background to communicate a message, or a flyer that is quick to read and easy to burn*

Example of Brainstorming GRASPS with Students, continued...

Name: ______________________________ Date: __________

Look at your ideas above. Choose one of the roles. Navigate through the following questions and determine if this role is right for you.

Role Chosen: Paul Revere's Horse

1. Describe me.	I did not belong to Paul Revere. He grabbed me off the street.
2. What feelings do I have?	I wanted to serve and rebel against the British. I was in the right place at the right time.
3. What information do I need to convey?	I need to convey that horses are critical to this war because we carry the men long distances, carry supplies, and allow the men some safety and repose.
4. What words or ideas might I include to get my point across?	Fight, important, companion, value, win, good life
5. What do I know about my audience? What type of information or persuasion might they need?	Many horses are afraid. There are long nights and not a lot of food and a lot of danger. But the solders deal with the same situations and we are a team fighting this war together.
6. What do I already know about the format? How might it look?	While this seems like a silly role of an animal, in reality animals are very intuitive. I am thinking that a horse would understand the emotions. So it could maybe wear a blanket or have a flag that communicates with patterns. Maybe it is a song, or a jingle, or a chant that the horses can "say" going into battle.

Template for Student Planning of GRASPS

Name: ______________________________ Date: __________

To be successful you will need to think carefully through the unit, have a clear view of what you want for the final product, and be certain of how you will get there. Complete the following sentence stems and make sure your ideas are aligned to the goals of the lesson that your teacher has provided.

Objective for this Project		
GRASPS Plan		
Goal: Problem or challenge to be resolved	■ The problem that exists is… ■ Therefore, we need to figure out how to…	
Role: The identity you will take on in the scenario and what you are being asked to do	■ To gain a different perspective of this situation, I am going to view it from the lens of…	
Audience: The people whose problem you are solving, and who you need to convince and communicate with	■ I am going to be presenting or performing in front of a certain type of people. This group will be… ■ Therefore, I need to consider…	

Template for Student Planning of GRASPS, continued...

Situation: The context of the situation and additional factors that could impede your resolution of the problem	■ The situation involves a lot of different factors including… ■ That could be a problem because… ■ That could help me by…	
Product/ Performance and Purpose: The product you will create or the performance you will engage in that will achieve the larger purpose	■ I am going to need to create…in order to fulfill my purpose of…	
Success Criteria: The standards, objectives, and guidelines that you will need to fulfill in order to communicate with your target audience	■ The goal my teacher established was… ■ My completion of GRASPS fulfills this goal because…	

Ideas for GRASPS Categories

Name: ______________________________ Date: ____________

Ideas for Roles and Audiences

candidate	**neighbor**
best friend	**forest ranger**
photographer	**inventor**
jury	**social worker**

Ideas for Products

Written	Oral	Visual
blog	dramatic reading	infographic
script	interview	diagram
position paper	song	photographs

Example of General Rubric for GRASPS

Name: ______________________________ Date: ____________

+ Examples and Explanation of What is Done Well	Standards for Success	– Examples and Explanation of What Could use Improvement
	Goal is focused and authentic	
	Role aligns with topic of study	
	Writing is appropriate for audience	
	Situation is detailed and information is accurate	
	Product is "authentic" and integrates multiple learning points	
	Overall demonstrates depth of knowledge and meets objectives established	

Writer's Notebook

Description

Writer's Notebook is a space where students can organize their thinking, brainstorm ideas, and learn to see themselves as writers. In fact, it is in the Writer's Notebook where students learn how to write (Fletcher, 2003). Writing is thinking, and by having a central location for students to hold their ideas, students will begin to see the patterns in their thinking, process their learning, and store ideas for further exploration. Traditionally, a Writer's Notebook is a place to hold one's ideas for future writing projects, practice using rhetorical devices, play with words, craft descriptive passages, engage in writing exercises, or generate ideas for further exploration.

These notebooks can also have discipline-specific purposes. For example, in math you may call it a Mathematician's Notebook. It would be used to hold formulas, conjectures, reflections on process, and examples of problem-solving. In a science class you may decide to call this a Scientist's Notebook. Students may use it to write observations and inferences, to organize their materials list for an experiment, and/or to collect questions for further inquiry. In a social studies class, you may use it as a space for students to ask questions, create running records of beliefs and perspectives held by various groups, or gather evidence for a particular historical argument.

Overall, a Writer's Notebook should be a place where students are asked to write regularly as well as review, revisit, and revise what they have written. This process of writing regularly will not only assist students in self-reflection but will also allow them to see various forms of writing, both formal and informal, used in the disciplines. Writer's Notebook can be housed in a binder with loose-leaf, could be a spiral notebook, or might be a Google Doc that students can organize using the Headings feature.

How and Why Would I Use This Strategy?

- To support students' writing process by organizing their thinking into the stages of the writing process
- To process learning by making connections and summarizing their learning
- To reflect on learning
- To list questions (and later record responses) for further inquiry
- To engage in writing exercises
- To encourage students to see themselves as writers
- To provide space for students to organize their learning and own their learning processes

How Do I Teach/Present the Strategy?

1. Introduce the concept of Writer's Notebook to your students. You may choose to call it a Scientist's Notebook, a Mathematician's Notebook, or a Historian's Notebook, if you prefer. Explain that the purpose of the Writer's Notebook is for students to organize their thinking and practice developing their writing skills. If you are using the Writer's Notebook for a more discipline-specific purpose, explain the purpose for that particular notebook. If you are using Google Docs to house the Writer's Notebook, ask students to create a document, share it with you, and use the first heading to put the date on the top of the entry. Ultimately, there are many purposes for a Writer's Notebook, and some of these more discipline-specific purposes can be found on page 161.
2. Model your own use of the Writer's Notebook by writing to respond to any prompts that you assign your students.
3. After students have included a few entries, be sure you return to the notebook periodically. You may ask students to review the content they processed or further explore ideas they have collected in their notebooks.

Connections to the Disciplines	Behaviors Targeted by the Strategy	Examples in Context
ELA	Brainstorm ideas; Process understanding of a text; Explore ideas for writing topics; Make connections among ideas; Generate questions for inquiry; Engage in practice-writing exercises	When writing a narrative, students may be asked to engage in writing exercises aimed at helping them craft detailed settings in their Writer's Notebook. You can also ask them to list each setting that would need to be described for their narrative (e.g., a classroom, a car, their home). You can invite students to find an image online that they would like to think about when they are describing. You can begin by asking for a word sketch of one element of setting and describing what they see, hear, feel, taste, and smell when at that particular place. You can then ask students to continue to develop the setting they selected or continue to develop additional setting scenes. Students may then select a piece of writing for a writing conference with you and receive feedback.

Connections to the Disciplines	Behaviors Targeted by the Strategy	Examples in Context
Math	Synthesize learning; Make connections among topics; Evaluate an approach to solving a problem; Explore concepts; Process learning	When studying triangles, you can ask students to list all the properties of triangles and describe those properties by writing the rules for triangles. By listing what they know to be true, students can assess their own learning or compare notes with another student to solidify learning, correct misconceptions, and fill gaps in knowledge. Later, you might ask students to return to their notebooks to study the properties of triangles and further solidify their learning and/or prepare for an assessment.
Science	Evaluate processes; Determine conclusions; Synthesize learning; Conduct experiments and/or labs; Summarize learning about content; Make connections among ideas	Students in a chemistry class may be asked to list everything they learned from a specific lab. They can then write more information about these topics by making connections regarding what they learned in the lab, what they have been studying in class, and what they have been reading in assigned texts. Graphic organizers can be used in Writer's Notebooks to organize information, but be sure to allow students freedom to brainstorm prior to suggesting or using an organizer.
Social Studies	Corroborate sources; Consider multiple perspectives; Organize evidence; List events and determine if they were a cause or simply preceded an event; Generate questions for inquiry	When studying Alexander Hamilton's role in the American Revolutionary War, you can ask students to write everything they know about his role, the events of the war, and the impact of the war. They may choose to write from his perspective. Next, you can have students write about Hamilton's role in the American Revolutionary War from Aaron Burr's perspective. This process could help them later form a thesis they can support with evidence. You can encourage students to capture questions in their Writer's Notebook for future research.

Examples for Writer's Notebooks in Each Discipline

Name: ____________________ Date: __________

Discipline	Purpose for Notebook
ELA	■ Practice the craft of writing ■ Engage in inquiry ■ Brainstorm during the writing process ■ Gather evidence to support claims ■ Practice using transitional words and phrases ■ Engage in writing exercises to build stamina
Math	■ Process learning ■ Apply formulas ■ Develop procedures to engage in problem solving ■ Reflect on current understanding ■ Craft questions to seek additional information
Science	■ Engage in inquiry ■ Apply learning from labs ■ Organize and categorize evidence ■ Record observations and make inferences ■ Synthesize learning
Social Studies	■ Engage in inquiry ■ Organize information ■ Gather and evaluate evidence ■ Consider additional perspectives

Listing

Description

A list is a set of ideas generated by the writer. Listing, then, is a versatile strategy that can help students hold their thinking about new ideas, brainstorm new ideas, and generate questions they plan to investigate. When used as a writing-to-learn strategy, listing can help students consider what they already know about the topic. These lists can be created using sticky notes, a notebook, loose-leaf paper, or through a variety of technology applications including Google Keep or a Google Doc (see page xvii in the introduction for more information about technology applications). Allow students to choose the format that works best for them.

Once lists are generated, you can ask students to revisit these lists for specific purposes. For example, in social studies, once students have listed all of the events they know surrounding a topic, you may ask students to return to the list and determine which events preceded others, or which were causes or effects. See page 164 for more details and additional discipline-specific ideas.

Specific types of lists may also be used to help make sense of a text and to use new vocabulary. See List-Group-Label and Semantic Mapping on page 48 for more information. Lists may also be used to help students manage their learning experiences. For example, students may work better listing all of their homework tasks before breaking down those tasks into smaller chunks.

How and Why Would I Use This Strategy?

- To help brainstorm ideas for a writing task
- To record what is already known about a topic
- To generate questions
- To reflect on learning
- To recognize the steps in a process
- To record information for later use

How Do I Teach/Present the Strategy?

1. Explain to students that a list is a set of ideas one generates to meet a specific purpose. You might share nonacademic examples of Listing that people use regularly, such as making a shopping list to record what they need from a store. You may also share common academic uses for lists, such as breaking down projects into smaller steps, listing ideas for an essay, or generating a list of questions for further study. Explain that lists can take many forms and that the purpose is to capture thinking and to revisit the lists at a later time. The purpose is not to worry about punctuation, spelling, usage, or grammar while listing.
2. Share ideas about where students might record lists or ask students to use one specific place to record their lists. You might ask students to write a list on a sticky note, on a piece of paper, in a notebook, or on a Google Doc. See page xvii for more information on the technology applications mentioned here.
3. Once students are aware of where and how to record their lists, explain the purpose you have for the list. You might ask them to list everything they know about a character in a text to prepare for a discussion or all the steps in solving a problem. You may ask students to list the results from an experiment or all of the events surrounding a particular event in history. See page 164 for more examples of how one might use a list in each discipline.
4. Additional application ideas include:
    a. Asking students to share their lists in order to gather ideas
    b. Providing time for students to revisit their lists for the purpose of adding more ideas
    c. Offering students a graphic organizer to help organize their lists
    d. Demonstrating how to revise lists when necessary, such as showing students how to break one long list into multiple, shorter lists
    e. Engaging students in a discussion using the ideas generated in the lists

Connections to the Disciplines	Behaviors Targeted by the Strategy	Examples in Context
ELA	Brainstorm ideas; Generate questions; List rhetorical devices and their impact on an audience	To solidify their understanding of rhetorical devices and their intended impact on the audience, students can use a Listing strategy while reading literary nonfiction. For example, while reading Patrick Henry's (1817) *Speech to the Virginia Convention,* students can generate a list of all of the rhetorical devices they notice while reading. They can later return to that list and note the impact of the device on the overall meaning of the text. Ultimately, they might rank the list in terms of which device is the most effective to help organize their thinking when drafting a claim for literary analysis. See the example on page 165.
Math	Make connections among topics; Evaluate an approach to solving a problem; Explore concepts	When learning new concepts, it's helpful to reflect on what is known, attempt to identify areas of confusion, and connect the new to the known. For example, when learning about systems of equations, students might list everything they already know about systems of equations to reflect on their current understanding before listing questions they might have. See the example on page 165.
Science	List steps in processes; Determine conclusions; Synthesize learning; Summarize learning about content	When learning about cell division, students can generate ideas by creating the following sublists: properties of cells, steps in the process, and elements of cells. Then they can review their notes to write a summary of what they have learned to solidify their understanding.
Social Studies	Organize evidence; List events and determine if they were a cause or simply preceded an event; Generate questions	When studying the Revolutionary War, students can list the events that occurred before, during, and after the war. Later, they can return to the list and determine the events that were causes and/or effects and the events that simply occurred before or after the war.

Example List for ELA of Rhetorical Devices in *Speech to the Virginia Convention*

List of Rhetorical Devices

1. *Diction*
2. *Comparison*
3. *Allusion*
4. *Parallel structure**

Star the most effective; prepare to defend decision

Example List for Math for System of Equations

Name: ______________________________ Date: ____________

What do I know?

- *Start with two variables; need to remove one*
- *Can be solved by substitution*
- *Need to find values in related equations*

How do I solve them?

- *Substitution*
  - *Start with one equation*
  - *Solve one variable*
  - *Plug the value into the second equation*
  - *Check the solution again*

Questions:

- *Does it matter where I start?*
- *How do I know where to start?*
- *What are the other methods to solve this problem? How do I know when to use them?*

Entrance and Exit Slips

Description

Entrance and Exit Slips are short, informal prompts that help students activate prior knowledge (Entrance Slips) and/or reflect on their learning (Exit Slips). They can be used to ask students open-ended questions or selected response questions. These prompts are designed to take less than five minutes to complete and are usually not graded, though they provide useful information about student learning (Fisher & Frey, 2004).

Entrance Slips typically ask students to reflect on their current understanding of the day's topic, make predictions about what they might read in the text, and ultimately prepare for the day's lesson. Exit Slips typically ask students to summarize the day's learning, make connections to help build their understanding, and reflect on learning.

How and Why Would I Use This Strategy?

- To assess student understanding of a concept or comprehension of a text
- To gather information about student learning to make instructional decisions
- To provide a space for students to summarize learning
- To help students make connections
- To provide application practice for new concepts
- To ask students to reflect on learning
- To provide a space for students to self-assess current understanding of a topic

How Do I Teach/Present the Strategy?

1. When planning to use an Entrance/Exit Slip, consider the lesson's objective and determine if and how your students would benefit from activating prior knowledge and preparing to enter the lesson or reflecting on their learning after the lesson.
2. Next, determine the format for the Entrance/Exit Slip. Would your goal best be met by asking students an open-ended response or a selected response question?
3. Then consider how your students will record this information. They might use an application such as GoFormative (see page xvii for more information on technology applications), index cards, or a reflective journal.
4. Present the prompt to students at the beginning of class, if you are using an Entrance Slip, and at the end of class, if you are using an Exit Slip. Possible example prompts are on pages 169–170.
5. When using an Entrance Slip, you might choose to use students' responses to engage in a discussion at the beginning of class. For example, in the ELA example in Examples in Context chart on page 168, the teacher asked students to complete a chart ranking whether they strongly agree, agree, disagree, or strongly disagree with statements related to the theme of a short story or novel and providing a rationale. Then students gather with other students who feel similarly and share their rationales. Alternatively, you might choose to gather information about how much the students know about a topic, just as the teacher in the social studies example did on page 168. This teacher asked students to list everything they remembered about the causes of World War I as a way to gauge their current understanding and shape the day's lesson.
6. When using Exit Slips, you might choose to quickly assess student knowledge, just as the math teacher did in the example on page 168, in order to place students in groups for the next day's lesson. You might also want to provide time for students to summarize their learning at the end of a lesson, just as the science teacher did in the example on page 168.

Connections to the Disciplines	Behaviors Targeted by the Strategy	Examples in Context
ELA	Make predictions; Reflect on learning; Summarize learning; Draw conclusions; Brainstorm ideas	Before beginning to read a complex text, it can be helpful to explore one's feelings about the major themes of the text. To do this, you can list statements that reflect the theme of the text and ask students whether they strongly agree, agree, disagree, or strongly disagree and ask them to provide a rationale for the rating. For example, when reading a text with a theme about technology, a statement on the anticipation guide might read, *Technology is in control of our society*. Once students have had a chance to respond, you can ask students to share their thinking about each statement as a way to launch into a class discussion about the themes.
Math	Apply concepts; Practice solving problems; Synthesize learning; Interpret vocabulary	After a lesson or two on quadrants, you can provide students with a problem to solve and ask them to share their reasoning for the approach they took to solve the problem. You can review the responses and group students based on their knowledge of the concept. Then, you can provide targeted instruction to the groups that were created.
Science	Summarize learning; Make connections; Apply concepts; Interpret vocabulary	After a lesson or a lab, ask students to summarize their learning so they can solidify their understanding. These summaries can provide you with information you can use to either reteach or expand on instruction.
Social Studies	Evaluate processes; Determine conclusions; Articulate ideas	When beginning a unit that includes topics students may have learned about in previous courses, it can be helpful for you to gain an understanding of how much students already know. For example, when starting a unit on World War I, you might ask students to list everything they remember about the causes of World War I. Gathering this information will give you an idea of how to shape the lesson or unit.

Example Prompts by Discipline

Name: ______________________________ Date: __________

Discipline	Entrance Slip Prompts	Exit Slip Prompts
General	■ List everything you know about _____ ■ Based on what we've studied so far, what do you think about _____? ■ Write down everything you know about _____.	■ Summarize what you learned about _____ ■ What questions do you have about _____? ■ What do you find confusing _____?
ELA	■ Brainstorm everything you know about _____. ■ Spend five minutes creating an outline to respond to the prompt: _____ ■ Make a prediction about _____ using evidence from the text.	■ How does the author's use of an unreliable narrator impact the meaning of _____? ■ Which rhetorical device did you find more compelling, _____ or _____? ■ Where are you in the writing process? List all the questions you currently have about your topic.
Math	■ Solve the following problems based on your current understanding of functions. ■ Describe your process in solving equations. ■ List everything you know about triangles.	■ Explain your rationale for the approach you took to solve the problem. ■ What is clear about today's lesson? What is muddy? ■ Rank your understanding of _____.
Science	■ What is your current understanding of _____? ■ What is your preliminary hypothesis? ■ Based on your reading, place the stages of Mitosis in the appropriate order.	■ How does what you learned today connect to your previous understanding of _____? ■ Summarize your understanding of _____. ■ What other data might you collect to determine if your hypothesis is correct?

Example Prompts by Discipline, continued...

Discipline	Entrance Slip Prompts	Exit Slip Prompts
Social Studies	■ List _____'s perspective on _____. ■ List evidence that would support the following claim: _____. ■ Read the following excerpt from _____. From whose perspective was this written?	■ Which viewpoint is absent from your current understanding of _____? ■ What questions do you have about _____? ■ Place the events surrounding _____ in order on the timeline.

Climbing and Diving

Description

Climbing and Diving (Urquhart & McIver, 2005) is a strategy that allows students to deepen their understanding about a topic through writing. Students are asked to list everything they know about a topic (Climbing) and then select one topic or idea from that list to explore further (Diving). This allows students to process their learning and/or brainstorm ideas before writing on a topic of choice, which helps deepen their understanding of the topic or idea. The strategy allows students to process their learning through writing and can also help them generate ideas for more extended writing tasks. For example, when students are engaging in an extended writing task and/or engaging in inquiry, they need the opportunity to brainstorm and think through the information they know. By providing students time to practice their writing while processing content, you will be able to improve students' capacity to learn as they are improving their writing skills (National Institute for Literacy, 2007).

How and Why Would I Use This Strategy?

- To allow students to restate content in their own words
- To help students identify ideas they feel they have mastered or that continue to challenge them
- To allow students to uncover questions they may have about the content
- To help students brainstorm ideas they would like to explore in extended writing tasks
- To assess students' current understanding and provide feedback on their learning

How Do I Teach/Present the Strategy?

1. After you have presented content, allow students to list everything they know and remember about the topic for ten minutes (Climbing). Students can record this information in a notebook or use a Google Doc.
2. Next, direct students to select a topic they would like to explore further (Diving). Encourage them to ask questions, rate their level of understanding (and explain why that is), or make connections to other material studied in class. See the chart on page 174 for prompts to help students "Dive" into the information they have learned.

3. This strategy may also be used to help students generate ideas for writing. To help students engage in Climbing and Diving to generate ideas for a topic, present students with a line of inquiry or a topic. Ask them to write a list of everything they might write about and/or all the questions they have related to that topic or line of inquiry for ten minutes (Climbing). Students can record this information in a notebook or use a Google Doc.
4. Next, ask students to read what they have written and select a topic to explore further (Diving). You might also ask students to share some of the ideas they have brainstormed with peers. Ask students to then expand their thinking about the topic they selected by writing for ten minutes. They can identify sources for additional information, cite any evidence they know that will support their thinking, and ask additional questions while "Diving." See page 174 to help students "Dive" into the list of ideas they have brainstormed.
5. You might choose to ask students to return to their lists and continue to "Dive" into the ideas they have listed throughout the unit of study and/or writing process.

Connections to the Disciplines	Behaviors Targeted by the Strategy	Examples in Context
ELA	Brainstorm ideas; Process understanding of a text; Explore ideas for writing topics; Make connections among ideas; Generate questions	When engaging in inquiry, students need an opportunity to organize the information they know so that they can determine what path their line of inquiry will take. When assigning a line of inquiry to students, you might ask students to brainstorm ideas for the line of inquiry. They could then organize this list from most to least compelling ideas before selecting a topic to "Dive" into. Students can then "Climb" again by brainstorming evidence for their idea and then "Dive" into that idea by listing additional questions, any sources for evidence, and explanations of their thinking. By regularly using the Climbing and Diving strategy during the inquiry process, students will be able to explore their thinking about their topic during each stage of the writing process.

Connections to the Disciplines	Behaviors Targeted by the Strategy	Examples in Context
Math	Synthesize learning; Make connections among topics; Evaluate an approach to solving a problem; Explore concepts	Students can use Climbing and Diving to process their learning near the end of a unit. For example, after learning about functions, students can "Climb" and list everything they know about functions. Once they have listed their ideas, they can write about one aspect of functions in more detail. They may rate their confidence in understanding, ask additional questions, or make connections between their new learning and concepts they feel they have mastered. Further, you may opt to review students' writing to help determine their current level of understanding.
Science	Evaluate processes; Determine conclusions; Synthesize learning; Conduct experiments and/or labs; Summarize learning about content	Students who are engaging in a lab to better understand circuits and electricity may "Climb" by listing their observations about electricity. They can then spend time "Diving" into an observation to better understand electricity. They may ask questions, make connections, or summarize what they think about electricity based on their current understanding.
Social Studies	Corroborate sources; Consider multiple perspectives; Organize evidence; List events and determine if they were a cause or simply preceded an event; Generate questions	When teaching students to recognize and interpret multiple perspectives on a topic, you might use any of the resources available at https://sheg.stanford.edu/history-lessons to provide students with multiple texts on the same topic. After students read a text set that includes multiple voices and perspectives, they can "Climb" by listing the perspectives they observe. They can then "Dive" by writing more about one of those perspectives including context, speaker, purpose, beliefs, and views. Students can then summarize their understanding of that perspective before "Diving" into another perspective on the topic.

Example Prompts

Name: ______________________________ Date: ____________

Prompts for "Diving" to Process Learning	Prompts for "Diving" to Generate Ideas for Writing
■ How might you explain this concept to a friend? ■ What questions do you have about the topic? ■ What content do you understand the most? ■ What information feels fuzzy to you? ■ What connections can you make between this topic and what we've learned in class? ■ What connections can you make between this topic and something you learned about in another context?	■ What evidence might support your line of thinking? ■ What questions might someone have if their viewpoint is different than yours? ■ What resources might help you investigate your questions? ■ What information might you need to gather? ■ What other ideas might you want to explore? ■ What do you already know about this topic?

Multiple-Text GIST

Description

The Multiple-Text GIST strategy (Manderino, 2007) supports students in synthesizing multiple texts in order to gain a deeper understanding of a topic. This strategy is adapted from the GIST strategy designed for single texts (Cunningham, 1982). Students need to work with multiple sources to develop a deeper conceptual understanding of a topic. However, students struggle to synthesize across multiple sources without scaffolding (Afflerbach & VanSledright, 2001; Hynd-Shanahan, Holschuh, & Hubbard, 2004). Multiple-Text GIST is a strategy designed to scaffold student thinking across multiple sources and source types. It is especially useful with documents that are contradictory. As students read each text, they write an integrative summary that builds as they read each text.

How and Why Would I Use This Strategy?

- To build prior knowledge
- To compare claims and propositions across texts
- To use norms for reasoning within the discipline (i.e., what counts as evidence) to evaluate claims

How Do I Teach/Present the Strategy?

1. Duplicate copies of the reproducible on page 178 or have students create a template in their notebook. If using Google Docs for this template, share a link so that students are prompted to make a copy.
2. Create a text set of four to eight sources on a topic. Sources can be contradictory, unique, or corroborate information from different viewpoints.
3. Read aloud the first text and model how to write a 20-word summary of the first text. It is helpful to model by thinking through the process aloud and not just sharing a prewritten summary you created.
4. Have students read the second text and write a 20-word summary of the first and second text. Continue to create summaries with students until they feel comfortable summarizing on their own.
5. Encourage students to share their summaries and project examples. If the second text contradicts the first text, ask students how they created their summary when the two texts were opposed. This is a good time to discuss the use of words like *despite, although,* and *however* in order to reconcile opposing texts.

6. Have students read the third text and write a 25-word summary of all three texts. Encourage students to discuss their accumulating summaries in small groups.
7. Have students read the fourth text and write a 30-word summary of all four texts. The word count is increased to accommodate the amount of text that needs to be summarized.
8. The process continues until students have read all of the texts. As the number of texts increases, you can increase the maximum number of words used in the summary.
9. At the end of the task, project examples of students' final summaries and discuss how students made sense of the overall text set.

Connections to the Disciplines	Behaviors Targeted by the Strategy	Examples in Context
ELA	Monitor meaning; Use prior knowledge; Infer meaning; Determine importance; Synthesize	Provide students with four or five literary nonfiction texts that offer multiple interpretations of a single work of literature.
Math	Synthesize; Analyze an approach to solving a problem; Determine patterns	Provide students with multiple texts that lead to a complete conceptual understanding of a topic. For example, you may present students with descriptions of different approaches to solving a problem, and Multiple-Text Gist will uncover any patterns in the approach to solving the problem.
Science	Synthesize; Analyze a scientific phenomenon; Integrate new information into existing theory	Have students summarize multiple texts that address a science topic that requires an in-depth explanation, such as electricity and magnetism.
Social Studies	Synthesize; Consider multiple perspectives; Apply a specific lens to understand a period in history	Provide students with an inquiry question and competing sources that address the question from multiple perspectives.

Example Multiple-Text GIST for History

Name: *Annette* Date: ____________

Based on documents from http://sheg.stanford.edu/montgomery-bus-boycott

You should summarize each document progressively as you read through them.

Text A *Textbook (The Montgomery Bus Boycott)*

Summarize in 20 words or less.

Rosa Parks refused to give up her seat on a public bus and was arrested. Dr. King led a city-wide boycott.

Text B *Letter from Robinson to the Mayor*

Summarize A + B in 20 words or less.

A year before Parks and King started the bus boycott, the Montgomery Women's Council demanded desegrated busses.

Text C *Bayard Rustin's Diary*

Summarize A, B, + C in 25 words or less.

The bus boycott led by King, after Parks refused to move, was widely practiced for months.

Text D *Highlander School*

Summarize A, B, C, + D in 30 words or less.

In 1954 a group of women in Montgomery demanded bus desegregation. Rosa Parks, trained for civil rights activism, started a large bus boycott in Montgomery led by Dr. King.

Text E *MLK*

Summarize A, B, C, D, + E in 35 words or less.

After a struggle by the Women's Council to desegregate buses in Montgomery, Rosa Parks, a trained civil rights leader, sparked a successful months-long boycott led by Dr. King.

Template for Multiple-Text GIST

Name: ____ Date: ___________

You should summarize each document progressively as you read through them.

Text A ____

Summarize in 20 words or less.

____

____

Text B ____

Summarize A + B in 20 words or less.

____

____

Text C ____

Summarize A, B, + C in 25 words or less.

____

____

Text D ____

Summarize A, B, C, + D in 30 words or less.

____

____

Text E ____

Summarize A, B, C, D, + E in 35 words or less.

____

____

____

Marathon Writing

Description

Marathon writing is a continuous writing exercise used to build students' writing skills and stamina. The strategy also promotes writing about content, which is key in helping students develop their writing skills (Graham & Perrin, 2007). In this strategy, students build writing fluency and stamina by writing about a given topic for increasing blocks of time, starting with two minutes, and gradually building the length of time spent writing to 20 minutes or longer. This strategy can also help reinforce conceptual understanding in the content areas while supporting students' writing fluency. Furthermore, practicing writing also supports students' reading development (Graham & Hebert, 2011).

How and Why Would I Use This Strategy?

- To reinforce content area learning
- To build writing fluency
- To build writing stamina
- To informally assess students' knowledge

How Do I Teach/Present the Strategy?

1. Provide students with a space to record their Marathon Writing entries. This could be a paper journal or notebook or a Google Doc. Determine how often you'd like to ask students to engage in Marathon Writing. You might decide to ask students to write daily, a few times per week, or weekly. Explain to students that you will be providing them with several prompts for their Marathon Writing sessions.
2. Provide students with prompts. These can be general in nature such as, *Describe your best friend,* or *Summarize a TV show you most recently watched,* or they can be content related, such as, *Describe how you approached solving the problem*, or *Summarize what we learned about potential and kinetic energy*. See more examples of Marathon Writing prompts on page 182.
3. Explain to students that they will write for the amount of time you specify. You can tell students that if they run out of ideas to write about, they can simply rewrite the other sentences they have already written to try and inspire new ideas.
4. Be sure to tell students that they will share what they have written with a partner once the time has expired.
5. Model this process by engaging in Marathon Writing with your students using think-aloud or by talking through a written product of your own.
6. Ask students to share their responses with a partner.

7. If you are using students' work as an informal assessment, you'll want to capture their writing by asking students to submit their journals or share a link to an electronic file. If you are not using the content as an informal assessment, students can be held accountable for the writing by sharing with a partner.

Connections to the Disciplines	Behaviors Targeted by the Strategy	Examples in Context
ELA	Imitate the style of a published work; Connect to independent novel; Brainstorm for a writing project; Write about general prompts to build fluency; Draw conclusions	One way to promote students' development of writing skills is to ask them to imitate the style of a published author. Marathon Writing prompts can be used throughout a unit of study to help students understand how an author's style impacts their message and to also help students develop their writing skills. For example, when reading Ray Bradbury, students will note that his writing style includes poetic prose and the use of vivid imagery, similes, and metaphors. Once students are aware of the author's style, they can be asked to use Bradbury's style when responding to a Marathon Writing prompt.
Math	Reflect on process; Summarize steps in solving a problem; Critique the reasoning of others; Engage in error analysis	Provide students with several problems and solutions. Ensure that some of the solutions are incorrect and represent common misconceptions students have. Students can select one of these problems as their prompt for Marathon Writing. They can then write about the process used to solve that problem, whether or not it was correct, and explain how to solve that problem correctly.
Science	Summarize understanding of concepts; Make connections among ideas; Explain how one theory builds on another; Describe the process in a lab or experiment	Marathon Writing prompts can be used to help students process the hands-on experiences they engage in during labs or experiments. Marathon Writing prompts can ask students to summarize the steps they took in their experiment or lab, describe the change that took place, richly describe their observations, explain their results, or reflect on how their lab/experiment helped solidify their understanding of a concept.
Social Studies	Cause and effect; Perspective; Use evidence to support claims; Analyze historical arguments	Marathon Writing can be used to help students unpack an argument a historian presents. While students are studying a historical account, they may be asked to answer a Marathon Writing prompt that asks them to write the claim a historian is using and then list and rank the evidence that author provides. This can help build students' writing fluency, help them see historical writing as arguments, and help them identify how historians use evidence.

Example Directions to Students

Name: ______________________________ Date: __________

Directions 1. Record the date in our Marathon Writing journal. 2. Read the prompt and make sure you understand what it is asking. 3. When I start the timer, be prepared to write to answer the prompt for two minutes. If you feel like you've finished before the timer stops, simply rewrite the sentences you have already recorded because we want to practice writing continuously for longer periods of time. And, rewriting may inspire new ideas. 4. When you have finished writing, we will share our thoughts with someone seated near us.
Prompt:
________________________________ ________________________________ ________________________________ ________________________________ ________________________________ ________________________________ ________________________________ ________________________________

Example Prompts for Marathon Writing

Name: ______________________________ Date: ____________

ELA	■ Write a description of your best friend in the style of Jonathan Swift. ■ Describe your favorite character in the novel you are reading. What makes them a great character? How does the author tell you about that character? ■ Which rhetorical element in the text did you find most compelling? Why? ■ Review the articles you read to answer your research question. Write a summary of the author's main points.
Math	■ Reflect on today's task. Rank your confidence in engaging in this task (1 = I totally get it; 2 = I'm kind of confused; 3 = HELP!). Then write down the process you engaged in to complete the task. What information do you need to help you feel confident in completing the task? ■ Create a list of questions we might include on our assessment for systems of equations. ■ I feel confident solving math problems when I … ■ Another approach I could have taken to solve this problem is..., but I chose this method because…
Science	■ Summarize the main concepts we learned today. What is confusing to you? List some questions you might have. ■ How do the results from today's lab connect to what we've been learning in class? ■ What do the findings of your experiment tell you about the concept we are studying? ■ How does Newton's third law apply to this example?
Social Studies	■ List the events which you think led to or caused the Great Depression. ■ Describe the Equal Rights Amendment from the perspective of Phyllis Schlafly. ■ Describe the Equal Rights Amendment from the perspective of Alice Paul. ■ Describe the context of the historical event we are studying.
General	■ Based on this image I have shared, write what you think is happening. ■ Describe the perfect meal, day, vacation, etc. (select one) ■ Summarize the plot of your favorite movie. ■ If you won $1,000,000, how would you spend the money?

Double-Entry Journal

Description

The Double-Entry Journal (Tovani, 2000, 2011) is a form of guided note-taking that helps students track their thinking and interact with text while reading. While similar in format to two-column notes, Double-Entry Journals are more flexible and allow students to respond to their reading in a variety of ways including: making connections, noting confusing parts, listing interesting facts or details, drawing a sketch, or defining difficult vocabulary words. Because they are versatile, Double-Entry Journals can be used to support student learning in all disciplines. By providing students with discipline-specific topics, you can scaffold students' apprenticeship to the disciplinary ways of consuming information. In addition, Double-Entry Journals can be helpful when students are listening to a lecture, viewing a documentary, or analyzing other non-print texts.

How and Why Would I Use This Strategy?

- To use writing to learn complex concepts
- To process thinking while reading complex text
- To conduct laboratory experiments
- To reflect on learning
- To connect text with additional learning

How Do I Teach/Present This Strategy?

1. Ask students to fold a piece of paper in half lengthwise or provide them with a copy of one of the Double-Entry Journal reproducibles on pages 188–192.

Example Double-Entry Journal for **Social Studies**

Title *Water: Stuff of Life*

What the Text Says	What I Wonder
1. Bad water—300 million Africans lack access to safe water. Page *1*	**1.** I wonder what caused the problem?
2. Government doesn't work. Page *3*	**2.** I wonder what the government of Malawi is like? I wonder why they don't do something?

2. Explain to students that on the left side of the paper they will copy sentences, words, or phrases from the text, noting the page(s) on which they were found. On the right side they will track their thinking about the information presented.
3. Create a discipline-specific focus. For example, a history teacher might say, "As you read, it is important to question the information presented and the arguments supporting it. How much does the author appear to know about this topic? Is the author presenting all sides of the issue? What information is missing?" Whatever your discipline, be direct about what you want students to record in the right column. See the examples on page 186.
4. Next, model the process for students. Read a section of the text aloud. As you read, write down a quotation or phrase from the text. For example, "In our text it says, '300 million Africans lack access to safe water.' I am going to note the page number, and on the right side I am going to write, 'I wonder how recent this information is? Africa is a big continent, so which specific areas or countries are being referred to?'"
5. Continue modeling your note taking on the left side, and your quotations, understandings, or connections on the right side, until you think that students understand how to proceed.
6. Invite students to work individually or in pairs to read the remainder of the selection and create notes and questions using their Double-Entry Journal. You may want to ask students to write an entry after each paragraph or page, depending on the format of the text.
7. When students have completed the reading, invite them to read their quotations and questions and use them as a basis for a class discussion of the reading.

Connections to the Disciplines	Behaviors Targeted by the Strategy	Examples in Context
ELA	Make predictions and other inferences; Explore author's use of figurative language; Monitor meaning while reading; Engage with rhetorical analysis	Double-Entry Journals can help students unpack an author's use of imagery and the ways in which imagery conveys the author's message. For example, in *The Great Gatsby* (Fitzgerald, 1925), the author uses imagery to communicate the amount of excess in Gatsby's life. Some students can track the imagery related to Gatsby while other students can track the imagery related to other characters in the novel. The culminating discussion can be a compare-and-contrast investigation regarding the author's message. See the example on page 187.
Math	Justify the steps taken to solve a problem; Identify rules in geometry; Solve proofs	When presented with a problem in context, students can unpack and justify the steps needed to solve the problem in the right-hand column. For example, when solving a system of equations problem, students can outline the process they would engage in and provide a rationale. Another option is for students to ask questions in the right-hand column for each step of the equation, and then exchange Double-Entry Journals with another student and respond to those questions.
Science	Identify the process or problem; Connect to scientific phenomena; Ask questions; Identify problem and solution	When reading a complex scientific text, students can note significant information in the text and then make connections to the scientific phenomena they are learning. For example, if students are learning about the Calvin Cycle, they might jot down notes of the process in the left-hand column, and in the right-hand column make connections to other biological concepts learned, such as energy transfer, food, and respiration.
Social Studies	Record observations and inferences; Note speaker; Note perspectives; Identify evidence in support of an argument	When reading a primary source such as a speech from the Virginia Convention, students can use the left-hand column to note what they find in the text. In the right-hand column they can label that evidence to determine whether it is the argument or evidence to support the argument. Students can then determine if the argument is solid and if the evidence is effective.

Examples of Disciplinary Strategies to Use with Double-Entry Journals

Name: ______________________________ Date: __________

ELA	■ Rhetorical Strategy ■ Quotation ■ Author's Purpose	■ Impact on Reader ■ Interpretation ■ Potential Biases
Math	■ Step in the Process ■ Rule ■ Information from Notes	■ Rationale ■ Proof ■ My Thinking
Science	■ Problem ■ Observation ■ Phenomena	■ Solution ■ Inference ■ Connection to Theory
Social Studies	■ Point of View ■ Argument ■ Quote from Text	■ Implications ■ Evidence ■ Evaluation of Perspective
General	■ Questions ■ What the Text Says ■ Information	■ Reflections ■ What I Wonder ■ Response Connection

Example Double-Entry Journal for ELA

Name: ____ Date: __________

By midnight the hilarity had increased. A celebrated tenor had sung in Italian, and a notorious contralto had sung in jazz ... A pair of stage twins, who turned out to be the girls in yellow, did a baby act in costume, and champagne was served in glasses bigger than finger bowls.

As you are reading *The Great Gatsby*, record examples of imagery found throughout the text. Then, explain what the examples of imagery help you understand about the characters. An example has been done for you.

Record the imagery you found. Include the page number.	The imagery helps me understand...
Teacher Example: "... hilarity had increased..."	Teacher Example: *The party is larger than life. It feels shallow, though.*

Template for Double-Entry Journal

Name: ______________________________ Date: ____________

Title: ____

What the Text Says	What I Wonder
1. Page ________	1.
2. Page ________	2.
3. Page ________	3.
4. Page ________	4.
5. Page ________	5.
6. Page ________	6.

Template for Double-Entry Journal

Name: ______________________________ Date: __________

Title: ____

Information	My Response/Connection
1. Page ________	1.
2. Page ________	2.
3. Page ________	3.
4. Page ________	4.
5. Page ________	5.
6. Page ________	6.

Template for Double-Entry Journal

Name: ______________________________ Date: ____________

Title: ____

What the Text Says	Why It's Important
1. Page ______	1.
2. Page ______	2.
3. Page ______	3.
4. Page ______	4.
5. Page ______	5.
6. Page ______	6.

Template for Double-Entry Journal

Name: ______________________________ Date: ____________

Title: ____

I Predict	What Happened
1. Page ________	1.
2. Page ________	2.
3. Page ________	3.
4. Page ________	4.
5. Page ________	5.
6. Page ________	6.

Template for Double-Entry Journal

Name: ______________________________ Date: ____________

Title: ____

New or Confusing Word	What I Think It Means
1. Page ________	1.
2. Page ________	2.
3. Page ________	3.
4. Page ________	4.
5. Page ________	5.
6. Page ________	6.

Cornell Notes

Description

The Cornell method of note taking is a form of two-column notes that allows students to collect information while listening to a lecture or reading a text and then go back and review the information they wrote once the lecture or reading task is complete. Students review and study their notes and record questions, main ideas, or make connections to materials in the left side of the graphic organizer. Finally, students review the notes again to write a summary of the information they gathered. The repeated review and reflection process helps students retain information (Pauk & Owens, 2011).

How and Why Would I Use This Strategy?

- To maximize student learning from lectures and complex texts by recording notes
- To build students' capacity to independently gather and study information from texts
- To build students' memory by separating main ideas from details

How Do I Teach/Present the Strategy?

1. Begin teaching this strategy by explicitly stating the purpose of using the Cornell method for note-taking. Explain to students that Cornell Notes help them record significant details, understand the relationship between ideas, and serve as a study aid. A template for student use is on page 195.
2. Next, guide students through Cornell Notes by modeling the strategy. It is helpful for students to see you complete the entire Cornell Notes process (Pauk & Owens, 2011). If you are modeling how to take notes while reading, set a purpose for reading the text and model your process of taking Cornell Notes while reading a selection aloud from the text. As you read, stop to:
    a. Record important ideas in the right-hand column. See page 195.
    b. Review/reread the notes.
    c. Determine the main idea of the notes and any questions you might have.
    d. Record the main ideas and any questions in the left-hand column.
    e. Summarize the notes on the bottom of each page.
3. After you have modeled the process, provide students time to continue the process on their own. Have steps a-e visible for students.
4. Once students have completed taking notes, remind them that they should review these notes to help them retain the information.

Connections to the Disciplines	Behaviors Targeted by the Strategy	Examples in Context
ELA	Engage in a lecture; Critique a published speech; Read complex literary nonfiction	Students reading literary criticism about poetry texts can use Cornell Notes to capture their ideas. Their purpose for reading can be to identify and explain the lens used for the critique and understand and retain information about the critique of the poem presented in the text.
Math	Engage in a lecture; Read math text explaining a statistical model; Determine how to solve and reason through a contextualized math problem	Students in a statistics class can use Cornell Notes when given a text that describes an ANOVA. Their purpose for reading is to identify the assumptions of the model, how to perform the model, and write an example of the model after they read the text.
Science	Engage in a lecture; Review instructions for a lab or experiment; Critique a scientific article	In Chemistry, when students are reading about complex topics, like hydrogen and covalent bonds, have them use Cornell Notes to collect and then reflect on important information they have learned about the topic.
Social Studies	Engage in a lecture; Unpack a complex historical argument; Review historical events/movements	In your U.S. history class, you can engage students in a multi-modal lecture on the Civil Rights Movement. To begin, you might share a PBS video and then some background information via a lecture. Finally, you might ask students to read primary and secondary source documents about the Civil Rights Movement. Throughout, students can record notes using the Cornell Notes format.

Template for Cornell Notes

Name: ______________________________ Date: ____________

Topic	
Main Ideas/Questions	Evidence and Details
Summary:	

Section 4

Collaborative Discussion Around Text

Contents for Section 4

Discussions allow students to take in and process new information. Using discussion strategies in the classroom creates a more active and engaging learning environment. Furthermore, collaborative discussions help students engage in collectivist learning practices that facilitate culturally responsive teaching practices (Hammond, 2015). Students are able to take ownership of their learning and gain a sense of responsibility alongside their peers. As with writing-to-learn strategies, discussion strategies can deepen students' ability to generate, process, organize, articulate, and elaborate on their ideas, thus deepening their understanding of complex disciplinary topics.

When given a clear goal, purpose, or outcome, students can leverage discussion strategies to engage more deeply with texts in the discipline, think through a line of inquiry, and synthesize their understanding of complex topics. Though sometimes discussions can be used as a way to assess student learning, the strategies we provide in this text are focused on using the tool of discussion to support students in processing, exploring, and expanding on their learning. The skills involved include brainstorming, elaborating on ideas, making connections, summarizing learning, synthesizing ideas, and engaging in reflection. Collaborative discussions can be a powerful and versatile tool if students are given the structure and scaffolding to engage effectively.

Taking the time to establish the roles, routines, and purposes of collaborative discussion within your particular classroom is critical. Students need practice and repetition. Students need to understand the goals for the lesson and your vision for what collaborative discussion should entail. Because students are still functioning within the context of school and classroom, they do not typically view themselves as leaders during collaborative discussion, even when you have relinquished control over to them (Meston, Galloway, & McClain, 2020). Rather, they tend to view these discussions as teacher-led, teacher-focused, and grade-focused, no matter the scenario. Therefore, establishing the purpose clearly and outright will help students understand their roles and responsibilities. Some recommended ideas include working with students to establish norms prior to discussion and troubleshooting issues immediately following discussion. In addition, demonstrate that you value your students' input by posting their learning goals as well as your own and reviewing the roles, responsibilities, norms, and goals prior to every discussion.

As mentioned in previous sections, this book will connect the structured activities we are sharing (often called strategies) to the strategic behaviors that students will engage in. In this section of the book, our focus is on supporting students in developing cooperative collaboration skills in order to gain a deeper understanding of the disciplines and the ways that members of each discipline communicate. Overall, our focus is on helping students deepen their understanding about complex concepts and gain ownership over their learning by engaging in collaborative discussions.

In the chart below, we have connected the strategy to the dominant strategic behavior that is developed when the strategies are used in the ways described in this text.

Strategic Behavior	Strategies that Support this Behavior
Expanding and Making Connections Among Ideas: When students have structured practice making connections, they are better able to connect new information to what they already know. When students make connections and reflect on their learning, it deepens their understanding and increases students' learning capacity (Connor-Greene, 2000).	Spider Discussion page 199 Value Line Up page 215 Save the Last Word for Me page 220 Accountability Pie page 242 30-60-90 page 251
Brainstorming: Brainstorming techniques promote students' creative thinking and idea generation (Al-Samarraie & Hj Hurmuzan, 2017). When connected to content in the disciplines, students can expand on their thinking and deepen their understanding of complex concepts and processes.	Discussion Web page 226 Anchor Jigsaw page 235

Spider Discussion

Description

The Spider Discussion is a student-led discussion format that builds students' understanding of what it means to be a collaborative, contributing member of a discourse community (Wiggins, 2017). The name of the Spider Discussion originated from Alexis Wiggins (2017). Wiggins made a chart of interconnected lines documenting when students were speaking and who took over the discussion at each turn, creating a web-like image.

It takes time and practice for students to be able to carry the discussion without your assistance. However, this strategy will support you in scaffolding for students the skills necessary to do so (Graff, Birkenstein, & Durst, 2008). These skills include teaching students how to communicate with each other, how to communicate within the discipline, how to use academic vocabulary, how to assess their own knowledge and understanding, and how to be patient with themselves in their pursuit of knowledge (Dweck, 2014). In addition, Spider Discussions offer a forum for students to work through misconceptions with their peers, thus promoting an atmosphere of collaboration (O'Brien, 2019; Shanahan, 2012).

Building towards a successful Spider Discussion is much the same as a spider's patient weaving of a web: the web will eventually be beautiful and interconnected, but it takes time to get there. While it might be human nature to change something that feels uncomfortable or unsuccessful, give this strategy time to develop. In addition, it can also be helpful to invite another teacher or an instructional coach into the room to co-teach. With another teacher, you will be able to have two smaller groups of 15 students rather than a large group of 30 students.

Also, it is interesting to note that students do not typically view themselves as the leaders during collaborative discussion (Meston, Galloway, & McClain, 2020). Because it takes place in the context of school and within your course, students still view these discussions as teacher-led, even if students are doing all the talking. Perspective is important. Take time to work with students to explore ways that their goals and yours can be honored throughout the process of collaborative discussion.

When and Why Would I Use This Strategy?

- To determine students' level of understanding of a topic
- To encourage students to learn from each other and see the value in peer academic relationships
- To facilitate a different mode of learning
- To develop students' ownership of their learning
- To support students' ability to self-assess
- To create cross-curricular connections within the STEM disciplines

How Do I Teach/Present This Strategy?

1. The first task is to teach students how to communicate with each other. When communicating in most disciplines, it is critical that students understand that attention to detail is critical with language. Practicing the skills of communicating with precision can be accomplished through a variety of collaborative exercises.

   Note: These activities can be done using Keva Blocks or building blocks of any kind. If you do not have blocks, students can do the same tasks by drawing a picture and describing it for another student to draw. Overall, students will quickly come to recognize the power of words!

   a. Activity Idea One: Place students in small groups of four. Two students are given "blueprints" that you provide and two students are given blocks. The students with the blueprints verbally explain what to build, and the other students try to follow the verbal directions without looking at the blueprints. Afterwards, students compare blueprints with the build and discuss what went right and wrong.

   b. Activity Idea Two: Place students in groups of two with the blocks. Make sure groups have areas in the classroom or school where they are unable to see other group's designs. The two students build one structure of their own choosing, take a picture of it, and then write up step-by-step instructions for how to build it. Then students dismantle their builds. They exchange instructions with another group and work to read the other group's instructions and build the structure. Then, they compare the built structure to the picture and discuss what went right and wrong.

   c. Activity Idea Three: Students can engage in additional tasks to demonstrate the power of vocabulary. This can be accomplished by asking students to communicate a message without using certain words or by only using certain words. This task does not need to directly relate to the discipline, and this step can also be accomplished with blocks. Imagine Activity Idea One or Two above with word banks that tell students that they must use words like "vertical," or "horizontal," or with word banks that tell students they cannot use the words "stack" or "attach" or "piece." Folding origami is a good idea here, too.

2. After engaging in one or more of the activity ideas above, bring students together for their first Spider Discussion to debrief the activity. This discussion is just to introduce the concepts of a collaborative discourse community. This Spider Discussion is called "Spider Zero" to communicate that it is not part of the typical Spider Discussion rotation, but instead is a "mock" session meant to teach the skills and procedures needed. There is preparation necessary for Spider Zero to go well.

3. First consider your groups carefully. The best Spider Discussions typically have about 15 students per group, if possible, sitting in a circle. For this first Spider Discussion, develop a line of questioning, as seen in the examples on pages 205–210. The examples in Resources are for math; however, the ideas can be modified for other disciplines. Overall, in the Spider Zero discussion, you want students to focus on how communication and vocabulary use were critical to their success as a team during the activity.

4. In this first discussion, you will be the moderator and the rapporteur, meaning that you will lead the discussion, ask the questions, and take notes on the conversation and who was speaking. This is to ensure that the first Spider Discussion is somewhat of a success and that students are confident in what the roles entail. See step 8 for more about the questions that you will develop for Spider Discussions.
5. Remember to be patient. Some groups are more talkative than others. Spider Zero is just one of the first steps toward fluid, student-centered, academic discussions. Having students open up with each other about what they built and what went right and wrong is important, as it develops vulnerability and a willingness to learn and listen.
6. After this first, more informal Spider Discussion, "Spider Zero," you will begin to establish the rules. For each Spider Discussion, there will be a moderator and a rapporteur. The moderator will be the person who facilitates the discussion using the sentence stems that you provide. For examples, view the math examples on pages 208–210. In addition, the Spider Discussion Conversation Stems (Graff, Birkenstein, & Durst, 2008) found in Resources on page 214 are a valuable tool to teach students how to elicit responses from others and remain respectful and attentive while others are responding.
7. During the Spider Discussion, the rapporteur will be taking notes about what is discussed, as well as populating the Spider Discussion Pie Chart Scoresheet, also called "Spider Pie," that you have created on Google Sheets. A sample pie chart is on page 213. The rapporteur does not verbally contribute to discussion unless it is necessary.
8. To prepare for each Spider Discussion, craft 5-7 questions that go from slight depth, to in-depth, to metacognitive and reflective. Spider Discussion metacognitive questions for all disciplines are in the Resources section on page 205, along with example Spider Discussion questions that are content-specific (pages 208–210). While the content-specific questions are for math analysis, they can serve as a model for developing questions in any discipline. Remember that questions should provoke thought and have more than one correct response so that students are able to engage in discussion rather than check a box of completion.
9. Provide students access to the questions a day or two in advance so that they can prepare their responses and have ideas ready for the Spider Discussion. A possibility is to have the questions in a Google document so that you can access the document history and see if students have reflected and changed their responses. In addition, during the Spider Discussion, students can be encouraged to take notes and elaborate on their thinking based on other students' responses and ideas.
    a. Be ready! The initial Spider Discussions may not last longer than 20 minutes. Know that all progress is good progress. Spider Discussions can exceed 75 minutes when students are used to them and know what is expected.
    b. Student preparation is critical. Students who are more engaged are often the same students who have responded to the questions in writing prior to the Spider Discussion. They are also the students who tend to score better on assessments because they have been more engaged with the unit overall.
    c. Get them talking! A "trick" is to place a metacognitive question first and last so that students who are struggling with the content will have an opportunity to speak at the beginning and at the end. Placing metacognitive questions first and last also encourages peers to bond while developing a personal connection to the material.

10. There is also a rubric that will be used to rate the discussion. There is a sample rubric in the Resources section on page 212. At the conclusion of each Spider Discussion, the rapporteur will share the Spider Discussion Pie Chart Scoresheet, the "Spider Pie," with their group, and provide additional feedback to the group based on the rubric scoring system. All students will then individually score the group based on the rubric. They will record their individual scores in the upper-left portion of their question sheet before submitting the question document. You will also provide a score, as will the moderator and the rapporteur. The ratings of all students will be averaged and then placed alongside your score, the moderator's score, and the rapporteur's score for comparison.
11. Spider Discussions should not impact students' grades. Students will begin to recognize that their preparation for and participation in Spider Discussions will directly impact their assessment grades and their overall understanding of content. One-on-one conferences with students showing them this data is helpful. Overall, however, it is up to your discretion as to how you use the scores:
    a. Will you track scores over the course of time for students to achieve a certain goal?
    b. Will you use the scores for extra credit?
    c. Will you show students their Spider Discussion participation in conjunction with their assessment grades to promote engagement?
    d. Will you use the scores to provide an incentive?

Connections to the Disciplines	Key Behaviors	Examples in Context
ELA	Articulate thoughts; Elaborate on others' ideas; Draw conclusions; Identify themes; Learn as a community	Spider Discussions can elicit some interesting responses if used in conjunction with anticipation guides like Value Line Up found on page 215. Students can be asked about how they would approach a situation or their perspective on a particular theme. Students might also enjoy using their Accountability Pie for a Spider Discussion end the sentence after discussion. Students can choose a character to blame for the struggle or problem in the text and defend their response with evidence.
Math	Identify confusion; Work through difficult problems; Rephrase solutions; Articulate ideas; Learn as a community	In the Resources section on pages 208–210, there are Spider Discussion materials from math analysis classes. They will be helpful for your planning. Students are often not used to collaborating in math. They are used to finding an answer and moving on. However, the Common Core asks for students to provide explanations and consider unique problem-solving methods. Spider Discussions work really well when students may already know an answer to a problem, but are unsure of how to explain their process or why they chose to use a certain method or equation. Also, some of the most successful Spider Discussion questions involve asking students to depict their thinking visually. Overall, when students are asked to explain and use math-specific vocabulary during Spider Discussions, they become more comfortable with content and, in our experience, their grades and confidence increase.

Connections to the Disciplines	Key Behaviors	Examples in Context
Science	Ask questions; Defend a stance; Use evidence to support a claim; Elaborate on thoughts and ideas; Collaborate to eradicate confusion	Consider having students read about science topics in student-friendly publications or trade books. After reading, invite students to ask questions about the topics and ideas they encountered. Students can only ask the questions, not respond to them or make statements, and you will record the questions. From these ideas, you can develop your Spider Discussion questions to get at the heart of any student misconceptions that you notice. Oftentimes, students struggle in science primarily because they hold inaccurate beliefs and thoughts about scientific material. Spider Discussions about lab work shift the focus to process and not just product. Students can talk through the process and the difficulties and uncertainties they faced. Students can work together with their classmates to discuss their results, thus engaging in problem-solving commentary and questioning.
Social Studies	Consider various perspectives and points of view; Use evidence to support a claim; Identify confusion and gaps in knowledge; Collaborate to eradicate confusion	A Spider Discussion is a great way for students to consider cause and effect relationships in social studies. Students can consider the most impactful effects of the Treaty of Versailles or causes of economic collapse during the Great Depression and its impact on the present day. Students can also be asked what society should have learned from particular historical events and how society has or has not heeded lessons learned from the past. Prompts such as *In what ways...* or *To what extent...* are often difficult for students to respond to. Spider Discussions are a way to support students in formulating ideas and knowing how to approach open-ended questions and prompts.

Example of Spider Discussion Metacognitive Questions for all Disciplines

Name: ____ Date: __________

Spider Discussion Metacognitive Questions for All Disciplines
What skills did you use?
What struggles did you face? At what points did you feel most confident?
How did you prepare for this discussion? Was it beneficial? What will you change for next time?
How will you prepare for the upcoming assessment? Why will you choose that learning and study method?
What were you visualizing? How were you using visualization to help your comprehension and understanding?
What was difficult?
Consider all of the units of the semester [list units]. Which unit was most challenging and why?
How have you taken your awareness of your "struggles" to help you when learning in this unit?
Which learning mode was most beneficial? Which was not helpful? Explain.
Where do you still have questions?
What language was easy to adapt into your explanations? What language is still difficult to grasp?
Consider the aspects of College and Career Ready. Determine which skills and characteristics you have developed the most throughout the course.
In what ways can your experience working on team projects support your continued learning?
Which skills and characteristics might you use going forward?
Connect what you learned in the past units to this one. How has your prior knowledge supported new growth?
Spider Discussions ask you to "talk" the discipline in order to support each other's learning. In what ways have language and cooperative learning been a critical part of learning and understanding for you?
Share with us the best thing you learned, realized, or remember from this course. What's the most interesting concept you learned? What's your favorite memory?
What goals can you set for yourself so that when you look back you can be proud of yourself?

Example of Spider Discussion Metacognitive Questions for all Disciplines, continued...

Spider Discussion Metacognitive Questions for All Disciplines
What keeps you going and motivates you?
As the content in this class gets more abstract, how do you keep the content anchored to reality?
What do you typically rely on to learn? Language, art, talking with others, reading, music, movement? How have Spider Discussions impacted your learning style?
How would you explain this concept to someone else?
What resources have you found most effective when you run up against the limits of your understanding?
What have been the most rewarding dimensions of this school year for you?
Fifteen years from now, a baby born today will be in high school. What advice would you give? What would you want them to learn and know?

Example of "Spider Zero" Discussion Questions for all Disciplines

Name: ____________________ Date: __________

Spider Zero Discussion Questions: Team Building*
1. What skills did you use during this activity?
2. What struggles did you face transforming a 3D object into written instructions?
3. Was the other team successful in interpreting your instructions?
4. What were the misunderstandings?
5. Why did we do this activity in [content area] class?
6. How did your understanding of [content area] concepts support you in this activity?
7. How did [content area] vocabulary support you or hinder you in the writing or building process?
8. How can you apply these skills outside of school?
9. Overall, what would you change about your experience?
***For each [content area], enter the name of your course, content, or discipline**

Example One of Spider Discussion Questions for Math Analysis

Name: ______________________________ Date: __________

The following examples have been drawn from a high school level math analysis class. However, there are metacognitive questions interwoven into the content-related questions to demonstrate how to find a balance between content-focused learning and student-centered learning. No matter your discipline, these resources will benefit your understanding of the overall strategy.

Trig Spider 2: My Powers have Doubled In collaboration with Daniel Landau
1. What was the easiest part of this unit? The hardest? Can you provide a specific example, problem, or learning style for each? 2. What are the similarities and differences among reciprocal, Pythagorean, and cofunction identities? 3. Explain the cofunction identity in terms of: a. SohCahToa b. Transformations of functions: af(b(x-c))+d c. Difference Formula 4. Discuss the correlation between your performance on the earlier quizzes and your preparation for and participation in the Spiders and Study Group. What ways of learning were successful for you? 5. What are two things you learned from this unit, and what is one question you still have? (Hint: Hang on to that question for the Study Group.)

Example Two of Spider Discussion Questions for Math Analysis

Name: ______________________________ Date: ____________

Vectors Spider: What the Vec? In collaboration with Daniel Landau
1. Overheard recently in math class: "I'm so glad we're back to regular math class." After the introductory Keva blocks activity, many of you said you preferred to learn math conventionally: the teacher talks, you take notes, and then you try the practice problems for homework. In what ways did the activity and Spider Zero Discussion influence your opinion about other ways to learn math?
2. What are some similarities between vectors and the parametric equations you noticed? What are some differences?
3. Given a vector with a known initial point and terminal point, explain the process of converting it into a linear combination of unit basis vectors.
4. Explain the relationship between unit vectors and trig functions.
5. Let's say you're the navigator in an RAF Mosquito speeding across the North Sea to rescue Niels Bohr from Sweden before the Nazi agents arrest him (true story). There's a serious crosswind blowing toward you from the left. The pilot wants to arrive to the correct destination on time. Explain to him the process of calculating the course and speed corrections.
6. How have you taken your learning about moving past "struggles and setbacks" from the Spider Discussions we have had and applied it to the current unit on vectors? How have you applied it in other classes or activities?

Example Three of Spider Discussion Questions for Math Analysis

Name: ______________________________ Date: __________

Limits Spider: To the Limits and Beyond! This Spider occurred during COVID, 2021. Some students were in-person partial days while others were learning remotely via Zoom. In collaboration with Daniel Landau
1. How has the partial return to in-person learning been going for you? Whether you have chosen to return to the building or continue to learn remotely, what has been surprising, rewarding, or disappointing? 2. If a limit is a finite y-value, how is it possible for a function to have a limit at infinity if x will never actually reach infinity? 3. Explain the differences in closure among the intervals of continuity that meet at the different types of discontinuities. 4. Use the concept of continuity to explain how the IVT can be used to guarantee that an equation has a solution. 5. Now that we have completed the unit on limits, what is the most important concept that you learned in this unit and why do you think so? How would you explain that concept to someone else? 6. Think about the changes in your life over the past 13 months. Some of these changes have been silver linings, or positive changes, that we could not have anticipated in March 2020. What are some of the positive things about life during Covid that you will either miss or plan to keep doing in the post-pandemic world?

Template for Spider Discussion Overview, Roles, Rubric, Scoring, and Scoresheet "Spider Pie"

Name: ______________________________ Date: ____________

Spider Discussion Overview: Collaborative Discussion for Learning Purposes
A Spider is a class discussion guided entirely by students to reflect on the unit and practice expressing [content area] concepts verbally. Each Spider is evaluated with a maximum score of 10 points. These points are not part of the course grade – they are simply a feedback mechanism to track growth over the course of the year. To earn all 10 points requires a hard-working, analytical discussion in which: 1. Everyone participates in a meaningful and substantive way and, more or less, equally. The loud or verbose do not dominate; the shy or quiet are encouraged. 2. The student who is speaking: a. takes risks and tries to express challenging ideas b. uses examples c. uses new vocabulary 3. Students listen carefully and respectfully to each other so that everyone is clearly understood and comments are not lost. Those who are not heard or understood are urged to repeat. 4. The discussion builds. There is an attempt to resolve questions and issues before moving on to new ones. Major points and complex issues are not brushed over or missed. 5. There is a sense of balance and order, with the focus on one speaker at a time and one idea at a time. The discussion is lively and well paced.
Spider Discussion Student Roles
During each Spider, two students will have specialized roles: 1. Moderator: a. initiates the discussion by introducing the topic b. maintains flow and balance by encouraging other students to participate c. asks a prompting question when the discussion lags 2. Rapporteur: a. does not speak during the discussion; monitors speaking using Spider Pie b. takes notes on the discussion with reference to the rubric c. gives feedback at the end on how well the discussion met the rubric criteria

Template for Spider Discussion Overview, Roles, Rubric, Scoring, and Scoresheet "Spider Pie", continued...

Spider Discussion Rubric

8-10 points

The discussion consistently met all of the criteria. Every student contributed meaningful ideas with examples and vocabulary, while everyone else listened and then followed up with productive questions and comments. The discussion gave students a complete understanding of the topic.

5-7 points

The discussion usually met most of the above criteria. Most students contributed relevant ideas with examples and vocabulary, while everyone else listened and then followed up with related questions and comments. The discussion gave students a pretty good understanding of the topic.

2-4 points

The discussion rarely met any of the above criteria. A few students contributed some ideas with minimal support while some people listened and then followed up with perfunctory questions and comments. The discussion gave students a basic understanding of the topic.

0-1 points

The discussion never met any of the above criteria. A few students contributed irrelevant ideas with no support while a few people listened and then followed up with random questions and comments, if any. The discussion gave students no understanding of the topic.

Spider Discussion Scoring

The score is not part of the course grade – it is a feedback mechanism to track growth over the course of the year.

The collective score will be determined by the following procedure:

1. Each participant will score the Spider individually and in secret – no consultation.
2. The scores will then be aggregated:
   a. The participating students' scores will be averaged.
   b. The rapporteur will recommend a score.
   c. The teacher will assign a score.
3. The Spider will earn the average of these three scores, rounded to the nearest tenth.

Template for Spider Discussion Overview, Roles, Rubric, Scoring, and Scoresheet "Spider Pie", continued...

Spider Discussion Pie Chart Scoresheet "Spider Pie"
A Google spreadsheet that records how often students participate in order to let students know if they were truly collaborative and inclusive of each others' thoughts and ideas.

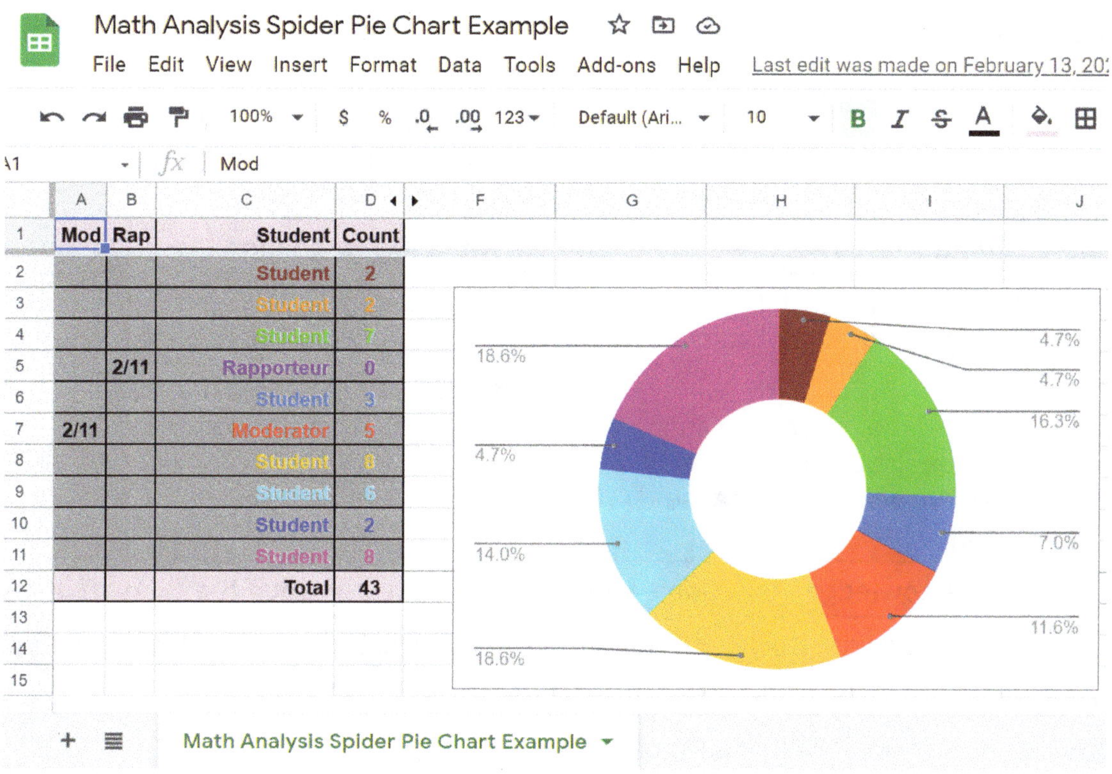

Example of Spider Discussion Conversation Stems for Students

Example of Spider Discussion Conversation Stems for Students (Adapted from: Graff, Birkenstein, & Durst, 2008)	
If you're in agreement, but want to add more:	**If you disagree:**
I really liked [student]'s point about [idea]. I'd like to add that [continue thought]. I see both [student] and [student]'s point about [idea], but I find myself agreeing more with [student] because [continue thought].	The claim that [student] made seems to overlook the idea that [continue thought]. I disagree with the argument that [idea] because [continue thought]. By focusing on [idea], it overlooks the deeper problem of [idea]. Think about it this way [continue thought].
If you agree and disagree:	**If you'd like to change the direction:**
I'm conflicted. On the one hand, I agree that [idea]. On the other hand, I'm not sure if [continue thought]. My feelings on [idea] are mixed. I do support the position that [idea], but I find the argument about [idea] equally persuasive because [continue thought].	So far, we've been talking about [idea]. But isn't the real issue [continue thought]? So [Student A] just said that [idea]. [Student B], what do you think?
If you want to acknowledge someone's idea:	**If you want continue the conversation:**
I appreciate what you said about [idea]. Let's all take a minute to think about that. I am hearing you say [idea]. Is that accurate? Could you repeat what you just said? That was interesting.	[Student] just shared the idea that [idea]. Does anyone want to add? What additional questions or comments do we have? Does anyone want to clarify that idea or add an example?

Value Line Up

Description

Value Line Up is a type of anticipation guide in which students are provided with real-life scenario statements based on the themes and topics of the upcoming unit. Students will make decisions regarding the order of the scenarios and provide reasons for their decisions. Through the Value Line Up process, students will be positioned as decision-makers (Silver, Strong, & Perini, 2007) and asked to consider themes and topics from a personal or disciplinary point of view. In other words, students will be asked to make decisions either based on what they value most or what the discipline values most. The true strength of this strategy is the discussion that takes place after students have ordered the scenario statements (Vacca, Vacca, & Mraz, 2011), as well as the personal and disciplinary perspectives that students consider throughout the process of ordering the statements.

There will be a wide range of responses, and while students should be encouraged to explain their reasoning, pushing students to cite evidence or develop an argument is not the focus. Rather, the goal is to cultivate students' more personal thoughts and reactions to the themes and topics of the lesson while encouraging them to listen to each other and consider all ideas within the context of the discipline (Buehl, 2011).

Students' Value Line Ups should be revisited during the unit. Students can change and shift their ordering based on what they have learned (Johns & Lenski, 2019). As Value Line Up is revisited, you can guide students to acknowledge the information that will be more valued in the discipline versus less valued. In this way, Value Line Up is a strategy that encourages collaborative discussion throughout the lesson while teaching students what information is important within the discipline. Value Line Up can also serve as a bridge between units to build on the topics, themes, and disciplinary concepts that will be revisited in the next unit or lesson (Vacca, Vacca, & Mraz, 2011).

When and Why Would I Use This Strategy?

- To encourage students' sense of personal ownership over the themes and topics of a unit and consider what they believe to be valuable information
- To collaborate and foster decision-making to prepare students for upcoming learning
- To support text-to-world and text-to-self connections.
- To develop students' ability to reflect and reevaluate their thinking based on new learning
- To position students as members of the discipline to make decisions about what is of value

How Do I Teach/Present This Strategy?

1. First, consider the topics and themes that are the main focus of the lesson, text, or unit and develop real-life scenarios that highlight those topics and themes.
2. The goal is to develop 10-12 one-sentence statement scenarios such as:
   - People who have too much ambition will hurt anyone who gets in their path to success.
   - Saving the rainforests is a critical element of controlling global warming.
   - Learning the formula for Pi and how to use it in problem solving for circles is the most valuable component of this unit.
   - Pythagoras is the most influential mathematician.
3. You can share these statements in worksheet format as seen on page 219, or you can encourage students to cut out the statements into strips and physically arrange them. The best way to approach this strategy is with Google slides. If each statement has its own slide, students can drag and drop them into order and make notes as to their rationale in the speaker notes section. Just ensure that students are prompted to make a copy of the slides so that each student has their own.
4. Students will put the statements in an order that is predetermined by you. You could ask students to order the statements from:
   - the decision they would probably make to the decision they are least likely to make
   - the topic they are most passionate about to the topic they are least passionate about
   - the idea they feel needs immediate social action to one that does not
   - the best application of a math concept to the most inaccurate application of a math concept.
5. The ideas for ranking and ordering are endless and truly depend on the discipline, the topics and themes, and the goals of the lesson.
6. After students have ordered the statements, have them share their ordering and reasoning in a small group prior to sharing with the entire class. Students will need to listen to each others' order choices and compare them to their own. If they are listening to another classmate and would like to change their own Value Line Up, they can. Change based on new learning or thinking is a part of this strategy.
7. The Value Line Up scenarios and ideas should be revisited and discussed throughout the lesson. The information that is valued in the discipline should be explicitly taught to students. For example:
   - In ELA, you will want to explain that the motivation behind someone's actions is a critical component of analysis.
   - In science, disproving and questioning are critical elements of understanding.
   - In math, being precise with language is important.
   - In social studies, every possible bias must be considered before you can consider the author's purpose.
8. Each time Value Line Up is revisited, students should be encouraged to make changes and to share their order and reasoning.

Connections to the Disciplines	Key Behaviors	Examples in Context
ELA	Develop text-to-self and text-to-world connections; Support decisions with reasoning; Change thinking based on new learning; Elaborate on theme across text; Form opinions; Analyze	In the tragedy *Othello,* students can engage in Value Line Up with a focus on the themes of racial prejudice and jealousy. These themes can be addressed with scenario statements that have been highlighted in the news. Students will order the statements from the worst offenses to the not-as-bad offenses. They can get into groups and do some research to try and determine the human characteristic or fault that drove the behavior. See page 219 for a Value Line Up for ELA.
Math	Provide reasoning; Analyze and synthesize ideas; Make decisions; Listen to the reasoning of others; Reflect on current and past learning	Value Line Up can be used when students are considering all that they will learn during a semester of mathematics. You can provide students with an equation and ask them to order problem solving approaches from most effective to least effective. Students can list their processes and approaches to solving in order to generate a class list. The students can also rank the approaches from simple to most complex and provide reasoning.
Science	Provide reasoning; Make decisions; Collaborate with peers; Encourage curiosity and personal connection; View material from a scientist's perspective; Consider misconceptions	In a unit on thermal isolation, students can put into order the materials they think will provide the most effective insulation to the least effective. They can reconsider these predictions as they engage with the experiment. Another idea is to make statements about certain scientific concerns. Students can order the concerns in terms of those that need immediate attention to those that can be addressed at a later time. Some examples include: ▪ overuse of antibiotics ▪ sustainable food ▪ clean drinking water ▪ protecting national parks ▪ microplastics Students can then begin to develop questions inquiring about the topics and ultimately research the topic of choice.

Connections to the Disciplines	Key Behaviors	Examples in Context
Social Studies	Make decisions after considering authorship and point of view; Consider cause and effect; Support decisions with reasoning; View material from a historian's perspective; Reconsider the idea of "truth"	In researching elections, students can prioritize topics that candidates should have or could be focusing on. Statements can be created that explain the topic and its relevance in historical context. For example, in 2019/2020, a major focus could have been the need for better access to educational technology during the COVID shutdown of schools. In terms of a topic like globalization, quotes can be pulled from websites like BrainyQuote www.brainyquote.com. Students can put the statements in order from strongly agree to strongly disagree and do some research about the quoted individual. Some examples follow: "Information technology has been one of the leading drivers of globalization, and it may also become one of its major victims." –Evgeny Morozov "Diversification and globalization are the keys to the future." –Fujio Mitarai "Where globalization means, as it so often does, that the rich and powerful now have new means to further enrich and empower themselves at the cost of the poorer and weaker, we have a responsibility to protest in the name of universal freedom." –Nelson Mandela

Example of Value Line Up for ELA

Name: ______________________________ Date: ____________

Value Line Up for *Othello*

Below you will find 14 real-life situations taken from the news and movie plots.

You have two goals:

1. Determine what emotion or human fault drives each action.
2. Assign each situation a number based on your ranking of them. There are fourteen situations. Let's use 1 for the "worst" situation and 14 for "not as horrible as #1."

A. To ensure their child goes to the perfect college, the parents pay someone to fake the test scores.

B. A person emotionally abuses their partner whenever they are alone in the house.

C. In order to win a gold medal in ice skating, the person has the competitor attacked and physically disabled.

D. A teenager convinces a friend, who is an A student and captain of the basketball team, to drink at the dance so that the friend gets caught and suffers.

E. A person fakes a pregnancy and then abducts the neighbor's baby and pretends it is their own.

F. A person stalks and threatens their partner's friend because they are jealous.

G. A student spreads gossip and rumors about another teenager, leading to the teenager's demise.

H. In order to keep their partner's undivided attention, they poison the partner's food causing them to be too weak to care for themselves.

I. A person becomes anorexic in order to feel accepted by others.

J. A person assassinates an iconic musical figure because they want the attention.

K. A person physically injures another person who will not accept their invitation to go on a date.

L. A teenager tackles their friend during lacrosse practice to try and injure them and gain their position.

M. After a teenager suffers a broken heart, they create a fake social media page to lure their former partner into a dangerous situation with a catfisher.

N. A person sabotages a coworker in order to get their position in the company, ruining the coworker's reputation and causing the coworker's family to leave them.

Save the Last Word for Me

Description

Save the Last Word for Me (Manderino, Berglund, & Johns, 2014; Short, Harste, & Burke, 1996; Vaughan & Estes, 1986) is a strategy that encourages students to select text and share the rationale for their choice with peers in a small group. The procedure of this strategy guides students to actively engage in close reading at a literal comprehension level before moving on to analysis, and ultimately, synthesis and whole class discussion. You will provide students with a purpose and lens for reading depending on your discipline and goals for the lesson.

Save the Last Word for Me encourages student collaboration and student voice. When the speaker in the small group shares the text they selected, each student in the small group has an opportunity to comment on the text segment before the speaker has an opportunity to comment. This procedure gives the speaker time to listen to others' ideas while further developing their own thoughts and commentary about their chosen segment. To wrap up each round, the speaker will share their thoughts and then turn it over to the next student in the group to be the speaker. The format of sharing creates a safe environment for leading, speaking, and learning.

When and Why Would I Use This Strategy?

- To encourage students to share ideas with each other and work through difficult text
- To provide space for students to choose their own content to discuss
- To support students in focusing on small parts of text carefully
- To develop students' ability to read text from a discipline-specific point of view

How Do I Teach/Present This Strategy?

1. Preselect a text and give students time to read it independently. Give students a purpose for reading by asking them to approach the text from a discipline-specific point of view. For example, in social studies ask students to consider bias; in ELA provide the prompt: Who gives advice to the main character and what does she do with it? See Examples in Context on pages 221–222 for additional ideas.
2. After students have independently completed the initial reading and marked up the text based on the purpose for reading, you can provide students with the template for Save the Last Word for Me found on page 223.
3. Instruct students to complete the template by choosing three of their marked text segments. Have students copy these segments into the template in a direct-quote format. You can also communicate with students the general amount of text you want them to choose for each segment (e.g., 10-15 words or less; 1-2 sentences). In

addition, remind students of the purpose or prompt so that they can narrow down which three segments they would like to choose. Some students may need to spend additional time reading and selecting segments.

4. Students then need to add their comments and thoughts about each of their chosen text segments to the template in the designated areas.
5. When this task is complete, place students in groups of four or five. To solidify the procedure, you may want to display the Save the Last Word for Me Procedure found on page 225 so that students can easily reference it throughout the lesson.
6. Choose one student in each group to begin. That student becomes the speaker and reads one of the text segments they have selected and written on their template. Only the text segment is shared at this time.
7. Each member of the group is then invited to comment on the first speaker's text segment and the speaker is encouraged to take notes about what their peers are saying about the segment.
8. When all students in the group have commented, the speaker who shared the quote offers their commentary about it. The comments may or may not be the same as the original thoughts or ideas written. The comments may or may not include the ideas of classmates. The other students in the group are encouraged to take notes about what the speaker is sharing.
9. The process continues by having another student become the speaker and share their segment. The process continues until all students have had a turn at being the speaker and have shared all of their chosen text segments. This means that each student may have a turn at being the speaker three times. It depends on your time constraints and how many text segments you would like students to work through.
10. At the conclusion of the lesson, students will be ready to synthesize, draw conclusions, and work through other difficult or confusing passages with a team of peers.

Connections to the Disciplines	Key Behaviors	Examples in Context
ELA	Collaborate to understand difficult text; Interpret text; Consider multiple points of view	When asking students to read *The Poet X* by Elizabeth Acevedo (2019), ask them to approach the text from the discipline-specific lens of looking for advice the character receives and how she responds to that advice. The prompt would read, "Who gives advice to the main character and what does she do with it?" Students can pull segments that provide the advice and then comment on how the main character uses that advice. To expand students' commentary, they can also explain whether they agree or disagree with the main character's decisions.

Connections to the Disciplines	Key Behaviors	Examples in Context
Math	Provide an explanation; Consider a problem- solving approach; Interpret graphical solutions to an equation; Use vocabulary to structure an explanation	Mathematical language can often be difficult for students to grasp, and yet being specific with language is critical to the discipline. When asking students to read through some of the instructional material in a math textbook or when asking them to read some lengthier problems, have students focus on the language. Save the Last Word for Me can be used to encourage students to notice, gather, and discuss the language and vocabulary in the text. Through the collaborative process of the strategy, students can connect the language and vocabulary to previous math learning or comment on how it differs from the meaning of the terms when used outside of the discipline.
Science	Analyze solutions; Consider problems; Access difficult and complex text; Critically consider a hypothesis; Develop cause and effect connections	Exploring and hypothesizing about cause and effect relationships is central to the discipline of science. When reading about data on vaccine reactions, students can use Save the Last Word for Me to catalog some of the effects of the vaccine. When they explain their reasoning, they can provide some ideas about potential causes for such a reaction. Alternatively, students can look for evidence to support a scientist's written hypothesis about why vaccines cause a reaction in one population more than another. Students can collaborate to determine if the scientist has strongly supported their hypothesis.
Social Studies	Determine point of view; Consider bias; Access difficult and complex text; Read with a critical lens	This strategy is helpful when working with sensitive topics because it breaks down information into manageable segments. One use for this strategy is in psychology when students are reading about topics such as coping with loss. Students can pull segments that resonate with them regarding steps in the process of coping. See an example page 224. Also, primary source documents can be difficult for students to access, but they are valuable and necessary texts in the discipline. Therefore, Save the Last Word for Me is a great strategy for supporting students in accessing primary source documents. When reading a primary source document, students can be asked to pull segments that seem to present the author's opinion about a topic. In their reasoning, students can explain why it seems to be an opinion versus a fact and how the opinion suggests bias.

Template for Save the Last Word for Me

Name: ______________________________ Date: ____________

Directions: As you read, make a light mark with your pencil next to three statements in the passage that you either agree with, disagree with, connect with, or wish to comment about. When you finish reading, write each statement in one of the boxes below. Then write your comments below it. You might include questions or thoughts you have about each of the quotes. When you finish, you will have the opportunity to discuss the text with a small group of your classmates.

Title: ______________________________

My first quote, page _______ My reasoning for selecting this quote:

My second quote, page _______ My reasoning for selecting this quote:

My third quote, page _______ My reasoning for selecting this quote:

Example of Save the Last Word for Me for Psychology

Name: *Beth* Date: ______

Directions: As you read, make a light mark with your pencil next to three statements in the text that *represent important steps in the process of Coping with Loss*. When you finish reading, write each statement in one of the boxes below. Then write your reasoning for choosing that statement. You might include questions or personal connections you have as well. When you finish, you will have the opportunity to discuss the text with a small group of your classmates.

Title: *Coping with Loss*

My first quote, page *228*
Any loss requires change and that change can be stressful.

My reasoning for selecting this quote:
An important part of the process is recognizing that change will occur. One needs to expect that loss will cause stress.

My second quote, page *229*
Hope operates through all five stages of grief.

My reasoning for selecting this quote:
There are five stages of grief. Hope is an important part of each stage.

My third quote, page *230*
What helped me most was talking to my family.

My reasoning for selecting this quote:
Talking is an important part of the process for coping with loss. Other important parts of the process include acceptance and seeking the comfort of others.

Save the Last Word for Me Procedure

Name: ____________________ Date: __________

Save the Last Word for Me Procedure
■ Students, make sure you have your *Save the Last Word for Me* organizer and a pen or computer to take additional notes. ■ The teacher will select a student in each group to begin the process. ■ The first student will be the speaker and read their first quote, but *not* comment about it. ■ Moving around the circle, each member of the group will take a turn in commenting about the speaker's quote. ■ When each student has had a chance to comment, the speaker who chose the quote may then share their comments about the quote. The commentary can be a combination of what was written originally by the speaker and/or a response to the other ideas that were shared by group members. ■ The next student will take a turn as speaker and will share their quote. Continue the process until all students have had a turn as the speaker. Take turns as speaker. Continue to share and comment until all quotes and comments have been made, or until the teacher calls an end to the activity. ■ Just remember, the person who shares the quote, the "speaker," needs to be the *last* one to make comments about it. Don't forget to Save the Last Word for them!

Discussion Web

Description

Discussion Web is a strategy that supports students in outlining both sides of an issue or argument before engaging in discussion (Alvermann, 1991; Barton, 1995; Duthie, 1986; Manderino, Berglund, & Johns, 2014; Swafford, 1990). Discussion Web fosters collaborative problem-solving and peer support. It also creates a concrete representation of what students have learned and the areas in which they still need to gather research and information. Seeing a visual of these knowledge gaps promotes student autonomy and reflection; they can see the next steps in the process. In addition, powerful learning occurs when students are able to consider and ultimately reconcile multiple perspectives and address all sides of an issue or argument. Discussion Web also provides structure for discussion and collaboration.

Before sharing ideas with the large group, students first meet with a partner, then a small group, and finally with the larger group. This procedure reassures students that they have peers who agree with their ideas and who will be able to share the responsibility of communicating those ideas with others. Discussion Web, as an organizer, gives students a way to succinctly outline an issue or argument. Discussion Web as a strategy supports students in determining their stance, reconciling multiple perspectives, and sharing their views during each discussion format.

When and Why Would I Use This Strategy?

- To promote students' ability to think critically
- To encourage students to consider multiple perspectives
- To develop students' ability to organize information in various ways
- To support students in using evidence to support a stance
- To promote collaboration and trust among peers

How Do I Teach/Present This Strategy?

1. Choose a topic that has the potential to generate opposing viewpoints. Provide students with research supporting both sides of the topic. Ensure that students have time to read, mark, and truly understand the information in the texts before working with the Discussion Web.
2. When students have a general grasp of the topic and an awareness of multiple, and potentially opposing views, distribute or share the template for Discussion Web on page 230. If you are distributing paper copies, it is helpful to have a copy of the template on both sides of the paper so that students have room to add ideas without erasing previous ones. For electronic copies, make sure students are always adding

ideas and not deleting ideas. The strikethrough option is helpful so that previous ideas can be read even if they are eventually ruled out. Various discipline-specific templates can be found on pages 231–234.

3. Pose a question to students related to the topic that stimulates opposing views. For example, if the topic is Manifest Destiny, the question you pose might be, "Do people have the right to conquer and control all land?" See additional ideas in Examples in Context on pages 228–229.
4. Have students work with a partner and use the provided texts to discuss and identify at least three responses for each side of the argument. Encourage students to provide thorough textual evidence to support their responses. Ensure that their thinking is recorded on the template for Discussion Web.
5. Then, have the pairs compare their responses with another pair. Tell the groups that their goal is to work towards consensus. Provide ample time for students to share and discuss what the texts are explicitly stating, what inferences can be made, and ultimately, the conclusions that can be drawn based on evidence. Make sure students are not deleting ideas. Rather, they can strikethrough ideas neatly and add additional ideas. It is important for students to see their thought processes and find value in all ideas.
6. Before moving forward, ensure that students have time to check their conclusions to ensure that they are accurately responding to the prompt and have evidence from the text to support the conclusions made. Check in with groups to make sure that they have taken a stance on the issue and that the members of the group have reached consensus on this stance.
7. As you speak to each group, determine how the classroom will be organized for the whole class discussion. Do you want students sitting across from each other in a debate-style setup, or would it make more sense for students to sit in a collaborative circle? Naturally, it not only depends on your goals for the lesson, but also on the number of students who have chosen each side or even on the number of students who are still unsure of their stance.
8. When discussion begins, pose the original question and tell students that they need to state their stance, provide one reason for that stance, and follow up with evidence from the texts in support of their reason.
9. Students will then respond by acknowledging other students' contributions and moving forward with a reason of their own. Discussion continues until all students have shared at least one piece of evidence.
10. Encourage students to complete a metacognitive written reflection of the process considering how they managed to reconcile their ideas, the text's ideas, and group member's ideas.

Connections to the Disciplines	Key Behaviors	Examples in Context
ELA	Defend an argument with textual evidence; Consider multiple points of view; Collaborate to form consensus	When students have a grasp of the characters in a novel and an awareness of the author's voice, a variety of questions can be posed for Discussion Web. Some potential questions to use for Discussion Web include: ■ What is the stronger motivator behind this character's actions: guilt or fear? ■ What is the attitude the author holds towards the idea of change: a benefit or a setback? If you have a final essay prompt in mind, this strategy is beneficial in getting students to think about those culminating themes. For example, if the essay prompt is questioning the ability to achieve the American Dream, the question for Discussion Web could be: ■ Which aspect of life gives a stronger feeling of achievement: strong, loyal relationships or money in excess?
Math	Think critically; Consider alternate solutions and approaches; Collaborate to reach consensus; Organize and apply data and information	Word problems often pose a struggle for students, especially when they include more information than the student needs. Therefore, Discussion Web can be used to support students in determining which information is relevant or not relevant to solving the problem. Another idea is to explore the ways that popular culture impacts students' beliefs about mathematics. Some common beliefs are: mathematics is too complicated; if mathematics is difficult, then I must not be good at it (Benoit, 2018). Posing these ideas, or other misconceptions that students have about mathematics, and asking students to find evidence in popular culture that supports these misconceptions, could bring students to a realization of the ways they can be negatively influenced by the media. ■ Ultimately, you can pose the question: Which messages are most damaging to your learning and appreciation of mathematics?

Connections to the Disciplines	Key Behaviors	Examples in Context
Science	Consider alternate points of view; Determine bias; Collaborate to reach consensus; Draw conclusions; Provide textual evidence to support a claim	In science, students' misconceptions about a topic or concept can be the greatest barrier to their learning (Shanahan, 2012b). Discussion Web can support students in eradicating misconceptions of threshold concepts by posing two solutions to a problem, one being the misconception. For example, in physical science, there is a misconception that the continents do not move. The question could be posed: ▪ Do continents move? Students can first discuss and provide reasons why the answer may be "yes" or "no." Then, they will be more invested in moving forward and researching to find out what scientists say on the topic. In physics, Discussion Web can be used to better understand misconceptions about weight, mass, and gravity in space when posing questions such as: ▪ Does gravity act on objects buried under the Earth? ▪ Is there gravity above Earth?
Social Studies	Determine point of view; Consider bias; Access difficult and complex text; Read with a critical lens	Decisions made throughout history can be explored through this strategy. When discussing Manifest Destiny, Discussion Web can be used to support students in researching the impact of Manifest Destiny with the question: "Do people have the right to conquer and control all land?" In the same unit about Manifest Destiny, students can determine which leaders would agree with the philosophy and which would disagree. You could offer the names of present-day leaders and challenge students to infer what these leaders would say about the topic. These exercises would encourage students to approach ideas from multiple perspectives.

Template for Discussion Web

Name: ______________________________ Date: ____________

Question

Reasons

No

Yes

Conclusion

Template for Discussion Web for ELA

Name: ______________________ Date: ____________

Question

Which aspect of life gives a stronger feeling of achievement: strong, loyal relationships or money in excess?

Textual Evidence

Strong, loyal relationships	Money

Concluding Ideas

Template for Discussion Web for Math

Name: ______________________________ Date: ____________

Mathematics Question

Which message is more damaging to your learning and appreciation of mathematics?

Reasons

Mathematics is too complicated	No effort should be needed in Mathematics

Conclusion

Template for Discussion Web for Science

Name: ______________________________ Date: __________

Before we begin researching this topic, know that a lot of people do not know the answer to this question. It is a common misconception. First, you will pair up and write down ideas for both sides. These ideas are from your own mind. Why do you think someone might think the continents move? Why do you think someone might think the continents do not move? Then, research the two sides and add information to the organizer.

Science Question

Do continents move?

Our Ideas

People may believe the continents move because...	People may believe the continents do not move because...

Research

Yes, continents move	No, continents do not move

Conclusion

After careful consideration, our overall conclusion is that...

Example of Discussion Web for Social Studies

Name: ______________________________ Date: ____________

Question

Do people have the right to conquer and control all land?

Reasons

Yes	No

Concluding Stance/Claim

Anchor Jigsaw

Description

Anchor Jigsaw is a process that supports student engagement through collaborative conversations with classmates (Vacca, Vacca, & Mraz, 2014). It is a powerful process because students are given the time to comprehend and share their ideas before moving into analysis and synthesis. Also, it provides time and opportunity for each student to share something unique with the group so that more reluctant students do not feel as though someone "took" their idea or said it "better" than they could. The process affords ownership, collaboration, and accountability for students. For teachers it provides multiple moments to determine students' understanding of concepts as well as their ability to analyze, synthesize, and use evidence. Students' ability to engage in collaborative conversations is developed over time, and Anchor Jigsaw supports that development.

When and Why Would I Use This Strategy?

- To support students' active engagement with text alongside peers
- To provide structure for students to discover the ways in which multiple ideas or concepts work together
- To encourage students to prepare to share their ideas with classmates
- To develop students' visual literacy skills using infographics for some of the text choices

How Do I Teach/Present This Strategy?

1. Create an essential question for the lesson such as: What is the impact of domestic violence? Or, what is the most thorough process for solving this equation? Put this question at the top of the template for Anchor Jigsaw that can be found on page 240. See Examples in Context on pages 238-239 for additional ideas.
2. Find an Anchor Text for the class and three to four Jigsaw Texts, depending on the number of students in a group. Label the Anchor text as "Anchor Text" at the top of the text and label each Jigsaw Text with "Jigsaw Text 1, Jigsaw Text 2," etc. at the top of the text.
    a. The Anchor Text can be a question, a picture, an infographic, a book excerpt, an article, or a video; basically, anything that will inspire students to think and collaborate. It is also the main, focal text of the lesson.
    b. Similarly, the Jigsaw Texts can be pictures, infographics, book excerpts, articles, video clips; basically, anything that will inspire students to see a unique perspective on the topic.

c. Consider that all students will need to independently access this material; the reading level should be appropriate for that goal. This strategy also provides you with an opportunity to differentiate text based on student need.

d. Some students may need their Jigsaw Text in advance or they may need to meet with you and talk through their ideas in order to feel comfortable moving forward. This strategy does not have to take place in a single class session.

3. Begin by distributing or sharing via Google Docs the template for Anchor Jigsaw, found on page 240. Make sure you have filled in the essential question prior to sharing the template. Talk through the essential question with students to clarify what it is asking and to answer any questions students might have about the essential question. Students need to understand the essential question so that they know the goals for the lesson. See page 241 for a social studies example.

4. Then, explain to students that they will complete the template for Anchor Jigsaw throughout the lesson. The goal for completing this template is not for complete sentences and perfect ideas, but rather a place to jot down notes and ideas. Students will bring together these notes and ideas in order to answer the essential question at the end of the lesson.

5. Divide students into small groups of 3-4 students. Four is ideal. Make sure you have a different Jigsaw Text for each group member. If you have students in groups of 4, you will need one Anchor Text and 4 different Jigsaw Texts. The entire class will have the same Anchor Text, and Student One in Group A will have the same Jigsaw Text as Student One in Group B; Student Two in Group A will have the same Jigsaw Text as Student Two in Group B, and so on.

6. Now, provide each group with the text labeled, "Anchor Text", at the top; students should each have their own copy through Google Docs or as a hard copy, so that they can annotate the text.

7. Provide students with time to independently read and comprehend the Anchor Text. The goal for this step is comprehension only. You may want to use an annotation strategy like Chunk and Go for this step, depending on the text and your goals for the lesson. See Section One on pages 18-22 for ideas.

8. After reading and annotating, ask students to write a few ideas that they want to remember from this Anchor Text at the top of their template.

9. Then provide each student in the group a different Jigsaw Text. This text should allow students to have a unique take on the Anchor Text or different information to add to the group discussion. Differentiate the texts to support what students need to be successful. Remember, Student One in Group A will have the same Jigsaw Text as Student One in Group B; Student Two in Group A will have the same Jigsaw Text as Student Two in Group B, and so on. However, within the same small group, no two students will have the same Jigsaw Text.

10. Give students time to independently read over their Jigsaw Text. Make sure students understand their Jigsaw Text by having them complete the sentence stem: "My Jigsaw Text is about (topic). It is telling me (summary of topic)."

11. For Round One, each student takes a turn explaining their Jigsaw Text to the group beginning with the sentence: "My Jigsaw Text is about (topic). It is telling me (summary of topic)." This summary step is important. Students jot down notes on their template as each group member shares their ideas.

12. After each student has shared their ideas about their Jigsaw Text with the small group, each student takes a few minutes to reread the Anchor Text and consider it in relation to their Jigsaw Text and their notes on the template. They then complete the sentence stem: "My Jigsaw Text connects to the Anchor Text because (explanation)" or, "My Jigsaw Text contrasts the Anchor Text because (explanation)."
13. For Round Two, students each take a turn explaining to the group how they think their Jigsaw Text makes sense in terms of the Anchor Text. You may prompt students to share an opinion they have formed, an explanation, an idea, a question, etc. This step can begin with students sharing their response to the sentence stem: "My Jigsaw Text connects to the anchor text because (explanation)" or, "My Jigsaw Text contrasts the Anchor Text because (explanation)."

    This is an analysis and synthesis step and it allows you to determine each student's level of mastery with the material being presented.
14. Group members continuously jot down notes and ideas in their template.
15. After each group member has shared their ideas in Round Two, the discussion opens up. The new focus for the group is to ensure that everyone's template is completed. This step allows students to revisit all of the ideas and continue supporting each other in a collaborative way.
16. Next, begin Round Three. In Round Three, students revisit the essential question as a small group in order to either form a consensus or to "agree to disagree." Either way, the small group will use the Jigsaw and/or Anchor Texts as evidence to support their ideas.
17. Finally, in Round Four, have each group share their stance with the class.

Connections to the Disciplines	Key Behaviors	Examples in Context
ELA	Determine theme; Elaborate on ideas; Synthesize evidence; Collaborate; Form consensus; Develop an argument	Students are reading a whole class text. As themes begin to emerge, students can explore the themes through Anchor Jigsaw. If students are reading *The Girl Who Fell from the Sky* by Heidi Durrow (2010), the essential question might be: *What is the impact of domestic violence?* They can read nonfiction Jigsaw Texts relating to mental illness, family dynamics, post-traumatic stress disorder, and/or abuse.
Math	Synthesize multiple representations of ideas; Use examples and nonexamples; Make connections; Ask questions	When students are navigating how to solve a new type of equation, the equation itself becomes the Anchor Text. Each student can be provided a problem that has been solved using that equation, with all work shown. Each solution contains an error that students will need to first identify and report and then correct and explain the correction. A possible essential question could be: What common mistakes do people make when solving math problems? In learning graphing solutions, students can be given data as the Anchor Text and then each Jigsaw Text can communicate the data in a different style of graph. In Round One, students will explain the type of graph and how to read the data. In Round Two, students will display their graph and explain why they think the graph format is a good form of communication for the data. A possible Essential Question could be: Do all graphical representations work equally well in communicating data and outcomes? Why? Why not?

Connections to the Disciplines	Key Behaviors	Examples in Context
Science	Read charts, graphs, and infographics; Use evidence to support ideas; Synthesize ideas	When looking at an interactive graph of the melting of the polar ice caps as an Anchor Text, you can provide each student with an article attributing the melting to different causes. In Round Two, students can share whether they agree or disagree with the conclusions drawn in the article. The Essential Question could be: What conclusions can you draw about the melting polar ice caps?
Social Studies	Recognize point of view; Analyze sourcing and bias; Synthesize primary and secondary sources; Understand the impact of context	When looking at a major social conflict that has continued for a duration of time, like discrimination, the Anchor Text can be an image depicting the struggle. Jigsaw Texts can be people's experiences, research about the reasons why people discriminate, and how to work towards solutions.

Template for Anchor Jigsaw

Name: ______________________________ Date: ____________

Essential Question:				
Main Ideas from Anchor Text				
Topics	Jigsaw Text 1	Jigsaw Text 2	Jigsaw Text 3	Jigsaw Text 4
Main Ideas				
Connection to Anchor				
New Ideas				

Example of Anchor Jigsaw for Social Studies

Name: *Dominique* Date: ____________

Essential Question: **Should college students who are exceptionally talented athletes, musicians, artists, or actors be allowed to accept money and sponsorships for their talents?**				
Anchor Text: *Image of a college athlete wearing a uniform sponsored by Nike.* Main Ideas from Anchor Text: ▪ *Other players on the team are wearing a different uniform since they are not sponsored by Nike* ▪ *That player makes money for playing and the other players do not* ▪ *How does the team feel about this?*				
Topics	Jigsaw Text 1: **Text Sample from Sports Illustrated Kids**	Jigsaw Text 2 **Images of college students at a sponsorship fair.**	Jigsaw Text 3 **Supreme Court decisions about this topic.**	Jigsaw Text 4 **Situations when young people have signed contracts that have hurt them.**
Main Ideas	*The article describes that before the college would make the money and now the student makes the money.*	*These are college students between the ages of 18-22 making huge financial decisions and selling their talents to the highest bidder.*	*It uses language like "modest" payments. Who defines these terms?*	*Music contracts often force teens to sing songs they don't want to sing and do things that they don't like.*
Connection to Anchor	*The team works together to make money to support their school's programs*	*Do these students have to hire financial advisors? How do they keep their money safe?*	*What if one student gets an offer from Nike and another from a small company?*	*What if the college student does not agree with Nike as a company? Isn't that a moral dilemma? And doesn't that hurt the collegiate sports culture?*
New Ideas	*I am just wondering if it causes problems among teammates. What is the social impact?*			

Accountability Pie

Description

Accountability Pie is a cause and effect based strategy that strengthens students' decision-making skills. The strategy supports students in creating a concrete visual that represents who or what is accountable for a certain event. Students must also assign the percentage of accountability that can be attributed to each possible cause. This strategy requires students to provide reasoning and evidence in support of their conclusions, critically evaluate information, and ultimately represent their decisions graphically through a pie chart. Accountability Pie positions students as decision makers because they are being asked to consider information from their own point of view (Silver, Strong, & Perini, 2007). Also, Accountability Pie solidifies students' understanding of cause and effect relationships within events.

Overall, the visual representation of information allows for ease of discussion, and the decision-making aspects of this strategy encourage students to listen to each other and defend their own conclusions with reasoning and evidence. Accountability Pie can be used before, during, or after reading; however, the strategy is intended to foster collaborative discussion no matter when it is used (Johns & Lenski, 2019).

When and Why Would I Use This Strategy?

- To support cross-curricular connections
- To encourage students to defend their decisions and conclusions with relevant information and evidence
- To develop students' abilities to collaborate with others
- To teach students various ways of representing and presenting their findings and conclusions
- To encourage students' personal connections to the content

How Do I Teach/Present This Strategy?

1. Provide students with a prompt asking who or what is accountable for a culminating event or situation.
2. Ask students to assign levels, or percentages, of accountability in the form of a pie chart divided into 3-6 segments. See Resources on pages 247–250 for pre-divided pie charts that serve as examples of Accountability Pie charts that can be used for this strategy.

3. Show students different examples of how a pie chart can be divided. Explain that students will assign higher percentages and thus larger segments of the pie to the people or events they think had a greater impact. Then explain to students that conversely, they will assign lower percentages and thus smaller segments of the pie chart to the people or events that they determine had less impact.
4. Model how this is done by creating and thinking aloud the creation of a pie chart for a sample topic, such as *Why I was late to school*, *Causes of accidents on the road*, or *My bad grade in history class*.
5. Provide students with texts and research to support their decision-making or let them find their own texts and research. This decision will depend on where you are in the unit and your goals for the unit. However, remember that students will need to use the texts and the research in order to come to their decisions.
6. It is important to know that the percentages of the pie do not need to be precisely accurate. If students are struggling with the mathematical concepts, you may want to provide pre-created pie charts for students to choose from, as found on pages 247–250. The headings and labels on the examples can be changed to reflect the topic that is the focus of your lesson.
7. It may be helpful for students to have a bank of characters, events, or topics to choose from based on the topics, themes, and readings.
8. Students will complete their charts and cite research or textual evidence to support the percentage of accountability assigned to each person/event that influenced the overall topic. For example, in ELA, students may assign accountability for the reasons behind Romeo and Juliet's deaths (Shakespeare, Mowat, & Werstine, 1992). In social studies, students may assign percentages of accountability for the people and events that brought greater acceptance for marginalized groups in society. See Examples in Context on pages 244–246 for additional ideas.
9. Students will need to share their Accountability Pie and defend their responses to their classmates.
10. To encourage extended collaboration, you may ask that students develop pie charts in groups of three. Another extension is to have the whole class deliberate and determine which pie chart is most representative of the information and research.

Connections to the Disciplines	Key Behaviors	Examples in Context
ELA	Consider multiple characters and points of view; Support decisions with explanations and evidence; Make decisions based on information; Build consensus with peers	When reading a novel that has controversy within the plot, such as *Romeo and Juliet* (Shakespeare, Mowat, & Werstine, 1992), Accountability Pie can be used to encourage students to closely analyze text and determine who should take accountability for the deaths of the main characters. Since multiple characters played a part in the deaths of Romeo and Juliet, including Romeo and Juliet themselves, students can consider which characters are more accountable than others and why. They can assign a percentage of accountability to each of the characters and further determine the characters' actions and decisions that warranted their allotted percentages. Once students determine the percentage of accountability that they would like to afford each character and have backed their decisions with textual evidence, students can use their pie charts to present or to begin to develop an essay. Students can also be asked to focus on events that lead to a certain outcome: ▪ What events lead to the demise of Hamlet? ▪ Which characters were the most impactful and why?

Connections to the Disciplines	Key Behaviors	Examples in Context
Math	Develop a graphic representation of information; Apply math learning to other content areas; Make decisions based on data; Analyze information	Math is the reason why this strategy is successful. Pie charts are effective at presenting information in an easy-to-access format. This strategy works with the language and tools of mathematics for the interpretation of information, yet the information students work with does not necessarily need to be numerical. Possible prompts may include: ■ Divide a pie chart into percentages of who/which you think are the top five people/events that society should hold accountable for national debt. ■ Divide up a pie chart into percentages determining who/what is accountable for successful space missions. ■ Divide up a pie chart representing the percentage of accountability that you assign to types of distractions that lead to car accidents. Another idea is for students to begin by predicting the percentages they think make sense when responding to a prompt, but then research the true percentages to check their predictions. An example of this type of prompt would be: ■ What are the best ways to hold students accountable for their own learning? ■ Predict the responses your classmates will have and assign a percentage to each. Then, interview your classmates and compare the data.

Connections to the Disciplines	Key Behaviors	Examples in Context
Science	Consider multiple points of view; Defend a decision based on evidence; Collaborate and critique with peers; Develop a graphic model to communicate findings; Determine cause and effect	In science, most environmental issues can be explored using this strategy. Students can assign percentages of accountability for the causes of the following: ■ global warming ■ deforestation ■ the loss of bees ■ food production ■ overpopulation In order for students to make educated decisions about percentages of accountability, they will need good resources and background knowledge on the topic. For science, Accountability Pie may be used as a culminating activity or an anticipatory guide. As an anticipatory guide, you can ask students to make predictions. When revisited at the end of the unit, students can add new learning to support or change their percentages. Because science discussions involve providing ideas to an audience of peers who will consider them critically, students can share their Accountability Pie and collaboratively decide on one or two pie charts that best represent the information and data available.
Social Studies	Critique and defend multiple points of view; Determine cause and effect; Support decisions with reasoning and evidence; Make decisions based on information; Build consensus with peers	Using the Accountability Pie that they create, students can engage in collaborative conversations considering the causes and effects of events throughout history. Primary and secondary source documents can be used as resources. Some sample prompts for Social Studies include: ■ Human Geography: Divide the pie chart into percentages of accountability for specific historical forces that have negatively impacted cultural patterns. ■ Psychology: Assign percentages of accountability for the developments that are supporting mental health recovery. ■ Government: Divide the pie chart into percentages of accountability for the rise of Communism over time.

Example of Accountability Pie for Social Studies

Name: *Sarah* Date: ____________

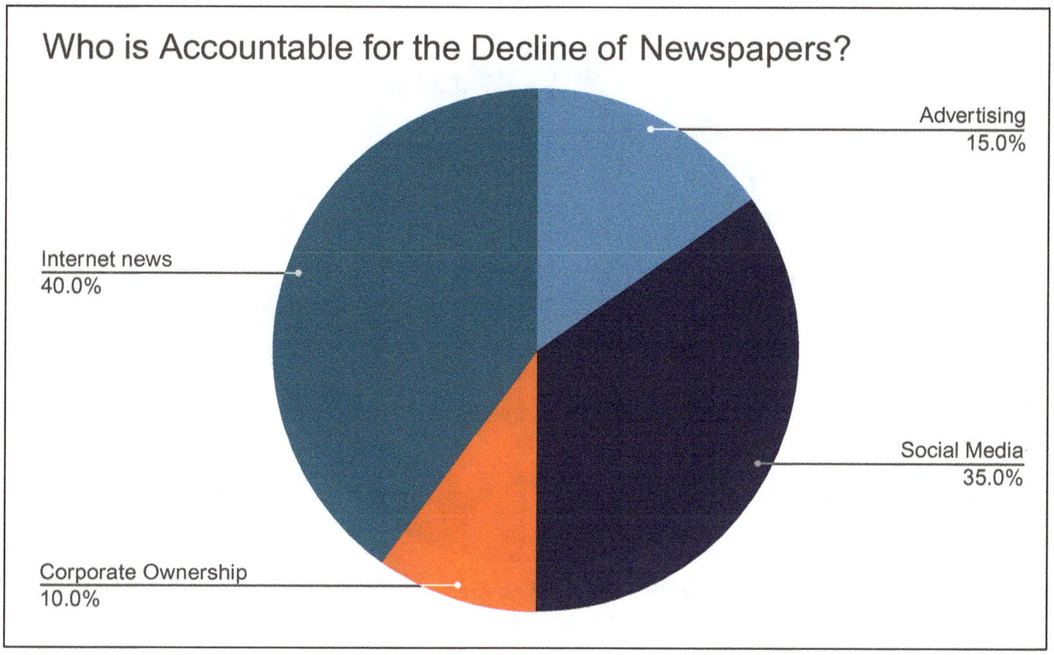

Conclusion: *Based on my reading and research, I think the primary reason why the newspaper industry is suffering is because the news is available on the internet.*

Template for Accountability Pie for "Who is to Blame"

Name: ______________________________ Date: ____________

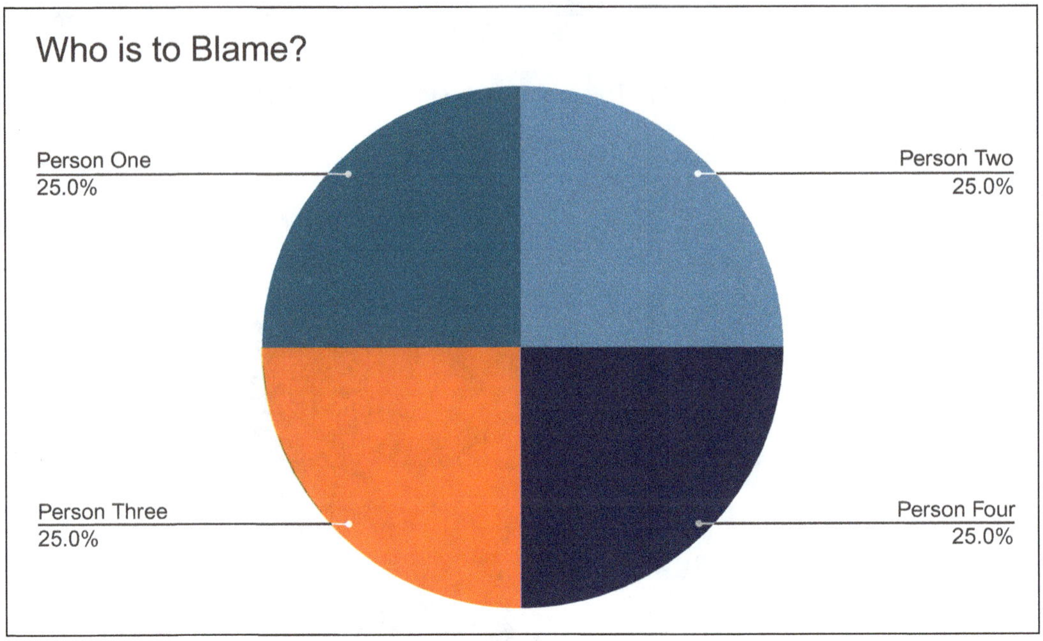

Conclusion

____

____

Template for Accountability Pie for "What is to Blame"

Name: ______________________________ Date: __________

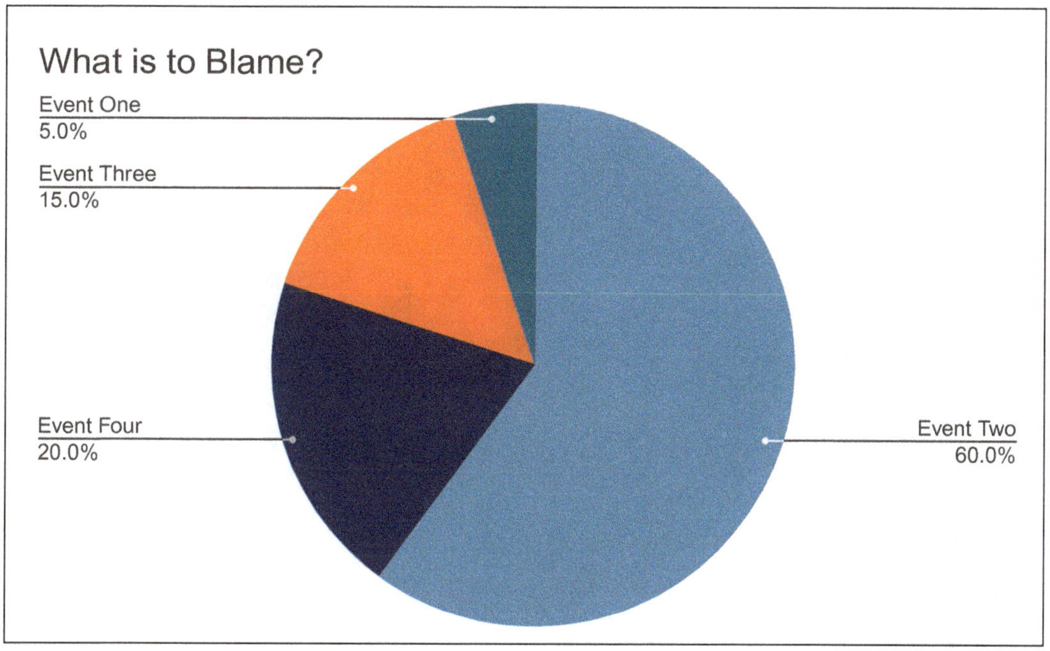

Conclusion

____

____

Example of Accountability Pie for "Who or What Deserves the Blame"

Name: ________________________________ Date: ____________

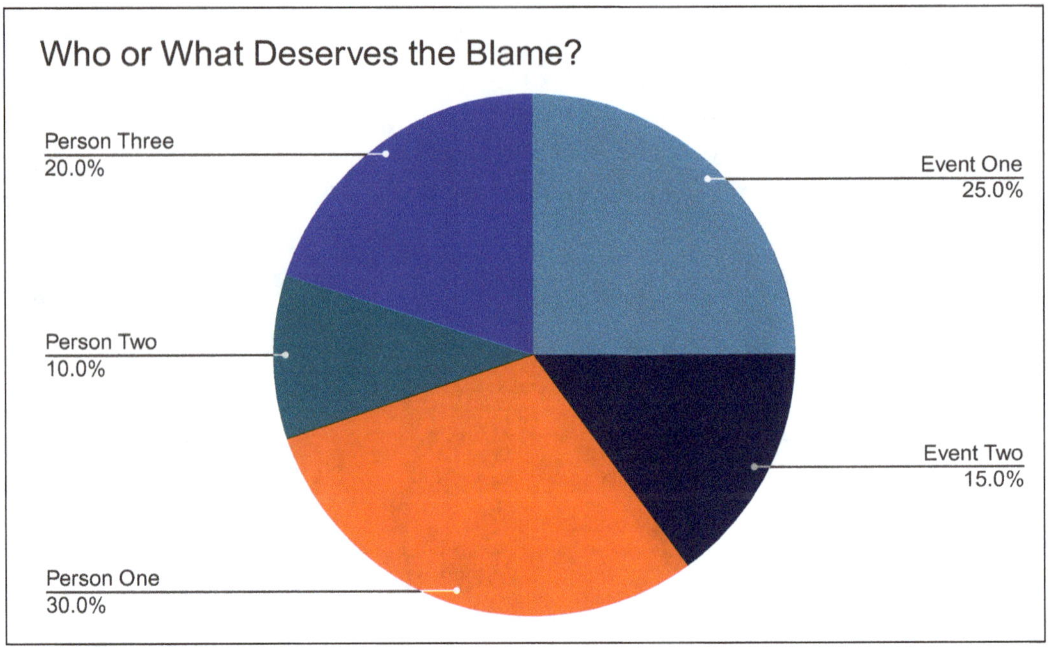

Conclusion

____

____

Description

The 30-60-90 strategy is a low-risk opportunity for students to verbally share ideas with each other and elaborate on their thinking through collaborative conversation. Like Anchor Jigsaw on page 235, this strategy provides each student an opportunity to speak. The 30-60-90 strategy was developed based on an understanding of the Sheltered Instruction Observation Protocol (SIOP) Model (Echevarria et al., 2016). The SIOP Model supports English Language Learners in developing academic vocabulary in an academic setting (McConachie & Petrosky, 2009; Zygouris-Coe, 2012b). One of the major components of the SIOP Model entails providing English Language Learners the opportunity to speak and practice vocabulary in a low-risk setting with peers (Krashen, 2004). The 30-60-90 strategy is designed to support these objectives, with English Language Learners and with all students. The numbers 30-60-90 refer to the number of seconds students are given to talk with their partner on a given topic.

When and Why Would I Use This Strategy?

- To support students in developing their ideas and understandings prior to whole-class discussion
- To provide students a chance to use discipline-specific language orally in order to incorporate the words into their lexicon
- To develop students' writing by allowing them to listen to others' ideas in order to elaborate on their own
- To support the development of academic language

How Do I Teach/Present This Strategy?

1. Determine the topic for each round.
2. Seek out a space or create a space that will allow your class to stand in two rows facing one partner (preferred) or two (if necessary). You can also have half of the class form the two speaking rows and the rest of the class create a listening outer circle, if necessary.
3. Students match up with a partner who is standing across from them. Tell students which row is Row A and which row is Row B. Explain that they will take turns speaking in increments of 30, 60, or 90 seconds and that you will be keeping the time. Explain that one person in the partnership will speak for the entire time while the other person practices active listening. Tell students that active listening involves nodding, saying "um hm," and looking in the general direction of their partner to indicate close, careful listening.

4. To support students in learning the process of 30-60-90, starting with a silly topic can be beneficial. Examples are, *What is your favorite place to eat?, When you have nothing to do, what do you do?,* and *Where is the best place ever?*
5. Another idea to support students in feeling comfortable with this strategy is to present the prompts beforehand and have students jot notes and ideas. Also, students can be given question stems or prompts that will support clarity of expression or elaboration during discussions such as *This reminds me of (idea), An example I can provide is (example),* or *This seems to connect to (connection).* See the example of 30-60-90 slides on page 255 for additional prompts for the speaker and listener as well as for set up and procedure.
6. For Round One, Row A is going to talk first. Explain by saying, "The students in Row A are going to speak on the topic for 30 seconds. Students in Row B must listen carefully and will be asked to recap what their partner said to them. Students in Row B can also support the Speaker when they run out of things to say by using prompts such as: *What made you think of that?*; *What examples can you provide?*; or *Does that connect to other things you have learned?* Then, we will switch and Row B students will speak."
7. After talking, or attempting to talk for 30 seconds, students in Row B must verbally recap, for about 10 seconds, what their partner in Row A has said, starting with a stem such as: *What I heard you saying was that (recap).* Then students in Row B will respond to the prompt for 30 seconds and students in Row A will offer a recap. A complete overview of the entire process is in the Example of 30-60-90 Slides on page 255. These slides can be projected during class for students to reference.
8. Students then rotate and change partners. Students in Row A move down one partner and the extra Row A person moves around to Row B. Then, a Row B person moves around to Row A. When rotating students, rotate in a clockwise fashion. A complete overview of the entire process is in the example of 30-60-90 on page 255. These can be projected during class for students to reference.
9. For Round Two, students in Row B respond to the prompt first with a different partner. They will have 60 seconds to speak on the topic while students in Row A practice active listening. After the 60 seconds, students in Row A offer a recap, for about 10 seconds, restating what they have heard: *What I heard you say was (recap).* Then, students in Row A respond to the prompt for 60 seconds and students in Row B will actively listen and offer the recap.
10. Round Two can be modified to 45 seconds if the topic requires less time. In addition, you can start the round by offering students a different topic. Or you can ask students to elaborate on a different aspect of the Round One topic. For suggestions see Examples in Context on pages 253–254.
11. After Round Two, students rotate again. Students in Row A move down one partner and the extra Row A person moves around to Row B. Then, a Row B person moves around to Row A. While the process may seem complex, students catch on quickly and will offer support with timing, turn-taking, and rotation.

12. For Round Three, you can choose to have students speak for 45 seconds, 60 seconds, or 90 seconds depending on your students' comfort and the needs of the topic. In addition, you can start the round by offering students a different topic or asking students to elaborate on a different aspect of the Round Two topic.
13. For Round Three, students in Row A respond to the prompt first. They will have 90 seconds, or whatever you have designated, to speak on the topic, while students in Row B practice active listening. After the 90 seconds, students in Row B offer a recap, for about 10 seconds, restating what they have heard: *What I heard you say was (recap).* Then, students in Row B respond to the prompt for 90 seconds and students in Row A will actively listen and offer the recap. After Row B has spoken, Row A will offer a 10 second recap starting with a stem such as: *What I heard you say was (recap).*
14. When the three rounds have culminated, you can bring the class together for a final writing product, discussion reflection, or small group conversation about the interesting things they heard.

Connections to the Disciplines	Key Behaviors	Examples in Context
ELA	Comprehend a text; Determine theme; Elaborate ideas; Consider evidence; Collaborate; Synthesize texts; Test predictions	After students have read a text, they can engage with 30-60-90 in order to discuss what they have read before joining in a whole-class discussion. This strategy can also help students in synthesizing text ideas and themes. For Round One, for example, students would discuss *Extremely Loud and Incredibly Close* by Jonathan Safran Foer (2006). For Round Two, students would discuss *Love is the Higher Law* by David Levithan (2010). And then in Round Three, students would attempt to bring the two texts together under a common theme or discuss common details between the two texts.
Math	Understand math vocabulary; Solve problems; Explain solutions	After students have solved a variety of equations, they can participate in 30-60-90 in order to explain to another student how they arrived at those solutions. Students can be provided with a vocabulary list and asked to use as many vocabulary words as possible during their explanations, and their partner can count how many of the words were used.

Connections to the Disciplines	Key Behaviors	Examples in Context
Science	Comprehend a text; Explain solutions; Ask questions; Determine faulty reasoning	When working with students on fallacious reasoning, you can have students create examples of a particular fallacy. During 30-60-90, they can present the fallacy to their partner and explain why it is fallacious reasoning and how it goes against scientific reasoning. In each round, students can trade fallacies, providing the opportunity to describe and listen to a variety of examples and situations.
Social Studies	Comprehend a media text; Corroborate evidence; Synthesize texts; Elaborate ideas	When learning about 9/11, students can watch the Discovery Channel's *The Flight that Fought Back* (2005). Prior to viewing, you can pose a question such as: "What characteristics determine a hero?" At a logical stopping point in the documentary, you can engage the class in a 30-60-90 rotation to discuss the documentary in terms of the question posed. At the conclusion of the documentary, students can discuss the topic in another 30-60-90 rotation with the same prompt or a different prompt such as: "In what ways has our world changed because of 9/11?"

Example of 30-60-90 for Rationale and Procedure to Share with Students

Name: ______________________ Date: __________

30 – 60 – 90 Discussion Procedure
Targeted Skills Student Voice; Comprehension; Elaboration; Collaboration; Listening Skills; Self-Assessment; Synthesizing; Analytical Thinking
30-60-90 ROUND ONE ▪ Match up with partner in two lines ▪ 30 seconds for students in Row A to talk; 10 seconds for Row B to recap ▪ 30 seconds for Row B to talk; 10 seconds for Row A to recap ▪ Rotate partners
30-60-90 ROUND TWO ▪ Match up with partner in two lines ▪ 60 seconds for students in Row B to talk; 10 seconds for Row A to recap ▪ 60 seconds for Row A to talk; 10 seconds for Row B to recap ▪ Rotate partners
30-60-90 ROUND THREE ▪ Match up with partner in two lines ▪ 90 seconds for students in Row A to talk; 10 seconds for Row B to recap ▪ 90 seconds for Row B to talk; 10 seconds for Row A to recap ▪ Rotate partners
30-60-90 Additional Ideas for Implementation ▪ 30-45-60 ▪ Students jot down ideas prior and add ideas through collaborative efforts ▪ Shift the times and when to change partners ▪ Work through the awkwardness ▪ Can pick any topic - warm up vs. full conversation ▪ Teach listening skills

Example of 30-60-90 for Rationale and Procedure to Share with Students, continued...

30 – 60 – 90 Discussion Procedure

30-60-90 Prompts for Speaker

1. When I think about this topic, the first thought that comes to mind is…
2. This reminds me of …
3. An example I can provide is…
4. This seems to connect to…
5. A visual that comes to mind is…
6. In my previous conversation, we thought…
7. Now I am thinking...

30-60-90 Prompts for Listener

1. Look in the direction of the speaker. Make eye contact, if and when possible.
2. Provide affirmative comments like: Um hmm I see. Interesting. And nod your head.
3. Provide ideas for clarification and elaboration like: Can you give an example? Can you explain that? Tell me more about… What made you think of that? How does that connect to other things?
4. Listen to what is being said to you and be ready to retell: What I heard you saying was...

Rotation:

Two Rows Partner Rotation: Everyone move down one and end cap students move to the other row.

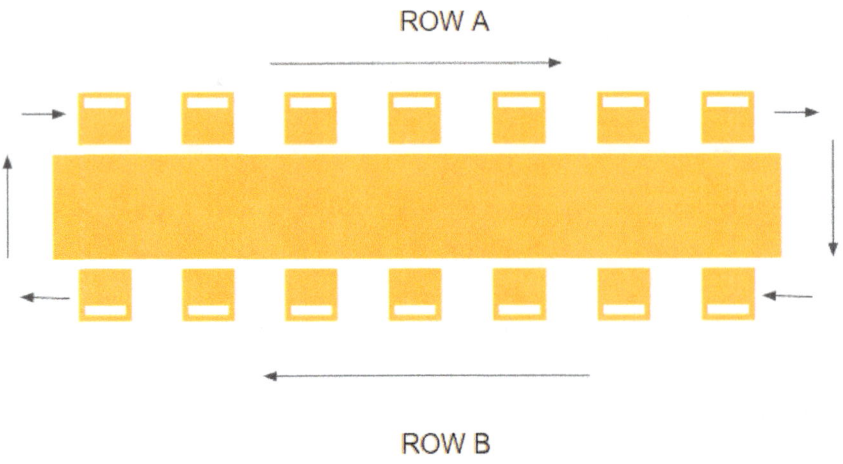

References

Acevedo, E. (2019). *The Poet X: A novel.* Large print edition. Waterville, Maine: Thorndike Press, a part of Gale, a Cengage Company.

Allen, J. (2004). *Tools for teaching content literacy.* Portsmouth, NH: Stenhouse.

Al-Samarraie, H., & Hj Hurmuzan, S. (2017). A review of brainstorming techniques in higher education. *Thinking Skills and Creativity, 27*, 78–91. doi: 10.1016/j.tsc.2017.12.002

Alvermann, D. (1991). The discussion web: A graphic aid for learning across the curriculum. *The Reading Teacher, 45,* 92–99.

Archer, A. L., & Hughes, C. A. (2011). *Explicit instruction: Effective and efficient teaching.* New York, NY: Guilford.

Arnold, K., Umanath, S., Thio, K., Reilly, W., McDaniel, M., & Marsh, E. (2017). Understanding the cognitive processes involved in writing to learn. *Journal of Experimental Psychology: Applied, 23*(2), 115–127. https://doi.org/10.1037/xap0000119

Assaf, L., Ash, G., Saunders, J., & Johnson, J. (2011). Renewing two seminal literacy practices: I-Charts and I-Search papers. *English Journal, 18*(4), 31–42.

Bar, V., Brosh, Y., & Sneider, C. (2016). Weight, mass, and gravity: Threshold concepts in learning science. *Science Educator, 25*(1), 22–34. https://files.eric.ed.gov/fulltext/EJ1110246.pdf

Barton, J. (1995). Conducting effective classroom discussions. *Journal of Reading, 38,* 346–350.

Bazerman, C. (1985). Physicists reading physics: Schema-laden purposes and purpose-laden schema. *Written Communication*, *2*(1), 3–23.

Beck, I. L., McKeown, M. G., & Kucan, L. (2013). *Bringing words to life: Robust vocabulary instruction.* New York, NY: Guilford.

Beers, K., (2003). *When kids can't read: What teachers can do.* Portsmouth, NH: Heinemann.

Beers, K., & Probst, R. (2016). *Reading nonfiction: Notice and note stances, signposts, and strategies*. Portsmouth, NH: Heinemann.

Bell, N. (2007). *Visualizing and verbalizing for language comprehension and thinking* (2nd ed.). Avila Beach, CA: Gander Publishing.

Benoit, G. (2018). Doctoral Thesis. Columbia University. Mathematics in popular culture: An analysis of mathematical internet memes. https://academiccommons.columbia.edu/doi/10.7916/D8BG45GT

Bialasik, J. E., & Martin, B. (2016). Cell phone plans. *Illustrative Mathematics.* Retrieved from https://tasks.illustrativemathematics.org/content-standards/tasks/469

Brown, M. D. (2007). I'll have mine annotated please: Helping students make connections with texts. *English Journal, 96*(4),73–78.

Brozo, W. G., Moorman, G., Meyer, C., & Stewart, T. (2013). Content area reading and disciplinary literacy: A case for the radical center. *Journal of Adolescent & Adult Literacy*, *56*, 353–357.

Buehl, D. (2011). *Developing readers in the academic disciplines.* Newark, DE: International Reading Association.

Buehl, D. (2014). *Classroom strategies for interactive learning* (4th ed.). Newark, DE: International Reading Association.

Burrell, K. I., & McAlexander, P. J. (1998). Ideas in practice: The synthesis journal. *Journal of Developmental Education, 22*, 20–30.

Burvall, A., & Ryder, D. (2019). *Intention: Critical creativity in the classroom*. Salem, OR: Blend Education.

Castles, A., Rastle, K., & Nation, K. (2018). Ending the reading wars: Reading acquisition from novice to expert. *Psychological Science in the Public Interest, 19*(1), 5–51. https://doi.org/10.1177/1529100618772271

Colorado State University. (2021). What is writing to learn? *The WAC Clearinghouse.* Retrieved from https://wac.colostate.edu/

Connor-Greene, P. (2000). Making connections: Evaluating the effectiveness of journal writing in enhancing student learning. *Teaching of Psychology, 27*, 44–46. doi: 10.1207/S15328023TOP2701_10.

Coxhead, A. (2000) A new academic word list. *TESOL Quarterly, 34,* 213–238. Retrieved from https://www.wgtn.ac.nz/lals/resources/academicwordlist/publications/awlsublists1.pdf

Cunningham, J. W. (1982). Generating interactions between schemata and text. In J. Niles & L. Harris (Eds.), *New inquiries in reading research and instruction: Thirty-first yearbook of the National Reading Conference* (pp. 42–47). Washington, DC: National Reading Conference.

Cunningham, J. W. (2013). Research on text complexity: The Common Core State Standards as catalyst. In S. B. Neuman and L. B. Gambrell (Eds.), *Quality reading instruction in the age of Common Core Standards* (pp. 136–148). Newark, DE: International Reading Association.

Crabtree, T., Alber-Morgan, S., & Konrad, M. (2010). The effects of self-monitoring of story elements on the reading comprehension of high school seniors with learning disabilities. *Education and Treatment of Children, 33,* 187–203.

Daniels, H., & Zemelman, S. (2004). *Subjects matter: Every teacher's guide to content-area reading.* Portsmouth, NH: Heinemann.

Dashner, J. (2010). *The maze runner.* New York, NY: Delacorte Press.

Di Domenico, P. (2016). High school teachers' disciplinary literacy knowledge. In R. D. Johnson, S. Vasinda, & S. Szabo (Eds.), Association of Literacy Educators and Researchers 38th Yearbook (pp. 49–70). Richmond, KY: Association of Literacy Educators and Researchers. Found at: https://www.aleronline.org/resource/resmgr/yearbooks/volume38_epdf.pdf

Discovery Channel. (2005). *The flight that fought back* [DVD].

Durrow, H. (2010). *Girl who fell from the sky.* Chapel Hill, NC: Algonquin.

Duthie, J. (1986). The web: A powerful tool for the teaching and evaluation of the expository essay. *The History and Social Studies Teacher, 21,* 232–236.

Dweck, C. (2014). *The power of believing that you can improve* [Video file]. Retrieved from https://www.ted.com/talks/carol_dweck_the_power_of_believing_that_you_can_improve?utm_campaign=tedspread&utm_medium=referral&utm_source=tedcomshare

Elish-Piper, L., L'Allier, S. K., Manderino, M., & Di Domenico, P. (2016). *Collaborative coaching for disciplinary literacy: Strategies to support teachers in grades 6–12.* New York, NY: Guilford.

Echevarria, J. J., Vogt, M. E., Short, D. J. (2016). Making content comprehensible for English learners: The SIOP Model. Boston, MA: Pearson.

Faggella-Luby, M. N., & Deshler, D. D. (2008). Reading comprehension in adolescents with LD: What we need to learn. *Learning Disabilities Research & Practice, 23,* 70–78.

Faggella-Luby, M., Graner, P., Deshler, D., & Drew, S. (2012). Building a house on sand: Why disciplinary literacy is not sufficient to replace general strategies for adolescent learners who struggle. *Topics in Language Disorders, 32,* 69–84. doi: 10.1097/TLD.0b013e318245618e

Fisher, D., & Frey, N. (2004). *Improving adolescent literacy: Strategies at work.* Hoboken, NJ: Pearson Prentice Hall.

Fisher, D., Frey, N., & Lapp, D. (2012). *Text complexity: Raising rigor in reading.* Newark, DE: International Reading Association.

Fletcher, R. (2003). *A writer's notebook: Unlocking the writer within you.* New York, NY: Harper-Collins.

Foer, J. S. (2006). *Extremely loud and incredibly close.* Boston, MA: Mariner Books.

Foley, J. A. (2019). *Sorry for your loss.* New York, NY: Quill Tree Books.

Frayer, D. A., Frederick, W. C., & Klausmeier, H. J. (1969). *A schema for teaching the level of concept mastery: Report from the project on situational variables and efficiency of concept learning.* Madison, WI: Wisconsin Research and Development Center for Cognitive Learning.

Gillis, V. (2014). Disciplinary literacy: Adapt not adopt. *Journal of Adolescent & Adult Literacy, 57,* 614–623. https://doi.org/10.1002/jaal.301

George Washington University & National Institute of Child Health and Human Development (U.S.), & National Institute for Literacy (U.S.). (2007). What content-area teachers should know about adolescent literacy. Washington, DC: National Institute for Literacy.

Golding, W. (2011). *Lord of the flies.* London, England: Faber.

Goldman, S. R., Britt, M. A., Brown, W., Cribb, G., George, M., Greenleaf, C., Lee, C. D., Shanahan, C., & Project READI. (2016). Disciplinary literacies and learning to read for understanding: A conceptual framework for disciplinary literacy. *Educational Psychologist, 51*(2), 219–246. https://doi.org/10.1080/00461520.2016.1168741

Gottfried, A. E. (1985). Academic intrinsic motivation in elementary and junior high school students. *Journal of Educational Psychology, 77*(6), 631–645.

Graham, S., & Perin, D. (2007). Writing next: Effective strategies to improve writing of adolescents in middle and high schools: A report to Carnegie Corporation of New York. Washington, D C: Alliance for Excellent Education.

Graham, S., & Hebert, M. (2011). Writing to read: A meta-analysis of the impact of writing and writing instruction on reading. *Harvard Educational Review, 81*(4), 710–744. https://doi.org/10.17763/haer.81.4.t2k0m13756113566

Graff, G., Birkenstein, C., & Durst, R. (2008). *They say, I say: The moves that matter in academic writing, with readings.* New York, NY: W. W. Norton.

Gray, W. S. (1925). Reading activities in school and in social life. In G. M. Whipple (Ed.), *The twenty-fourth yearbook of the National Society for the Study of Education, Part I* (pp. 1–8). Bloomington, IL: Public School Publishing.
Hall C., & Barnes M. A. (2017). Inference instruction to support reading comprehension for elementary students with learning disabilities. *Intervention in School and Clinic. 52*(5), 279–286. doi:10.1177/1053451216676799
Hamilton, E. R., & Stolle, E. (2016). The importance of disciplinary literacy. *Colleagues, 13*(3), 29–31. doi: http://scholarworks.gvsu.edu/colleagues/vol13/iss1/9
Hammond, Z. L. (2015). *Culturally responsive teaching and the brain.* Thousand Oaks, CA: Corwin Press.
Harste, J. (2014). The art of learning to be critically literate. *Language Arts, 92*(2), 90–102. Retrieved from www.ncte.org/library/NCTEFiles/Resources/Journals/LA/0922-nov2014/LA0922Art.pdf
Harvey, S., & Goudvis, A. (2007). *Strategies that work: Teaching comprehension to enhance understanding.* Portsmouth, NH: Stenhouse.
Heimlich, J. E., & Pittelman, S. D. (1986). *Semantic mapping: Classroom applications.* Newark, DE: International Reading Association.
Herber, H. L. (1970). *Teaching reading in the content areas.* Englewood Cliffs, NJ: Prentice Hall.
Henriquez, C. (2014). *The book of unknown Americans.* New York, NY: Knopf.
Hickey, W. (2013, March 25). The 12 most controversial facts in mathematics. *Business Insider.* New York, NY. Retrieved from https://www.businessinsider.com/the-most-controversial-math-problems-2013-3
Hillocks, G. (2011). *Teaching argument writing, grades 6–12: Supporting claims with relevant evidence and clear reasoning.* Portsmouth, NH: Heinemann.
Hoffman, J. V. (1979). The Intra-Act procedure for critical reading. *Journal of Reading, 22,* 605–608.
Hoffman, J. (1992). Critical reading/thinking across the curriculum: Using I-Charts to support learning. *Language Arts, 69*(2), 121–127.
Hoyt, L. (2009). *Revisit, reflect, retell: Time-tested strategies for teaching reading comprehension* (updated ed.). Portsmouth, NH: Heinemann.
Huntley, M. A., Marcus, R., Kahan, J., & Miller, J. L. (2007). Investigating high-school students' reasoning strategies when they solve linear equations. *Journal of Mathematical Behavior, 26,* 115–139.
Hynd-Shanahan, C., Holschuh, J. P., & Hubbard, B. P. (2004). Thinking like a historian: College students' reading of multiple historical documents. *Journal of Literacy Research, 36,* 141–176.
IRA/NCTE Joint Task Force on Assessment, International Reading Association, & National Council of Teachers of English. (2010). *Standards for the assessment of reading and writing.* Newark, DE: International Reading Association.
Johns, J. L., & Berglund, R. L. (2011). *Strategies for content area learning* (3rd ed.). Dubuque, IA: Kendall Hunt.
Johns, J. L., & Lenski, S. D. (2019). *Improving reading: Strategies, resources, and common core connections* (7th ed.). Dubuque, IA: Kendall Hunt.
Johns, J. L., Lenski, S. D., & Berglund, R. L. (2006). *Comprehension and vocabulary strategies for the elementary grades.* Dubuque, IA: Kendall Hunt.
Johnson, D. D., & Pearson, P. D. (1984). *Teaching reading vocabulary* (2nd ed.). New York, NY: Holt, Rinehart, & Winston.
Keene, E. O., & Zimmermann, S. (2007). *Mosaic of thought* (2nd ed.). Portsmouth, NH: Heinemann.
Kleon, A., *Newspaper blackout.* New York, NY: Harper Perennial.
Krashen, S. D. (2004). *The power of reading: Insights from the research.* Portsmouth, NH: Heinemann.
Lee, C. D., & Spratley, A. (2010). *Reading in the disciplines: The challenges of adolescent literacy*. New York, NY: Carnegie Corporation.
Lee, H. (2006). *To kill a mockingbird.* New York, NY: Harper Perennial Modern Classics.
Lenski, S. D., Wham, M. A., & Johns, J. L. (1999). *Reading and learning strategies for middle and high school students*. Dubuque, IA: Kendall Hunt.
Lenski, S. D., Wham, M. A., & Johns, J. L., & Caskey, M. M. (2011). *Reading and learning strategies for middle and high school students* (4th ed.). Dubuque, IA: Kendall Hunt.
Levithan, D. (2010). *Love is the higher law.* New York, NY: Knopf.
Lind, N. (2019). *We speak in storms.* New York, NY: Philomel Books.
Manderino. M. (2007, November). *Integrating the visual: Strategies for student synthesis.* Paper presented at the annual meeting of the National Reading Conference, Austin, TX.
Manderino, M., Berglund, R. L., & Johns, J. L. (2014). *Content area learning: Bridges to disciplinary literacy* (4th ed.). Dubuque, IA: Kendall Hunt.

Malatesha J. R. (2005) Vocabulary: A critical component of comprehension. *Reading & Writing Quarterly, 21*(3), 209–219. doi: 10.1080/10573560590949278

Marzano, R. J., Pickering, D., & Pollock, J. E. (2001). *Classroom instruction that works: Research-based strategies for increasing student achievement.* Alexandria, VA: Association for Supervision and Curriculum Development.

Marzano, R. J. (2004). *Building background knowledge for academic achievement: Research on what works in schools.* Alexandria, VA: Association for Supervision and Curriculum Development.

McBride, L. (2014). *We are called to rise.* New York, NY: Simon and Schuster.

McConachie, S. M., & Petrosky, A. R. (2010). *Content matters: A disciplinary literacy approach to improving student learning.* San Francisco, CA: Jossey-Bass.

McKenna, T.J. & Zieminski, C. (2020). Phenomena for NGSS: Creating the next generation of student engagement. Retrieved from https://www.ngssphenomena.com

Meston, H. M., Galloway, E. P., & McClain, J. B. (2020). "They're the ones who hold the answers:" Exploring educators' and students' conceptions of academic conversation. *Journal of Adolescent & Adult Literacy, 64*, 409–419.

Moje, E. B. (2008). Foregrounding the disciplines in secondary literacy teaching and learning: A call for change. *Journal of Adolescent & Adult Literacy*, *52*, 96–107.

Narter, D. (2013). Pencils down: Is mimicking the behaviors of "good readers" bad for good readers? *English Journal, 102* (5), 63–68.

National Center for Education Statistics & National Assessment of Educational Progress (NAEP) & Education Testing Service (U.S.). (2015). *NAEP reading report card for the nation and the states.* Washington, DC: National Center for Education Statistics, Office of Educational Research and Improvement, U.S. Department of Education.

National Governors Association Center for Best Practices & Council of Chief State School Officers (NGA Center & CCSSO). (2010). *Common Core State Standards: Appendix A.* Washington, DC: Author.

Nist, S. L., & Hogrebe, M. C. (1987) The role of underlining and annotating in remembering textual information. *Reading Research and Instruction, 27*(1), 12–25. doi: 10.1080/19388078709557922

Nokes, J. D. (2008). The Observation/Inference Chart: Improving students' abilities to make inferences while reading nontraditional texts. *Journal of Adolescent & Adult Literacy, 51*, 538–546.

O'Brien, T. (2019). *Overcoming peer learning phobia: It's time to release the reins and let students evolve their own thinking.* Boston, MA: Harvard Business Publications. Retrieved from https://hbsp.harvard.edu/inspiring-minds/overcoming-peer-learning-phobia

Pauk, W., & Owens, R. J. Q. (2011). *How to study in college.* Boston, MA: Wadsworth, Cengage Learning.

Paivio, A. (2006, September). *Dual coding theory and education.* University of Western Ontario. Draft chapter for the conference on "Pathways to Literacy Achievement for High Poverty Children," The University of Michigan School of Education.

Pearson, P. D., & Gallagher, M. C. (1983). The instruction of reading comprehension. *Contemporary Educational Psychology, 8*(3), 317–344.

Pearson, P. D., & Johnson, D. D. (1978). *Teaching reading comprehension.* New York, NY: Holt, Rinehart, & Winston.

Popp, J. S., Di Domenico, P., & Makhlouf, J. (2021). Teachers' perspectives about students' productive textual engagement in social studies. *Reading Horizons: A Journal of Literacy and Language Arts, 60*(1), 25–53. Retrieved from https://scholarworks.wmich.edu/reading_horizons/vol60/iss1/3

Porter-O'Donnell, C. (2004). Beyond the yellow highlighter: Teaching annotation skills to improve reading comprehension. *English Journal, 93*(5), 82–89.

Reynolds, J. (2019). *Long way down.* New York, NY: Simon & Schuster.

Reynolds, J. (2020). *Look both ways.* New York, NY: Simon & Schuster.

Reynolds, J., & Novgorodoff, D. (2020). *Long way down.* New York, NY: Simon & Schuster.

Riess, H. R. (2018). *The empathy effect: Seven neuroscience-based keys for transforming the way we live, love, work, and connect across differences*. Boulder, CO: Sounds True.

Sadoski. M. (1992, Spring). Imagination, cognition, and persona. *Rhetoric Review*, *10,* 266–278. http://www.jstor.org/stable/465487

Sammons, L. (2011). *Building mathematical comprehension: Using literacy strategies to make meaning.* Huntington Beach, CA: Shell Education.

Salinger, J. D. (1979). *The catcher in the rye*. Boston, MA: Little, Brown.

SAT Practice Test #6. Copyright © 2016. The College Board. Retrieved from https://collegereadiness.collegeboard.org/pdf/sat-practice-test-6.pdf

Schoenbach, R., Greenleaf, C., & Murphy, L. (2012). *Reading for understanding: How reading apprenticeship improves disciplinary learning in secondary and college classrooms.* San Francisco, CA: Jossey-Bass.

Shakespeare, W. (1992). *Romeo and Juliet.* In B. A. Mowat & P. Werstine (Eds.), *Folger Shakespeare Library.* New York, NY: Washington Square Press.

Shanahan, C. (2012a). How disciplinary experts read. In T. L. Jetton & C. Shanahan (Eds.), *Adolescent literacy in the academic disciplines: General principles and practical strategies* (pp. 69–90). New York, NY: Guilford.

Shanahan, C. (2012b). Learning with text in science. In T. L. Jetton & C. Shanahan (Eds.), *Adolescent literacy in the academic disciplines: General principles and practical strategies* (pp. 154–171). New York, NY: Guilford.

Shanahan, C., Shanahan, T., & Misischia, C. (2011). Analysis of expert readers in three disciplines: History, mathematics, and chemistry. *Journal of Literacy Research, 43*, 393–429.

Shanahan, T., & Shanahan, C. (2008). Teaching disciplinary literacy to adolescents: Rethinking content-area literacy. *Harvard Education Review, 78*, 40–61.

Shanahan, T., Fisher, D., & Frey, N. (2012). The challenge of challenging text. *Educational Leadership, 69,* 58–62.

Shelley, M. W. (1994). *Frankenstein.* New York, NY: Dover.

Short, K. G., Harste, J. C., & Burke, C. (1996). *Creating classrooms for authors and inquirers* (2nd ed.). Portsmouth, NH: Heinemann.

Shusterman, N. (2017). *Scythe.* New York, NY: Simon and Schuster.

Silver, H. F., Strong, R. W., Perini, M. J. (2007). *The strategic teacher: Selecting the right research-based strategy for every lesson.* Alexandria, VA: Association for Supervision and Curriculum Development.

Small, D. (2010). *Stitches: A memoir.* New York, NY: W.W. Norton.

Stahl, S. A., & Fairbanks, M. (1986). The effects of vocabulary instruction: A model based meta-analysis. *Review of Education Research, 56*, 72–110.

Swafford, J. (1990, July). *Discussion strategies for improving reading and writing to learn.* Paper presented at the World Congress on Reading, Stockholm, Sweden.

The National Children's Book and Literacy Alliance. (2021, September 30). Retrieved November 20, 2021, from https://thencbla.org/.

Tovani, C. (2000). *I read it, but I don't get it: Comprehension strategies for adolescent readers.* New York, NY: Stenhouse.

Tovani, C. (2011). *So what do they really know? Assessment that informs teaching and learning.* New York, NY: Stenhouse.

Taba, H. (1967). *Teacher's handbook for elementary social studies.* Reading, MA: Addison-Wesley.

Templeton, S., Johnson, F., Bear, D. R., & Invernizzi, M. (2010). *Vocabulary their way: Word study with middle and secondary students.* New York, NY: Pearson.

Thompson, D., & Rubenstein, R. (2000). Learning mathematics vocabulary: Potential pitfalls and instructional strategies. *Mathematics Teacher, 93*, 568–574.

Urquhart, M., & McIver, V. (2005). *Teaching writing in the content areas.* Alexandria, VA: Association for Supervision and Curriculum Development.

Urquhart, A. H., & Weir, C. J. (2016). *Reading in a second language: Process, product and Practice.* New York, NY: Routledge.

Vacca, R.T., Vacca, J. A. L., & Mraz, M. (2011). *Content area reading: Literacy and learning across the curriculum* (10th ed.). Boston, MA: Pearson.

Vacca, R. T., Vacca, J. A. L., & Mraz, M. (2014). *Content area reading: Literacy and learning across the curriculum* (11th ed.). Boston, MA: Pearson.

Vaughn, J., & Estes, T. (1986). *Reading and reasoning beyond the primary grades.* Boston, MA: Allyn & Bacon.

Vaught, S. (2006). *Trigger.* London, England: Bloomsbury Publishing.

Weisberger, M. (2020). An aurora that lit up the sky over the titanic might explain why it sank. *Live Science.* Retrieved from https://www.livescience.com/titanic-sunk-by-aurora.html

Wiggins, A. (2017). *The best class you never taught: How spider web discussion can turn students into learning leaders.* Alexandria, VA: Association for Supervision and Curriculum Development.

Wiggins, G., & McTighe, J. (2012, February). Understanding by design professional development workbook: UbD design guide worksheets. *Wordpress.* Retrieved from https://grantwiggins.files.wordpress.com/2012/02/wiggins-mod-m-grasps-and-roles.pdf

Wiggins, G., & McTighe, J. (2004). *Understanding by design professional development workbook.* Alexandria, VA: Association for Supervision and Curriculum Development. Retrieved from http://nvsd44curriculumhub.ca/wp-content/uploads/2017/09/GRASPS-Instructions.pdf

Wineburg, S. S. (1991). Historical problem solving: A study of the cognitive processes used in evaluation of documentary and pictorial evidence. *Journal of Educational Psychology, 83*, 73–87.

Wisconsin Department of Public Instruction. (2012). *Literacy in the disciplines and disciplinary literacy: A place for both.* Retrieved from http://standards.dpi.wi.gov/files/cal/pdf/literacy-disciplines.pd

Wolf, M. (2018). *Reader, come home.* New York, NY: Harper Collins.
Zaboi, I., Salaam, Y., & Pasha, O. T. (2020). *Punching the air.* New York, NY: Balzer and Bray.
Zygouris-Coe, V. (2012). Disciplinary literacy and the common core state standards. *Topics in Language Disorders, 32,* 35–50. doi: 10.1097/TLD.0b013e31824561a2
Zygouris-Coe, V. (2012, March 18). "What is disciplinary literacy and why aren't we talking more about it?" In S. Ebbers (Ed.), *Vocabulogic: Bridging the Verbal Divide.* Retrieved from vocablog-plc.blogspot.com/2012/03/what-is-disciplinary-literacy-and-why.html
Zywica, J., & Gomez, K. (2008). Annotating to support learning in the content areas: Teaching and learning science. *Journal of Adolescent & Adult Literacy, 52,* 155–165.

Printed in the USA
CPSIA information can be obtained
at www.ICGtesting.com
JSHW051448051123
51414JS00001B/1

9 798765 706992